Dante and the Limits of the Law

DANTE AND
THE LIMITS OF THE LAW

Justin Steinberg

The University of Chicago Press

Chicago and London

Justin Steinberg is associate professor of Italian literature in the Department of Romance Languages and Literatures at the University of Chicago. He is the author of *Accounting for Dante: Urban Readers and Writers in Late Medieval Italy*.

The University of Chicago Press, Chicago 60637
The University of Chicago Press, Ltd., London
© 2013 by The University of Chicago
All rights reserved. Published 2013.
Printed in the United States of America

22 21 20 19 18 17 16 15 14 13   1 2 3 4 5

ISBN-13: 978-0-226-07109-1   (cloth)
ISBN-13: 978-0-226-07112-1   (e-book)

DOI: 10.7208/chicago/9780226071121.001.0001

Library of Congress Cataloging-in-Publication Data

Steinberg, Justin.
    Dante and the limits of the law / Justin Steinberg.
        pages cm
    Includes bibliographical references and index.
    ISBN 978-0-226-07109-1 (cloth : alk. paper) — ISBN 978-0-226-07112-1 (e-book)
1. Dante Alighieri, 1265–1321—Knowledge—Law.   2. Law in literature.
I. Title.
    PQ4432.L3S74 2013
    851'.1—dc23

                                                                    2013016609

⊗ This paper meets the requirements of ANSI/NISO Z39.48-1992 (Permanence of Paper).

Contents

Acknowledgments

Looking back, it seems unlikely that this book would have been written had the legal historian Julius Kirshner not been my colleague at the University of Chicago. Our initial conversations about legal and literary fictions first led me to conceive of a book about Dante and the law, and those conversations have continued to enrich my thinking throughout the process of researching and writing it. Through Jules, moreover, I came into contact with a vibrant group of scholars of legal culture, including Emanuele Conte, Massimo Meccarelli, Sara Menzinger, Giuliano Milani, and Massimo Vallerani. For the continued dialogue and debate that has arisen among us, I am truly grateful. In particular, many of my ideas about "limits" in Dante's work stem from the discussions with participants in the seminar "Intorno all'eccezione," organized in Bologna in the spring of 2008. Later on in the writing of the book, I was able to sharpen my ideas by presenting research in a seminar for the Law and Humanities program at the University of Rome (Roma Tre). I am thankful for having had this and similar opportunities to publicly share my work.

All the while my fellow *dantisti* have ensured that I not lose sight of the primary aim of this project: to illuminate Dante's texts. I would like to single out Albert Ascoli, Zyg Barański, Ted Cachey, Giuseppe Mazzotta, and Nancy Vickers for continuously making me aware of the stakes of the exception for Dante's poetics, as well as for his politics. I owe a special debt of gratitude to Ron Martinez, who commented on the entire manuscript at various stages in its development. Numerous other colleagues and friends over the years have generously read draft chapters and/or pointed me toward valuable sources. It gives me great pleasure to thank for their crucial insights Elizabeth Anderson, Roberto Antonelli, Robert Buch, Paolo Cherchi, Rita Copeland, Bradin Cormack, Daisy Delogu, Unn Falkeid, Paolo Falzone, Anna Fenton-Hathaway, Antonia Fiore, Bob Fredona, Christiane Frey, Paul Gehl, Claudio Giunta, Graham Hammill, Laurence Hooper, Andrew Horne, Lorna Hutson, Isabella Lazzarini, Michèle Lowrie, Joe Luzzi, Simone Marchesi, Andrea Massironi, Guido Mazzoni, Christian Moevs, Vittorio Montemaggi, John Najemy, David Nirenberg, Diana Robin, Marco Ruffini, Eric Santner, Claudia Storti, Giacomo Todeschini, Anna Wainwright, and Raffaella Zanni. Finally, I greatly benefited from the perceptive comments of the editors at the University of Chicago Press, including those of Randy Petilos, Alan Thomas, and Renaldo Migaldi.

A small portion of chapter 1 appeared as "Dante and the Laws of Infamy" in *PMLA* 126.4 (2011), 1118–26, and is reprinted by permission of the copyright owner, the Modern Language Association of America. Sections of chapter 2 were revised from "*Arbitrium*: Judicial Discretion and Poetic License in *De vulgari eloquentia* and *Purgatorio* 27," originally published in *Critica del testo* 14.2 (2011), 179–98.

Introduction

Dante's literary-theoretical framework is simultaneously and manifestly a legal one.[1] His engagement with the law is most evident in the *Commedia*, where he imagines the afterlife as a highly regulated administrative body—complete with an elaborate network of local laws, hierarchical jurisdictions, and rationalized punishments and rewards. The normative structure of Dante's otherworld continues to influence the collective imagination. Damnation is no longer specific enough; today it seems natural to ask: "Which circle in Hell?"

Unlike his contemporary, the poet-jurist Cino da Pistoia, it is improbable that Dante had any formal training in civil and canon law, and his sporadic references to specific legal texts are concentrated in doctrinal works such as *Convivio* and *Monarchia*. On the other hand, as a convicted criminal and former public official, Dante was immersed in the legal culture of his day, and the *Commedia* is permeated with contemporary juridical rituals of everyday experience: deterrent and retributive punishment; testimony and confession; litigation and sentencing; special privileges, grants, and immunities; amnesties and pardons; and a variety of forms of oaths and pacts. These enactments of the life of law—not his explicit citations of legal doctrine—represent the poet's most profound statements about law and justice.[2]

In Dante's singular imagining of divine justice, limit cases play a central role. Indeed, though it may seem paradoxical, Dante creates this elaborate normative geography in order to explore its *exceptions*. The rules of the game are quickly assimilated by readers, but are just as quickly overturned: pagans are saved, the damned are pitied, oaths are broken, and punishments are unprecedented. Even the narrative itself may be viewed as an exception, a singular privilege granted Dante to traverse the otherworld, immune from the laws of his own construct.

Just as we now take into account the "period eye" when analyzing historical artworks, it is important to historicize similarly the reflexive habits of judgment that Dante's readers would have brought to his poetry, especially in their perception of norms and exceptions. Before the concentration of legislative authority in the modern centralized state, the suspension—or, more accurately, the "derogation" or setting aside—of a specific norm was viewed as an organic element within the legal order. Even when imperial rescripts or papal dispensations were in violation of positive law (*contra ius*), they were expected to remain faithful to higher norms, namely the foundational, "constitutionalist" tenets of the *ius commune* and the dictates of natural law. These extraordinary yet regulated exceptions were in fact necessary to the juridical order, serving to ensure its universal reach and adaptability by balancing the demands of justice with the authority of law. From this perspective, the exception guaranteed the law's continued applicability, saving it from becoming a dead letter when confronted with unforeseen cases.[3]

The main distinction between our modern exception and its medieval form is that the former is political while the latter was jurisprudential. Today, governing authorities invoke the exception by suspending the legal order for the preservation of the sovereign state. In the medieval legal system, overseen by a cadre of university-trained lawyers, the exception expressed the continued relevance of the legal order. For these jurists, who considered themselves "oracles" of the law and who depended on the legitimacy of the legal order for their livelihood and status, the suspension of that order for the necessity of the state was unfathomable. In lieu of this "state of exception,"[4] they relied on a system of individual exceptions to reconcile the validity of their legal corpus with the contingencies of life.

In line with a medieval legal perspective, Dante deliberately embeds certain incongruities within his normative system of punishments and rewards so as to call attention to its "system of exception."[5] But centuries of commentary have sapped these interpretive challenges of their vitality. When scholars encounter anomalies to the laws of Dante's literary creation, such as the salvation of the pagan suicide Cato, they tend to search for doctrinal answers that safeguard and reconfirm its normative structure. Invoking a historical document, a literary precedent, or a theological argument, they explain—or rather explain away—any apparent contradictions. In this way the extraneous case is reabsorbed within rational, all-inclusive laws. This defensive approach to the exception ultimately derives from a post-Enlightenment conception of the law. From that perspective, law is synonymous with legislation, so any phenomenon at odds with a given legal code is deemed illicit. Unconsciously guided by this legalistic approach, the modern critic anxiously seeks to find a precedent for the problematic case, thereby familiarizing and domesticating it.

In modern annotated editions of the *Commedia*, the reader is thus presented with two possibilities when confronting an interpretive crux: either the apparent abnormality is fit back into the rules of the otherworld or it is justified by pointing to divine omnipotence. Reducing the reader's interpretation to a choice between ordinary procedure or state of exception, this critical approach keeps the reader's discretion to a bare minimum. Yet Dante is deeply invested in the role of discretion in both law and art. Nor does he construe God's power as being absolutely released from the "laws" of the established order. For him, the exception can be bound by the rule of law and the rule of law can tolerate the exception. Sustaining this faith in "judgment calls," the poem encourages readers to think through these individual exceptions, to explore their contours as part of a collectively shared enterprise rather than delegating them to an amorphous sovereign decision.

Today, for example, when we witness the devils' refusal to allow Dante and Virgil into the infernal city at the Gates of Dis, the critical apparatus accompanying the text informs us that this is only a temporary setback (one illustrating, among other things, a crisis of faith on the part of Dante's character). We are already aware of and focused on the foretold solution to the impasse. But Dante spreads the refusal at the gates over two cantos (*Inferno* 8–9) in order to call attention to it as a pressing *problem*. Accustomed to the ambiguities arising from multiple, competing jurisdictions, medieval readers would have no doubt recognized the inherent drama of a scene of interregional travel in which the authority of a writ of safe passage is threatened. These situations of conflict, negotiated in narrative form, can still contribute to the aesthetic vitality of the work—but only if we turn away from the notes and reclaim our right to judge.

The limits of the law can be understood in a variety of ways. Above all, the law sets boundaries to human actions and punishes transgressions of such limits. These include the limit that Ulysses fails to heed (*Inf.* 26.108) and the "segno" (mark) that Adam and Eve "trespass" (*Par.* 26.117). But what happens when the public authorities charged with enforcing these limits fail to respect them, such as when figures such as Pope Boniface or King Philip the Fair of France overstep their authority? In his depiction of Boniface's exploitation of the sacraments and Philip's disregard of natural law, Dante exposes the vulnerability of a system of constraints when the offices instituted to uphold them are no longer treated as sacrosanct.

Yet even these expressions of tyrannical illegitimacy were, for Dante, more a symptom than a cause. He located the primary threat to the legal order elsewhere: in the disintegration of the cultural fabric that had long supported the law. The jurisdictional struggles between Church and Empire, together with the wars ravishing the Italian peninsula, had taken their toll on the elemental *fides* (trust) among citizens. When public opinion was tainted by partisan politics, when corrupt public officials had eroded the public trust, when the privileges of the clergy and nobility were treated as commodities, and when longstanding models of economic behavior were no longer respected, the ordinary course of positive law became just another legitimized form of violence. Detached from a shared cultural-political ethos, the law revealed its limits in the sense of its *limitations*. When, in *Purgatorio* 6, Dante compares Florence to a sick woman who changes "legge, moneta, officio e costume" (laws, coins, offices, and customs; 146) every time she tosses or turns in bed, he targets not the arbitrary suspension of the law but the arbitrariness of the laws themselves.[6]

Dante seeks in the *Commedia* to restore the common values, exemplary narratives, and disciplining practices that exist at the boundaries of the law. His poem is meant to occupy the interstices between law and life, to provide the moral and aesthetic preconditions necessary for the law to thrive. These "emergency poetics" form the cultural tissue beneath, beyond, above, and beside the law (see the descriptions of the individual chapters below). They foster a commitment to the law irrespective of its enforceability. In this light, the dismissal by modern critics of Dante's fealty to the reign of the Holy Roman Emperor as nostalgic and detached from historical reality reveals our own "limitations." Where such estimations equate the vigor of law with its enforcement, Dante understood that compliance with the law depended more on an imaginative attachment to the ideal of an universal "imperador" (emperor) who "in tutte parti impera" (rules in all parts; *Inf.* 1.124, 127) than in actual force.

Our understanding of the interconnectedness of legal and literary fiction-making still owes much to Ernst Kantorowicz's brilliant studies of this phenomenon. In particular, a resurgence of interest in political theology has led literary scholars to fruitfully reexamine Kantorowicz's epochal *The King's Two Bodies: A Study in Medieval Political Theology*,[7] especially by focusing on the readings of Shakespeare with which he opens the book.[8] Yet where Kantorowicz begins *The King's Two Bodies* with Shakespeare, he concludes his reconstruction of how the abstractions of the secular state emerged from medieval theological and juristic sources with a chapter on Dante. For Kantorowicz, Dante was just as important a theorist of political theology as Shakespeare was; he argues that Dante's concept of "man-centered kingship" anticipated Renaissance scholars' fascination with the "Dignity of Man," especially in *Purgatorio* 27 where the poet achieves "sovereign status" when Virgil crowns him lord over himself.[9]

Contemporary scholars focus more on Kantorowicz's use of Shakespeare than on his reading of Dante, and the preference is telling. Despite Kantorowicz's attempts at turning Dante into an anticipatory precursor of (early) modernity by reversing the chronology of his narrative, Dante stubbornly resists that characterization. As medievalists have long recognized,[10] the fundamental weakness of Kantorowicz's account of the theological origins of the modern state is his anachronistic focus on sovereignty, including his projection of Shakespearean modernity onto his readings of Dante and medieval law. Literary scholars tend to reproduce this slanted genealogical perspective, whether they focus on the absolutist or the constitutional possibilities of Kantorowicz's political theology.[11]

Laying aside the question of origins, my work turns to Dante's representations of justice as a means for understanding the role of imaginative constructs before the emergence of the modern state. Insisting upon the validity of a *ius commune* in the absence of an emperor or national monarch, Dante and the jurists created fictions that in many ways were the king's *only* body. Thus while Kantorowicz reads medieval legal fictions as legitimizing the early modern sovereign, in Dante's time it was the fiction of the sovereign as *lex animata* (law animate) that legitimized the continued creativity of the law. Not surprisingly then, Dante imagines the poet not as a sovereign who is above the law in the act of creation,[12] but rather as an activist judge, one who ingeniously adapts the law in order to keep it alive.

Like Kantorowicz, Carl Schmitt, the most prominent theorist of political theology, views the influence of theology in modern politics as unidirectional: through a process of secularization, religious thought and practice were transformed into the metaphysical basis of governance. For example, in Schmitt's oft-invoked account of the divine miracle as a model for the sovereign's right to suspend the law, we move from early modernity to Enlightenment, from theism to deism (on the road to atheism), from monarchy to liberal democracy, from decisionalism to proceduralism, and from religion to politics.[13] In this genealogical account, the theological beliefs of the medieval and early modern periods are presented as stable and straightforward.

Yet rather than the original source of the political, the metaphor of the miracle was itself always already politicized. As we will see in more detail in chapter 3, the monarchic view of the miracle, in which God intervenes in the laws of his own creation, was a late development in medieval thought, emerging out of theological voluntarism. This "absolutist" perspective on miracles clashed with a more standard "constitutionalist" understanding of them, one shared by theologians such as Thomas Aquinas. That view of the miracle held that while it was certainly an extraordinary event, it remained entirely bound by the principles of the ordained universe of nature and grace. The distinction between ordained and absolute accounts of divine action had tangible implications for the legitimacy of the pope's plenitude of power (especially when he "miraculously" issued privileges *contra ius*). In this light, when the angel miraculously descends to aid Dante and Virgil at the Gates of Dis, the extraordinary event cannot simply be explained with reference to God's omnipotence—we need to understand precisely which type of divine power the angel's intervention represents. Only then can we unlock its implications for how Dante viewed the relationship between the ruler (divine or secular) and his laws.[14]

Politics and theology thus are dynamically interdependent in the *Commedia*. One important clarification is necessary, however, before we can begin our exploration of Dante and the law. My intention in these chapters is not to "humanize" Dante's otherworld by depicting it as fallible or heterodox. We need to keep in mind throughout this discussion that God's justice and human justice necessarily differ. At the same time, as Beatrice makes clear in *Paradiso* 4, the divine cannot be communicated to human intellects except by analogy. Inevitably drawing on models of earthly justice in the construction of his otherworld, Dante cannot disassociate his creation from the legal ambiguities inherent in these borrowed structures. Indeed, the dialectical nature of the poem, its function as a narratological *quaestio*, depends on such a negotiation of differing viewpoints: it is to be expected that a journey through a juridical landscape would provoke questions about the foundations of law and political authority. Or, to put it another way, the ultimate theological orthodoxy of the poem does not preclude the experience of legal ambiguity in the course of the narrative.

My ultimate claim, then, rests on the conviction that the particular justice reserved for souls in the afterlife is not intended to be interpreted absolutely, but instead dialectically, even critically, and in relation to recognized forms of earthly justice. One thing, at least, I hope to make clear: the pitiless approach to the damned that modern scholars ascribe to medieval justice in general, and Dante's justice in particular, is off the mark. (If anything, such a conception has more in common with the sardonic realism of the devils than the fraught, inquiring justice of the *Commedia* at large.) After all, it is widely recognized that both the topography and the administrative structure of Hell represent a perverse, surreal vision of a corrupt Italian city. Why would such an infernal city be ruled by anything except an equally infernal legal order? I argue that the nightmarish terror of infernal justice derives from its strict interpretation of the law and its inability to fathom the exception: in other words, its "rigid justice" (*Inf.* 30.70). In challenging readers with a series of difficult "cases," Dante invites them onto the bench with him—and no one is excused from their responsibility to judge.

* * *

The structure of this book follows the four "edges" of the law that Dante explores: beneath, beyond, above, and beside. Each of these different perspectives centers on a specific legal concept: *infamia*, the role of personal reputation in legal cases; *arbitrium*, the prevalence of judicial discretion in the medieval legal system; *privilegium*, the problem of immunity and "singular" laws; and *pactum*, the question of how an informal or "naked" pact is binding. These legal concepts are not only frequent themes or motifs in the poem; they arise ineluctably from its basic constitutive elements (the shaming punishments, the discretional interrogation of the shades, the exceptional journey, and the informal agreements with the guardians of the otherworld). Ultimately, these global structures raise issues about the law's artifice that are critical for Dante's poetics as well, such as the tension between legal and literary verisimilitude treated in the first chapter.

Chapter 1 ("Beneath the Law: *Infamia*") examines the role of legal disgrace in Dante's work and its influence on his realistic style, his "mimesis." Unlike in our contemporary legal system, disgrace held official weight in medieval law. Dante's own indictment was based on evidence provided by *infamia facti* (infamy of fact). His sentencing and punishment then officially diminished his legal capacity, thereby creating an *infamia iuris* (infamy of law). I argue that, beginning with his post-exilic *Convivio*, Dante continuously explores this terrain of the social imaginary "beneath" the law, critiquing its presumptions but also seeking to reshape it according to his poetic vision. The poetics of reputation are especially notable in his treatment of sodomy in the *Commedia*. As an often notorious yet necessarily hidden sin, sodomy foregrounded the repercussions of using what "everyone knows" in legal decisions. In his portrayal of sodomites, Dante creates a form of realism based on the intransigent detail that counters the longstanding reliance on verisimilitude in courtroom procedure. Outside the city walls and under a new moon, Dante discovers that nothing is what it seems, and this revelation of the actual lives of Florence's most outstanding citizens, such as his own beloved teacher Brunetto, highlights the disconnect between the realistic social "picture" of society and the inescapable detail.

In addition to recognizing and ratifying social infamy, the law could also *produce* it by publically branding the condemned (*infamia ex genere poenae*). I read the aesthetic principles of the *contrapasso* (countersuffering) as a reflection on this ability of institutions to effect what they say through shaming punishments. In the "creative" punishments of Mohammed and Bertran de Born, as I show, Dante investigates the capacity of public authorities to transform a declarative statement into a legal reality.

In chapter 2 ("Beyond the Law: *Arbitrium*") I focus more directly on the law's "creativity," moving from the presuppositions beneath the law to the unanticipated legal and literary cases "beyond" it. In particular, I take issue with Kantorowicz's reading of the coronation scene atop Mount Purgatory as an allegory for the poet as sovereign. While I agree that Dante employs legal formulas to describe his artistic investiture, he models his newly achieved freedom on judicial discretion rather than, as Kantorowicz argues, on sovereign will. In Dante's time, *arbitrium* referred to a judge's discretion and was viewed by contemporaries as essentially rule-bound and normative. When Dante characterizes his poetic license as an "arbitrio" (*Purg.* 27.140), it follows that he is not imagining a "negative freedom" in the modern liberal sense. Instead, his license entails a circumscribed liberty that is necessarily justified, case-based, and beholden to higher norms.

Dante's character achieves this regulated poetic freedom through the reeducation he undergoes during the journey. In contrast to scholars who view the journey as a learning curve in which the Pilgrim must purge himself of pity for the damned, I argue that his progress teaches him how to better judge on a case-by-case basis. In *Inferno* he trains his estimative sensibility by playing the role of inquisitorial judge, investigating the truth of crimes and measuring the credibility of the damned as witnesses. At times, however, he appears to overstep his mandate, such as when he tortures certain of the damned to produce a confession (Pier della Vigna, Bocca degli Abati). In order to offset these potentially capricious judgments, Dante's character must ascend Purgatory and, by experiencing a program of moral exempla, internalize the values and norms of tradition. In light of this disciplinary mechanism, in which art and violence often converge, I argue that the disappearance of Virgil after the coronation scene does not symbolize Dante's individualistic liberation from tradition. On the contrary, I show, it represents the successful interiorization of a system he is now free to adapt.

Dante consistently treats the extraordinary grace of the Pilgrim's journey as if it were a legal privilege, such as an imperial rescript or a papal dispensation. Chapter 3 ("Above the Law: *Privilegium*") illustrates how the poet uses his own exemption—to pass through the afterworld alive—to question what it means to be "above" the law. Each time the infernal guardians test Dante's writ, they raise the issue of the ruler's relation to his laws. Can the unprecedented exception of the journey be reconciled with a stable and lawful conception of providence? Does the authority of the grant reside in God's capacity or his justice—in the constituted order, or in the sovereign's absolute decree?

Dante also contrasts his specific privilege to travel through the otherworld with the general immunities and privileges enjoyed by the clergy and the nobles, who too often acted as if they were "above" the law. In his depiction of the hypocritical Jovial Friars, the poet exposes the injustice of exempting individuals from the collective burdens of a community when nothing is demanded in return. In *Paradiso*, his noble ancestor Cacciaguida similarly contrasts the commodification of the rights of citizenship, now based more on social wealth than on duty, with the former military commitment to self-sacrifice. (That profound sacrifice is not unlike the one the poet endures in his exile for the "common good" of writing the *Commedia*.) Ultimately, I demonstrate, Dante seeks to refound the "privilege" of his poetic vocation on shared obligations rather than on individual rights.

Dante's various exchanges with the souls of the otherworld, in which he typically promises them worldly fame or recent news in return for information, exist in a kind of legal limbo. Neither in direct contrast with nor explicitly sanctioned by divine justice, they occupy an ill-defined space "beside" the law. In chapter 4 ("Beside the Law: *Pactum*"), I examine medieval contract law as a framework for understanding the "deals" Dante's character makes with the souls he encounters on his journey. In contrast with modern contract law, Roman and medieval law did not recognize consent as the primary mechanism for "binding" a given contract. Instead, economic transactions had to fit into preexisting schemas or molds in order to be recognized as enforceable (otherwise they remained simple promises, or what lawyers referred to as "naked pacts"). The transactions of *Inferno* expose the limits of shared standards and models as a way of forming binding agreements in light of the radical otherness of the devils and the damned. Such limit cases raise the question of what, if anything, can "dress"—or make binding—a contract when traditional schemas no longer apply.

Dante faced a similar contractual crisis as a poet. Excluded by exile from participating in traditional literary institutions, Dante needed to find new ways to "dress" his unconventional poem. Received literary genres, not unlike contractual types, could not keep pace when his vernacular literary practice moved beyond municipal poetry and its performative context. From monumental lyric poems such as "Tre donne intorno al cor mi son venute" to the addresses to the readers in the *Commedia*, Dante struggles to redefine the contract between author and reader.

Given the obsolescence of traditional categories, why did Dante entitle his work a "comedy"? In many ways the *Commedia* is itself a naked pact, unmediated by collective molds and schemas. The only "dress" Dante can furnish for his poem must be directly negotiated with readers, as when he swears by his *Commedia* to the truth of the monster Geryon. We see a similar breakdown in conventions in the pacts made with the devils, in which the epic values of Virgil's *Aeneid* are rendered "quaint" in the face of a total war with the enemies of God. Despite this descent into a state of nature, I argue, Dante's insistence on naming his poem and classifying it as a "comedy" is in fact a heroic act of cultural conservation—an attempt to salvage conventional schemas, not abandon them.

The book concludes with a brief examination of Dante's fantasy of homecoming in *Paradiso* 25. Near the end of both the poem and his life, the poet's fading hope for a reconciliation with his fellow citizens provides a final devastating instance of the limits of the law.

1

Beneath the Law
Infamia

Of the limits to the law discussed in this book, *infamia* was the one that affected Dante most deeply. When he was convicted in absentia of graft and sentenced to perpetual exile, he suffered a loss in official status that would have placed him "beneath" the protections of the city statutes. In addition to this legal form of infamy, *fama* in the sense of common knowledge was increasingly considered juridically relevant in Dante's time. According to contemporary records, the common "fama" was responsible for prompting the initial investigation into Dante's crimes.

In this chapter I will examine Dante's continued engagement with fame and infamy, from the early exilic work *Convivio* to the central cantos of *Paradiso*. For Dante, fame and infamy operate within the politics of reputation—of one's self and one's texts. They also play key roles in the representation and reproduction of social reality. In crucial passages in his work, Dante seeks to expose the mechanisms by which *fama* and *infamia* perpetuate a seemingly self-evident image of society. The famous realism of Dante's *Commedia*, for instance, assumes a more dialectical and polemical shade when viewed in light of the contemporary legal context, especially in terms of the growing reliance of lawyers and judges on *fama* in constructing a plausible likeness of an event. His mimesis is not only a diachronic development of an artistic trend, but also a synchronic challenge to the ways in which legal authorities harnessed the social imaginary of "what everyone knows." In lieu of this naturalizing picture, Dante celebrates the estranging detail.

Exile and Disgrace

In the fall of 1301, the government of Florence dispatched Dante Alighieri and two other envoys to the papal court in Rome. The mission capped a period of intense political activity for Dante, including a stint the preceding year as one of the six priors of the city (the highest office in the Florentine government). His diplomatic charge was to block, stave off, or at least mitigate the intervention of the French prince, Charles of Valois, in the factional struggle between the White and Black Guelphs. Charles had been sent as a mediator on behalf of Pope Boniface VIII.

When he was a prior, Dante had approved the expulsion of the most violent leaders of both the White and Black Guelphs. His political allegiance, however, was to the former—or perhaps more accurately, was set against the Blacks. Under the leadership of the arrogant and violent nobleman Corso Donati, the Black party was allied with Pope Boniface and his French troops. In the decisions he took as prior and, immediately after his term, in local assemblies, Dante had forcefully rejected the pope's claims of jurisdiction over Florentine affairs.

Dante's mission was unsuccessful; Boniface apparently had little interest in a truce. In early November 1301, Charles entered Florence with five hundred troops, nominally as a peacemaker. He was accompanied, however, by Corso Donati and other exiled Blacks who, in addition to committing outright acts of violence, immediately removed the current priors and installed priors of their own choosing. In this tumultuous political climate, Dante was accused of political corruption along with four other prominent Whites. Since he refused to return from his ambassadorship to answer these charges, he was heavily fined, exiled, and eventually sentenced to death should he set foot in Florence again. He never did.

We tend to think of Dante exclusively as a political exile. But he was also a convicted criminal who bore the disgrace of a guilty verdict. The Florentine *podestà* had sentenced him in a regular tribunal and through valid procedures—not as an enemy of the state, but as a corrupt public official. After failing to appear in court for charges of fraud, extortion, and other crimes connected to his term as prior of the city, Dante was convicted in absentia on January 27, 1302. Sentenced to two years of exile, he was also fined an exorbitant five thousand florins, ordered to repay any illicit gains within three days or risk confiscation of his property, and banned from public office for life. For refusing to heed these penalties and other summonses, in March of 1302 he was ultimately sentenced, along with fourteen other former Guelph officials, to death by fire. In 1311, an amnesty offered to a number of exiled White Guelphs expressly denied pardon to Dante and his sons. In 1315, a final condemnation designated Dante as a Ghibelline insurgent "rebel," who was to be beheaded if he came within the commune's purview.[1]

Given the severity of these punishments, it is easy to understand the animosity and sense of betrayal that suffuses Dante's writing. In early post-exilic works such as *De vulgari eloquentia*, for instance, he bitterly evokes the conditions of his banishment while ridiculing Florentine localism. In the Latin epistles, he tellingly identifies himself as "Dante Alighieri, a Florentine, and an undeserving exile." Most significantly, in the *Commedia*, Dante draws upon his personal experience to construct a critique of human judgment vis-à-vis God's judgment. Many of the damned he places in Hell belonged to Florence's most respected and illustrious citizenry, the elite members of the populace who had originally judged him. The poet reverses the earthly hierarchy of judges and judged by revealing the former's adherence to a moral universe driven by power and money, which he often represented as the infiltration of the Church in secular politics and its collusion with the emergent French monarchy. To cite just one example of Dante's textual revenge against his judges: In the Heaven of Mars, Cacciaguida decries "lo puzzo / del villan d'Aguglion" (the stink of the peasant from Aguglione; *Par.* 16.55–56), a reference to the jurist Baldo d'Aguglione, who had authored the amnesty of 1311 that excluded Dante and his sons. With marked symmetry, Dante accuses Baldo of "barattare" (committing graft; 57), the same crime with which the poet was charged on earth.

Despite the trauma of his banishment, there was apparently at least one thing worse for Dante than exile: infamy. In the "Letter to a Florentine Friend," written around 1315, Dante refuses a newly proposed amnesty that might let him return to his city. His reason is the ignominy that would follow his return: he refuses to be counted among the infamous. As he states in the letter, he will neither pay a settlement to those who unjustly accused him nor suffer, as a common criminal, the "stigma of oblation."[2] Unless he can return without diminishing "fame Dantisque honori" (Dante's fame and honor)—the only time in the Epistles Dante names himself— the poet will find his bread, and contemplate the stars and universal truths, elsewhere.

Why did Dante prefer exile to a tarnished reputation? Certainly, shame punishments had profound ramifications in a "face-to-face" society such as medieval Florence, and affected one's social, political, and economic status. But his reluctance to accept the proposed amnesty was not solely based on social pride. After fifteen years of exile, he had established himself as a "preacher of justice" by explicitly distinguishing between truth and appearance,[3] using his own undeserved punishment as a primary example. The dramas of judgment in the *Commedia* continuously call into question the institutional mechanisms of infamy and the instability of its juridical foundation. If Dante were to accept a settlement and submit to these degrading rituals, he would implicitly acknowledge and ratify the laws of public opinion and, in doing so, delegitimize the mission of his life's work. The cost for Dante of reintegration under these terms would be to discount the aesthetic, epistemological, and even metaphysical basis of his masterpiece.

Forms of Infamy

Dante's reluctance becomes more comprehensible when we consider the special legal repercussions of medieval infamy. Legal writers of the period distinguished primarily between two types of infamy: *infamia iuris* (infamy of law) and *infamia facti* (infamy of fact). The sources of *infamia iuris* were law and legal procedures. *Infamia facti* referred to social infamy deriving from the opinion of the community.

Glossators of Justininian's Digest defined *infamia iuris* as a privation or diminution of *fama*—*fama* signifying, in this usage, positive reputation or civic honor (*existimatio*).[4] As a legal sanction incurred for a transgressive act, this type of infamy damaged a culprit's legal capacity, disqualifying him or her from specific rights. Above all, it targeted one's juridical credibility (*fides*). Individuals labeled by public authorities as infamous lost the right to sue for damages; to accuse a non-infamous citizen of a crime; to act as a representative or advocate for others; to testify; and even, in the most extreme cases, to draft a valid last will.[5]

Civil lawyers organized the sources of infamy cited in the *Digest* (esp. *Dig.* 3.1–2) into three basic subcategories.[6] First, infamy was incurred *per sententiam* (by sentence) when a culprit became infamous after conviction and sentencing in a regular trial. Second, infamy was incurred *ipso iure* (by law) when a culprit was considered infamous from the very moment of having committed a crime, even in the absence of a regular trial and sentence. Debased professions and scandalous acts violating the sexual and moral norms of the community, such as adultery and sodomy, automatically defamed "by law." Third, infamy *ex genere poenae* (from punishment) resulted from submission to degrading corporal punishments, such as public scourging, exile, imprisonment, and forced labor.[7] These punishments marked the culprit with infamy even when conviction for the crime did not in itself normally defame.

The civil lawyers responsible for creating this tripartite schema (*per sententiam, ipso iure,* and *ex genere poenae*) strove to construe infamy as a predominantly legal phenomenon and to distinguish this juridical form from its looser counterpart, *infamia facti*.[8] For the most part, civilists limited their discussions of *infamia facti* to those few cases treated explicitly in the *Corpus iuris civilis*, such as when a son was disgraced by his father in his will. But the social origins of disgrace were never far from the surface. For example, many of the categories of undesirable persons defamed by *infamia ipso iure* were the same ones excluded by *infamia facti* from testifying in court. Further, civil lawyers acknowledged the porous border between social and legal disgrace when they used terms such as *notare* (to mark) and *macula* (blemish) in defining infamy. Visible to the entire community, the blemish of infamy depended as much on public shame as on legal censor. For this reason, it would often remain even after a punishment was rescinded or a sentence repealed, like the scar from a wound.[9]

In canon law, on the other hand, the applications of *infamia facti* were more expansive. Church authorities could not ignore the scandal created when members of the clergy openly engaged in illicit behavior. In the wake of the Gregorian reforms, canon lawyers elaborated a doctrine affirming the juridical relevance of what "the people of a certain city . . . commonly consider, judge, or perceive" about a person or event.[10] In this usage, *infamia facti*, *mala fama*, or often simply *fama* referred to the common hearsay about a crime, and was considered a verifiable form of public knowledge, situated between self-evident fact and untenable rumor. Social infamy could be invoked to initiate a criminal investigation, justify the torture of a suspect, and even to facilitate a conviction when direct evidence was otherwise lacking.[11]

The legal use of *infamia facti* gained prominence in the decretals of Innocent III (1160–1216), and was sanctioned by the Fourth Lateran Council in 1215.[12] For the reformist pope, a proactive approach to infamy was necessary to control the "clamor" about a crime. Innocent's concern was with the damage that manifest transgressive behavior on the part of the clergy could wreak on his Church's credibility. By incorporating and codifying *fama* within canon law, Innocent and his lawyers attempted to head off the destabilizing effects of ill fame, mediating the reality depicted by the Church and the one observed daily by its parishioners. In the ritual of *purgatio canonica* (canonical purgation), for example, the Church authorities attempted to reestablish their representation of the world by compelling the defamed priest to publicly swear his innocence. What counted in this ritual was not legal truth—since to be eligible for purgation the charges against the priest needed to be already dismissed—but the social fact of his purity.[13] By the same logic, if no infamy arose from an offense, Innocent found that there should be no prosecution, expanding on the idea that "the Church does not judge hidden offenses."[14]

While Innocent III used *fama* to turn the machinations of justice inward, to purge the Church leadership of any disgraces, jurists and judges working in communal Italy turned it outward, to more effectively prosecute local subjects and punish criminals.[15] The "popolo" governments of late medieval Italy, ruled primarily by elected members of various guilds, drew much of their fragile authority from the public enforcement of justice. As a result, any undiscovered crime and any unpunished criminal could be perceived as a threat to their legitimacy—a notion captured in the oft-quoted maxim: "It is in the interest of the republic that no crimes go unpunished."[16]

Infamia facti was a crucial instrument in the emergence of a public penal order because of the role it played in the inquisitorial procedure, a new method of prosecuting crime. According to Roman law, there was no case without an accuser; public authorities could not initiate an investigation of a crime unless a victim came forth. In this transactional vision of justice, the primary role of institutions was to mediate private conflict.[17] In the inquisitorial procedure (not to be confused with its radicalization in the later Inquisition of Heretical Pravity), however, judges investigated crimes on their own initiative, as part of the normal functions of their office. Originally sanctioned by Innocent to combat the potential scandal of wayward clerics, it quickly gained popularity with secular judges. Albertus Gandinus, a contemporary of Dante's and an active judge in various Italian cities, promoted the streamlined inquisitorial method as the most efficient way to get to the truth of a crime: "Since it does not require many formalities, guilt can be established more easily."[18]

The legality of this innovative procedure was maintained through the fiction that *fama* itself could accuse a defendant. As Innocent III put it: "It is not so much that the judge is himself the accuser; rather it is as if *fama* were accusing and clamor denouncing."[19] Standing in for the voice of the injured community, "fama deferente" (or "fama denunciante") quickly became an established feature in legal proceedings. City judges could use these formulations to inquire about a crime or charge a defendant even when no complaint had been lodged. Simplifying the process of legal discovery was not the only effect *infamia facti* had on the legal system. It also lessened the burden on whoever chose to "denounce" a crime: in existing accusatorial procedure, the complainant had been responsible for providing evidence and was normally bound to suffer a penalty, the *pena talionis*, if the case ended in acquittal. *Infamia facti* eliminated that impediment to prosecution.

Both *infamia facti* and *infamia iuris* touched Dante's life directly. As revealed in the transcription of his sentence, his crimes were denounced by public report ("fama publica referente") and he was thereafter investigated according to inquisitorial procedure ("per inquisitionem").[20] His ban from holding public office was a classic defamatory punishment, and his perennial exile could also be construed as infamy *ex genere poenae*. Yet the primary source of his legal infamy was the charge itself, *baractaria*. Although conventionally translated in English as graft, the term referred more generally to the misuse of public funds. As with other crimes harming Florence's *bene commune* (common good), *baractaria* was considered legally defamatory not only in doctrine but also in practice. Its severity can be measured by the fact that, as part of his sentence, Dante's name was to be recorded in the city statutes in order to underscore and perpetuate his infamy in the collective memory ("ut perpetua fiat memoria").[21]

Dante may not have conceived of his public disgrace in the exact technical terms employed by contemporary legal scholars, but he understood its consequences viscerally, from experience. His writings are invaluable to scholars for illustrating what documents cannot: the effect *infamia* had on an individual after the trial was over. His trenchant critique of earthly justice cannot be separated from his deeply personal investigation into the mechanisms of infamy. With the many unexpected sentences of divine judgment dramatized in the *Commedia*, Dante insists that the distinction between celestial citizens and infernal exiles cannot be based on *doxa*—on what people think they know.

Scholars have long singled out Dante's mimesis as a turning point in the history of literary forms. Yet his innovative poetics also need to be understood as a reaction to how the iconology of *fama*—the image a community has constructed around an individual or social group—influences questions of justice. The realism of the *Commedia* responds to prevailing forensic narratives by rebuking their reliance on verisimilitude. Dante's realism insists on the details of the individual cases over and above the likely or probable picture that *fama* suggests. Breaking with the rhetorical tradition of imaginatively reconstructing a plausible account of a crime, he invents a realism of estrangement.

At the same time, Dante does not simply reject legal infamy and community justice outright, as it might appear from a post-Enlightenment standpoint. Instead, he situates his literary creation in the space between notoriety and gossip, between sight and voice—the same space that those jurists seeking to verify the "clamor" of the populace with legal regulations sought to occupy. After all, in many ways the *Commedia* is itself an infamy-making machine, carefully identifying the damned by name, birthplace, and the essential circumstances of their biographies. When Guido da Montefeltro responds to Dante's inquiry about his identity "without fear of infamy" ("sanza tema d'infamia"; *Inf.* 27.66), his words are thus loaded with unintended irony. The distance from the moment of Guido's enunciation to that of our reading testifies to the success of the *Commedia* in establishing infamy across time and space. Indeed, Dante's masterpiece, the "carmi" (*Par.* 17.111) he fears will offend the powerful, can be viewed as a modern version of the *carmen famosum*, the libelous defaming song outlawed in Roman law. Dante's slanderous takedown of public authorities challenges their exclusive right to defame.

Infamia per sententiam: Dante's Conviction and Authorial Credibility in *Convivio* 1

The first repercussion Dante would have suffered from his verdict and sentence was a loss of credibility. In the law, a loss of reputation rendered an individual's testimony unreliable—*infamia* was closely connected with *intestabilitas*. This privation of juridical credibility carried over into other, less formalized forms of trustworthiness as well. Persons labeled untrustworthy by the state and disgraced in the eyes of their neighbors were de facto barred from patronage networks and economic transactions, since they were no longer able to pledge their good name—a fatal blow to their "credit."[22] *Infamia* marginalized Dante's word, just as exile did his person.

In Book One of *Convivio*, written only a few years after his conviction, Dante explores the relationship between reputation and credibility, *fama* and *fides*. In what serves as a prologue to the unfinished collection of poems and allegorical self-commentary, Dante begins by "purging" the work, presented metaphorically as the communal bread at a banquet, of possible "blemishes" ("macule")—possible objections to its style and structure.[23] Self-reference, the first blemish, violates the rhetorical precept forbidding the poet to speak about himself. The second blemish concerns the style of his commentary to the poems, which seems unnecessarily difficult and complex. Once he addresses these two accidental blemishes ("macule accidentali"; 1.5.1), Dante turns to a more substantial flaw: the bread he offers his readers is made of coarse oats, not wheat—that is, composed in the vernacular instead of in Latin.[24]

In the course of Dante's response to these anticipated objections, it becomes clear that they are considered blemishes on his work not absolutely and abstractly, but dialectically and in relation to the author's recent legal disgrace. In the legal writings of the time, *infamia* was continually defined, in fact, as a blemish or *macula*. Similarly, as we have seen, the public denial under oath of an infamous act was known as a *purgatio*. In purging his text of supposed imperfections, Dante uses the same language as if he were clearing his name of a public stain.

Yet Dante's references to the specific infamy he incurred through criminal conviction remain implicit, almost repressed. The institutional origin of the poet's damaged standing infiltrates the literary discussion only intermittently and symptomatically, often surfacing where it is least expected. For example, Dante argues early on that speaking about oneself in certain circumstances is necessary in order to defend oneself from "grande infamia": "When great infamy or danger cannot be avoided except by talking about oneself then it is permissible."[25] The poet uses Boethius as an example, explaining that the philosopher was compelled to defend himself against "the perpetual infamy (*perpetuale infamia*) of his exile, by showing it to be unjust."[26] The parallel with Dante's historical circumstances could not be clearer. Yet when he turns to justifying his own work, Dante speaks not of his exile but of the potential infamy that could arise from a misinterpretation of his love poems. He substitutes the public shame of criminal conviction with the more private shame of falling victim to erotic passion.

We have to wait until nearly the end of the first book, in the midst of an apparently unrelated discussion about the inherent goodness of the vernacular, for the juridical nature of Dante's infamy to be revealed. At this point in the treatise, Dante is concluding his explanation of why he wrote the work in the vernacular and not in Latin. The last reason given is the natural love he feels for his native tongue. This "perfect" love, Dante specifies, derives from the natural proximity the author feels to the vernacular as well as from the vernacular's proper activity, which we know from an earlier chapter is "to make manifest a conceived meaning" (1.10.9). In order to illustrate this Aristotelian notion of proper activity, Dante cites the capacity of the fox to smell, of the greyhound to run, and of man to practice the virtues. Among these virtues, he writes, justice is the most fully human, and is loved even by its enemies, just as its opposite, injustice, is hated by all.

Although the comment that injustice is hated seems offhand and irrelevant to the argument, Dante extends it, illustrating what he means by "injustice" with an additional gloss: "Sì come è tradimento, ingratitudine, falsitade, furto, rapina, inganno e loro simili. Li quali sono tanto inumani peccati, che ad iscusare sé de l'infamia di quelli, si concede da lunga usanza che uomo parli di sé, sì come detto è di sopra, e possa dire sé essere fedele e leale" (As, for example, treachery, ingratitude, falsehood, theft, rapine, fraud, and the like. All of these are such inhuman sins that to exonerate himself from the infamy incurred by them it is granted through long custom that a person may speak of himself, as has been said above, and may declare himself faithful and loyal; 1.12.10–11). By discussing such crimes at length,

Dante reminds readers of his initial justification for speaking about oneself, thus supplying a crucial forensic context for the "perpetual infamy" against which he must defend himself. Only in retrospect does that connection between rhetorical vices and legal crimes become evident.

Dante treats the consequences of his legally imposed infamy somewhat more explicitly in the process of purging the second "blemish" of his work: the "durezza" (difficulty; 1.3.2) of the commentary. In a famous passage describing the effects of his exile, he laments that many people have lost respect for both him and his writings after encountering him in a state of need:

> Ah, if only it had pleased the Maker of the Universe that the cause of my apology had never existed, for then neither would others have sinned against me, nor would I have suffered punishment unjustly—the punishment, I mean, of exile and poverty. Since it was the pleasure of the citizens of the most beautiful and famous daughter of Rome, Florence, to cast me out of her sweet bosom— where I was born and bred up to the pinnacle of my life, and where, with her good will, I desire with all my heart to rest my weary mind and to complete the span of time that is given to me—I have traveled like a stranger, almost like a beggar, through virtually all the regions to which this tongue of ours extends, displaying against my will the wound of fortune for which the wounded one is often unjustly accustomed to be held accountable. Truly I have been a ship without sail or rudder, brought to different ports, inlets, and shores by the dry wind that painful poverty blows. And I have appeared before the eyes of many who perhaps because of some report had imagined me in another form. In their sight not only was my person held cheap, but each of my works was less valued, those already completed as much as those yet to come.[27]

Dante ascribes his loss of status to an unjust sentence as well as to two specific repercussions of his punishment, "essilio e povertate" (exile and poverty). These de jure and de facto aspects of his infamy have combined to diminish the trustworthiness of his texts, which now require extensive commentary to regain a measure of authority.

To dissect how the public has processed his work, Dante focuses on the role of appearances. For him, what everyone knows is intimately connected to what everyone sees, either with their vision or in their mind. *Fama* quickly turns into *infamia* when there is a disjunction between what the public has imagined and what now appears in their sight. When the poet's future readers see him standing before them in a state of need, forced to display his "wound of fortune" to all, they lose respect for the man and his works. The injustice of being blamed for one's fortune derives from Boethius, but the figure of the visible wound is Dante's contribution. It speaks to the shame of being *seen* as guilty, of spectacles of humiliation, and of the permanent stains, *macule*, that remain in cultural memory long after the initial crime has taken place.

By describing his infamy as a wound rather than merely a stain or blemish, Dante summons to mind his attackers—the ones who inflicted such a blow. Rather than the effect of arbitrary fortune, then, the defaming "wound" reveals a relation of force. Specific agents emerge from behind the neutral institutions of infamy and a politics of labeling that creates victims as well as guilty subjects.

In blaming his banishment on the "pleasure of the citizens," Dante also seems to acknowledge the role played by *fama publica* in his eventual conviction. However, in his initial critique of public reputation as a criterion of judgment, he does not start in immediately with his undeserved infamy, or *mala fama*, as one might expect. Instead, he first dissects the basis for the positive reputation he previously enjoyed, his former *bona fama*. Demonstrating how "esteem inflates things with respect to the truth" (1.1.6), he represents the source of good reputation as the biased evaluation of a friend's good deeds: "A good reputation (*la fama buona*) is principally engendered by good thoughts in the mind of a friend, and this is how it is first brought to birth; for the mind of an enemy, even though it receives the seed, does not conceive. That mind which first gives birth to it, both to make its gift more fair and for the love of the friend who receives it, does not confine itself within the limits of the truth, but oversteps them" (1.3.7).[28] This overvaluation is embellished each time it passes from one person to another, until the final result is an "image" of the person's worth that exceeds reality: "Anyone who wishes, then, can clearly see that the image generated by *fama* alone is always greater, no matter what kind it is, than the thing imagined is in its true state" (1.3.11). The erroneous judgment of Dante and his work is produced not just by what the public sees now, but also by what they have formerly seen in their mind's eye; both perspectives are skewed and partial.

Dante's critique has various elements in common with what was written about *fama* in contemporary legal writing. Civil and canon lawyers shared Dante's reservations about the instability and uncontrolled dissemination of *fama*, peppering their discussions with maxims such as "fama facile oritur" (*fama* arises easily) and "ad dictum unius sequitur multitudo" (the crowd follows the pronouncements of one). When both the judge Gandinus, in the *Tractatus de maleficiis*, and the poet Dante, in the *Convivio*, cite *Aeneid* 4.174–75 regarding the dangerous mobility of *fama*,[29] it is clear that they are navigating common ethical territory: the epistemological status of *fama* is troubling for jurist and poet alike. At the same time, the similarity of their attacks on the reliability of public perceptions belie a competing interest in regulating—and justifying their right to regulate—common talk.

When Dante turns his attention from the causes of his formerly inflated reputation to those of his current debasement, from *fama* to *infamia*, he correspondingly shifts focus from the errors of imagination to those of sensory perception. At the beginning of chapter 4 of the first book, Dante gives three reasons why "a man's presence makes him less worthy than he really is" (1.4.2): the first is immaturity of mind, the second is envy, and the third is human impurity (the universal blemish of original sin). The first is the most relevant for Dante's exploration of *fama/infamia*. Dante draws a stark contrast between mundane sensory perception and true insight into the proper function and end of things: "The majority of men live according to the senses and not according to reason, like children; as such they do not understand things except simply by their exterior, and they do not perceive the goodness of things, which is ordained to a proper end, because they keep shut the eyes of reason which penetrate to a vision of it" (1.4.3). Because of this deficiency in reason, when the populace encounters a discrepancy between what they have heard about someone's *fama* and what they observe before them, they treat what they had heard as a lie and, judging according to their senses alone, disparage the person they had previously esteemed.

The social phenomenon behind the production of *infamia* thus stands in a chiastic relation to the processes responsible for creating *fama*. *Fama* arises out of an individual observation and then circulates, through word of mouth, until it becomes a collective image. *Infamia* results when an individual perceives a contrast between that collective image and what he or she can observe directly with the senses. Instead of retaining one and rejecting the other, Dante attempts to explain why *both* ends of this relay are marred by errors in perception. In doing so, he implicitly erodes the juristic distinction between *scientia* and *fama*, vision and voice.

To fully comprehend Dante's exploration into the mechanisms of popular opinion, we need to contrast his discussion of the immature mind with later comments about the populace's lack of discernment. As part of his defense of the "substantial blemish" of writing in the vernacular, Dante disputes the notion that the vernacular is inferior. He blames that notion on the "contemptible men of Italy" (1.11.1) who demean their own vernacular. As with his discussion of the origins of *infamia*, he sets up a contrast here between purely sensible sight and rational vision: "Just as the sensitive part of the soul has eyes by which it apprehends the difference in things with respect to their external coloring, so the rational part has its own eye by which it apprehends the difference in things with respect to how they are directed to some end: and this is discernment."[30] Because they are blind to the teleological nature of this Aristotelian cosmos (in which the proper activity of the vernacular is clarity of expression), most men are reduced to following the judgment of others. They rely on the public outcry ("grido"; 1.11.4) to distinguish good from evil and truth from falsehood. The "populari persone" (common people; 1.11.6), whose occupation in a trade prevents them from developing "l'abito di vertude" (the habit of virtue; 1.11.7), are the most reliant on and vulnerable to public rumor. Unable to think for themselves, they blindly follow the belief that their vernacular is inferior to others.

With his analysis of the passivity of popular opinion, Dante continues to denigrate the role of exterior vision in the formation of a *sensus communis*, instead privileging an inner sight that, guided by reason, perceives a reality structured by proper activities and ends. This contrast, between outward appearances and inward reality animated by reason, anticipates the hermeneutical approach undertaken in the rest of the treatise. In the remaining books, the author will reveal the "vera sentenza" (true meaning) of the poems, which no one can see because they are hidden underneath the veil of allegory (1.2.16). In particular, he claims that the love object of the poems, the *donna gentile* (noble lady), should be understood allegorically as a personification of philosophy rather than as a flesh-and-blood woman. Dante had already introduced the *donna gentile* in his first experiment in self-commentary, *Vita nova*. In that work, she functions as a love interest who appears after Beatrice's death and momentarily leads the poet into unfaithfulness, in thought if not in deed. In the *Convivio*, however, Dante reimagines this episode as an allegory for the philosophical studies he undertook as consolation for losing his beloved.

Many readers of *Convivio* have found it difficult to accept Dante's assertion that the figure of the *donna gentile* was originally intended to personify philosophy rather than represent a genuine love interest. But the author may have expected, and indeed invited, such skepticism. In juxtaposing the interpretive questions of his poems with those of his alleged crimes, Dante problematizes the relationship of what everyone knows to what everyone sees. In both of these interpretive cases he suggests the fallibility of the self-evident. Challenging readers to believe that, despite appearances, he did not betray Beatrice, he tacitly erodes the certainty of the criminal charges against him.

Infamia ipso iure / infamia facti: Verisimilitude and Sodomy

First visible in the Epistle and in *Convivio*, the dialectic relationship between infamy and justice remains a prominent concern for Dante throughout his postexilic corpus. He returns to the problematic of *fama/infamia* with particular force near the end of this literary trajectory, in the central autobiographical cantos of *Paradiso*. In one tense, culminating episode, Dante's character finally learns both the explicit details of his impending exile and the purpose behind his otherworldly journey. His ancestor Cacciaguida bears the news, foretelling how any outcry of guilt, however undeserved, will cling to the injured party: "La colpa seguirà la parte offensa / in grido" (*Par.* 17.52–53). But this Anchises-like figure also charges Dante with a compensatory higher mission: to reform society by relaying what he saw and heard in the otherworld. That is to say, he must write the poem we are reading.

Even more than in *Convivio*, Dante's defamatory poetics are meant to rectify his damaged reputation. Exposing the hypocrisy of those on high, Cacciaguida tells him, will not only serve as bitter medicine for his contemporaries, it will bring him "honor" (*Par.* 17.135) in posterity. Specifically, Cacciaguida exhorts the Pilgrim to make his otherworldly vision manifest: "tutta tua visïon fa manifesta" (128). This visualization of "hidden crimes" will challenge and destabilize what had previously seemed so evident in the collective imaginary (in terms of innocence as well as guilt). The depiction of souls recorded in the *Commedia* will in this way directly intervene in the "fama" (138) about these persons, revising popular assumptions about their status and credibility. Ultimately, the *Commedia* will function as a cry or "grido" (133) that damages the powerful while it simultaneously—almost as a felicitous side effect—remedies the outcry responsible for the author's disgrace.

Gherardo Ortalli has suggested that the *Commedia* can be viewed as a giant collection of defaming portraits,[31] similar to the depictions of criminals painted on the city walls in Dante's time. As in these officially sanctioned portraits, Dante portrays the shades in ironically emblematic fashion with respect to their sins, and often identifies them by their full names. Yet contemporary viewers of Dante's *pittura infamante* would have been startled by his revisions to the accepted canon of the disgraced. When Ciacco reveals in canto 6 of *Inferno* that some of Florence's most respected citizens are among the damned, he is also announcing a guiding principle of the work: that neither the sentences of the damned nor of the saved can be predicted by common opinion.

Where famous souls have been banished to the deepest recesses of Hell despite their reputation and status, a number of unexpected personages are uncovered among the saved. An adulterer (Solomon), an adulteress (Cunizza), a prostitute (Rahab), two heretics (Siger and Joachim), and two pagans (Trajan and Ripheus) all manage to elude God's Book of Infamy. Those blessed souls are the very same marginal figures who, according to earthly justice, would have been considered infamous "instantaneously," *ipso iure*, without a trial or sentence.[32] With this otherworldly redistribution, Dante exposes how, without any intervening procedure, social norms could be wrongly taken for legal findings. Because of the blurred line between public knowledge and the law, known malefactors were simply presumed guilty without ever being tried for a particular act. In this instance, the role of law was to reinforce and institutionalize the prior judgments of a community—to ratify rather than impose. In contrast to infamy by sentence, then, infamy by law was primarily descriptive rather than normative. But what rendered this description so convincing in the first place? What made it so "manifest" that it required no further demonstration?

The normally disgraced persons whom Dante counts among the saved in the *Commedia* are well studied, and consequently no longer startle readers. Yet the poet no doubt intended his distribution of damned and saved to jolt his contemporaries, and in several passages he accompanies these revelations with admonishments against rash judgment. In *Paradiso* 20, for example, after his presentation of the noble pagan Ripheus—damned by Virgil, saved by Dante—the Eagle warns: "E voi, mortali, tenetevi stretti / a giudicar: ché noi, che Dio vedemo, / non conosciamo ancor tutti li eletti" (And you mortals, hold back from judging, for we, who see God, do not yet know all the elect; *Par.* 20.133–35). Critics examining this passage tend to focus on how it foregrounds the moral dilemma at the heart of Dante's endeavor—that the *Commedia*, more than any other literary work before it, relies on the art of judging another. Yet it is important to recall that the imperial Eagle does not condemn judgment per se, but rather the practice of rushing to judgment based on presumptions of fact.

Dante has in his critical sights a particular mode of evaluation, one based on likelihood and probability. He is especially suspicious of the practice of using previous behavior to predict future guilt, an approach to justice encapsulated in the legal presumption *semel malus semper malus* (once a criminal, always a criminal). Dante's underlying critique comes to the fore in Aquinas's outburst against rash judgment in *Paradiso* 13:

> Non sien le genti, ancor, troppo sicure
> a giudicar, sì come quei che stima
> le biade in campo pria che sien mature;
> ch'i' ho veduto tutto 'l verno prima
> lo prun mostrarsi rigido e feroce,
> poscia portar la rosa in su la cima;
> e legno vidi già dritto e veloce
> correr lo mar per tutto suo cammino,
> perire al fine a l'intrar de la foce.
> Non creda donna Berta e ser Martino,
> per vedere un furare, altro offerere,
> vederli dentro al consiglio divino;
> ché quel può surgere, e quel può cadere.

> (And let not people be too sure to judge, like one who appraises the oats in the field before they are ripe: for I have seen all the previous winter long the thornbush appear rigid and fierce, but later bear the rose upon its tip, and I have seen a ship run straight and swift across the sea for all its course, only to perish at last when entering the port. Let not dame Bertha and messer Martin believe, because they see one stealing, another offering, that they see them within God's counsel, for that one can rise up, and this one can fall. *Par.* 13.130–42)

Unaware of the hidden content of an individual's conscience, the proverbial Bertha and Martin base their judgment on what someone has done (stolen or made an offering) in the past. They fill in any blank spaces with what the picture *should* look like, basing such suppositions on mere glimpses. The examples of the late-blossoming rose and the sudden shipwreck reprove those leaps to judgment, and demonstrate that the specifics of a case cannot be reduced to probable scenarios.

In the reference to the falsely-accused thief, Dante evokes the archetypal Christian rebuke to presumptive justice: the moment when Jesus pardons the repentant thief on the cross. In legal discourse, in contrast, the infamy of habitual thieves was often assumed as "probable cause" to deviate from procedural protocol; their disreputable status effectively placed them "beneath the law." Yet within a narrative of conversion, the innocence of such people, however implausible, must always be presumed, since the movement of the will, that "yes and no you do not see" (*Par.* 13.114), does not follow the laws of normally predictable phenomena.

Dante emphasizes hermeneutical profundity in this passage, articulating the imperative to "fish for the truth" (*Par.* 13.123) deep beneath the surface of appearances. This reminder brings us back to the contrast between vision and reality that characterizes the poet's treatment of *fama* and *infamia* in *Convivio*. The implicit association between linguistic and legal judgment I suggested was at play in *Convivio* rises again to the surface in these cantos of *Paradiso*.

Aquinas's critique of presumptive justice culminates in a long gloss to a phrase he uttered three cantos earlier, about the biblical king Solomon. Aquinas had singled out Solomon for his wisdom, unparalleled among the illustrious teachers of theology presented in this Heaven of the Sun: "se 'l vero è vero / a veder tanto non surse il secondo (if truth is true, no second ever rose to see so much; *Par.* 10.113–14). But how, wonders Dante, can Solomon's wisdom surpass that of the two most perfect human beings ever created, Adam and Christ? Proceeding in scholastic fashion, Aquinas distinguishes from wisdom in its own right and regal prudence, the wisdom necessary to judge one's subjects. Only in the latter acceptation is Solomon's wisdom without peer. Aquinas's explanation is logically impeccable, but without this virtuosic example of self-commentary, the underlying meaning of his speech would have remained opaque, both to Dante's characters and to his readers. By framing the question of culpability within a linguistic gloss to a purposefully ambiguous expression, Dante locates the meaning of human actions deep within the recesses of authorial "intenzion" (*Par.* 13.105).

Aquinas's theoretical account of God's justice retrospectively illuminates an earlier encounter in Dante's journey: the improbable salvation of Buonconte da Montefeltro. In presenting the details of Buonconte's ultimate fate in *Purgatorio* 5, Dante creates a limit case that challenges the practice of prejudging known malefactors. In this group of the late repentant, Dante encounters the souls who suffered violent deaths and only turned to God in the last moments of their lives. Many of Dante's readers would have recognized the mercenary captains encountered on the slope of ante-purgatory, and many too would have heard of their propensity for violence. Indeed, these violent inclinations reemerge when the souls recount their blood-filled final moments on earth. Yet despite all precedents and previous offenses, only one detail is required to save them, as exemplified in the narrative of Buonconte.

Buonconte was killed at the battle of Campaldino, fighting for the Ghibellines of Arezzo. (Dante fought on the side of the Florentine Guelphs.) We learn that after Buonconte's death an angel and a devil fought over his soul, much like how St. Francis and the Devil had fought over the soul of Buonconte's father, Guido, in *Inferno* 27. In contrast with that episode, however, in which the devil proved himself an excellent logician, this time the angel is the better lawyer, and wins possession of the soul. Frustrated with the outcome of the case, the demon laments that Buonconte, despite his record of violent behavior, gets off on a technicality, on account of a single "lagrimetta" (little tear; *Purg.* 5.107). The demon's lament is not misplaced. What saves Buonconte is indeed an implausible detail. He dies uttering the name of Maria, with a "little tear" in his eyes, and with his hands making the sign of the cross. Thus, while the father Guido provides a concrete illustration of moral shipwreck at the end of his journey, the son Buonconte exemplifies the late blossoming rose, exiting life with the flower of Maria on his lips. Dante drives home the power of such details in the unlikely story that follows.

Buonconte's body was never recovered, and was apparently the object of much speculation. Furious at losing Buonconte's soul, the demon covers the valley in fog and calls forth a violent rainstorm. Buonconte's body is swept away by the ensuing current and buried beneath the riverbed of the Arno. None of this elaborate description is in any way expected, probable, or verisimilar. Buonconte realizes this when he tells Dante: "Io dirò vero, e tu 'l ridì tra' vivi" (I will tell the truth, and you retell it among the living; *Purg.* 5.103). Dante is thus a witness twice over—first for the circumstantial evidence he and others observed on the battlefield at Campaldino, and then for the unseen reality of what actually happened to the body.

The odd, seemingly extraneous interlude revealing the outcome of Buonconte's missing corpse underlines the dangers of relying on a likely or verisimilar reconstruction of an event. Verisimilitude had, of course, played an important role in forensic narrative since ancient times, and its potential uses would have been familiar to Dante and his contemporaries through the works of Cicero and Quintilian. For these authors, it was the responsibility of advocates to relay the facts of a case within a vivid, credible narrative in order to convince a jury of their version of events. They dealt, as orators, in the realm of the probable, relying on the *circumstantiae* of the case to supplement direct evidence and to construct an argument that would enforce their credibility (and produce a conviction). In addition to information about the time, place, and manner of the crime, these "artificial" proofs often highlighted the character of the accused, including his or her family, nationality, sex, status, education and lifestyle. Marshalling together these identifying marks, the orator created an argument that would place his audience at the scene of the crime, rendering them virtual eyewitnesses to its easily imagined reenactment. The details that rendered such a narrative plausible or convincing depended in large part on the perceived stability of character, and on the reliable categories of *dignitas* and *persona*.[33]

In medieval theories of evidence, verisimilar *fama* migrated from a mode of persuasion practiced by orators and advocates to a means of discovery employed by judges.[34] The foundational text medieval lawyers used to justify the probative value of such evidence was *Digest* 50.17.114: "In obscure things one usually considers what is more likely (*verisimilius*) or what happens for the most part (*quod plerumque fieri solet*)." Drawing on this citation, Gandinus argued that for obscure crimes, a suspect of ill repute (*mala fama*) could be tortured on the basis of hearsay, as the past behavior of such a man suggested he could have plausibly (*verisimilius*) committed, or at least possessed knowledge of, the crime.[35] Gandinus therefore advised judges to evaluate the "circumstances" of a suspect—his friends, the locales he frequented, his habits, and his reputation among neighbors—in order to form an opinion about the likelihood of his guilt. In canon law, ecclesiastical judges were similarly instructed to discover whether the *verisimilis suspicio* (verisimilar suspicion) implicating a suspect was derived from biased or reliable sources. Originally, this verisimilar *infamia* served only as a means to compel a prelate to swear an oath of innocence. Yet by the thirteenth century, common fame had been elevated to the status of a *presumptio probabilis* (probable presumption), powerful enough to initiate a criminal investigation or aid in conviction when full proof (*plena probatio*) was wanting.

The oft-discussed mimesis of the *Commedia* assumes renewed significance when examined through the lens of forensic verisimilitude.[36] Rather than being read as a literary-critical milestone on the teleological path ending in modern realism,[37] it can be appreciated for its critical engagement with another, competing form of representation. In response to the employment of verisimilitude in legal contexts, that is, Dante creates a realism based on the intransigent detail—a realism of the improbable. Throughout the otherworldly journey, his eschatological perspective on past actions reveals a reality different from the one assumed in *Dig.* 50.17.114. His reality comprises the less likely events that occur outside of "for the most part." Namely, Dante rejects the practice, inherited from the rhetorical-juridical tradition, of "profiling" suspects. (As we have seen, that representational style was incompatible with Christian conversion.) His brand of illusionism, however, seeks not to reconfirm the self-evident, but instead to expand the collective sensibility of what could perhaps be. To reconfigure such stubborn unconscious assumptions, Dante must first dissolve the cohesive social picture that filters his readers' experiences of the world and sanctions its hierarchies. For this project, his best weapon was the implausible yet ineluctable detail.

Dante's realism of estrangement, and its relation to the social poetics of *fama*, are conspicuously on display in his treatment of the sodomites in *Inferno* 15–16. The sinners in these cantos inhabit the circle of the violent, in the subcircle of the violent against God. This subcircle is further divided among those who sin against God directly (the blasphemers); against his "offspring," nature (the sodomites); and against his "grandchild," art (these are the usurers, who sin against productive work). All three categories are subjected to the same horrifying punishment. They are scorched by an eternal rain of fire, albeit to different degrees—the blasphemers must lie flat on the burning sands, the usurers are sitting, and the sodomites run in continuous circles (if they halt even momentarily, they must endure the punishment of the blasphemers for a hundred years). The rain of fire is an especially appropriate torment for the sodomites since, according to the account in Genesis, God visited the same punishment upon the inhabitants of Sodom and Gomorrah. In other words, this punishment is the only one in Dante's poem that is based on a "historical" event. The poet-as-judge withdraws in these cantos to let God's art of justice (visible both in the rain of fire and in the embankments providing shelter from the fiery downfall) speak for itself.

In canon law, the manner in which God first investigated and then avenged the transgressions of Sodom and Gomorrah had served as a model for earthly justice at least since Gratian's *Decretum*.[38] In particular, God's handling of the notoriety of the sodomites functioned as a touchstone in legal treatments about *infamia facti*.[39] Innocent III, for instance, repeatedly references the ill repute of Sodom and Gomorrah in his discussions about the probative value of *fama*, especially this passage from Genesis 18.21: "I will go down now, and see whether they have done altogether according to the cry of it, which has come unto me; and if not, I will know." In his encyclicals, the pope cites that biblical episode as a precedent authorizing the inquests set in motion by *fama*. The fact that an omniscient God descended from the heavens to verify for himself ("descendam et videbo") the outcry ("clamor") about Sodom's depravity demonstrates that local bishops are obliged to investigate whenever the "public outcry or *fama*" of a priest's transgressions "reached the ears of his superiors."[40] (Dante's own sentence claims that he was prosecuted according to inquisitorial procedure after the "fama publica" about his crimes had "reached the ears and notice of the court."[41])

Like the divine judge of Genesis 18.21, Dante's character descends in *Inferno* 15–16 to a simulacrum of Sodom. But unlike in the biblical narrative and its juridical commentaries, what he discovers there is not what he expected: "Siete voi qui, ser Brunetto?" (You're here, sir Brunetto? *Inf.* 15.30). This passage, in which the Pilgrim is surprised and dismayed to find his revered teacher in Hell, has been justly celebrated for its pathos. But its importance to understanding the link between representation and justice in Dante's system has yet to be fully investigated. In the scene, the Pilgrim addresses his teacher with the deferential second-person "voi" form and the honorary title "ser." With these remnants of former esteem, the poet signals the violent dissimilarity between someone's public persona and how they act in specific circumstances (especially when no one can see them, such as at night, "under a new moon"; *Inf.* 15.19). Dante's defaming poetics can be grasped in synthesis in this contrast between semantic deference and the haunting deixis of *qui*.

The legal context of Genesis 18.21 can also shed light on a major crux of this canto: the lack of a historical basis for condemning Brunetto. Dante scholars have long sought in vain for corroborating evidence that Brunetto and other famous damned souls in this circle were known by contemporaries to have engaged in sodomy.[42] But such notoriety would run counter to the poet's primary aim in these cantos: to demonstrate that the verisimilar picture constructed around an individual is unreliable as forensic proof. On the contrary, Dante deliberately selects some of Florence's most outstanding citizens to exemplify the sin of sodomy, and even sacrifices the reputation of his teacher Brunetto for the sake of his argument. While the canon lawyers writing about God's descent to investigate the rumors about Sodom were concerned with attenuating potential scandal—protecting the separateness and charisma of their class—Dante's depiction is meant to scandalize. Outside the city's gates at twilight, Dante's character stumbles across an illicit subculture, and what he witnesses firsthand utterly contradicts any probable reconstruction of events. By uncovering these hidden crimes, the poet violates the inner circle of the credible, eroding the distinction between individuals traditionally considered suspect and those of intact reputation.

Dante's understanding of the representational potential of *fama* can also help us better grasp the seemingly paradoxical tension between his character's positive treatment of Brunetto and the poet's placement of his teacher in Hell. More than any other "sympathetic sinner," Dante's character treats Brunetto with respect and apparently genuine admiration and affection. When the two meet, he extends his hand to touch his master's burnt face, and then lowers his head in reverence as they walk together. In almost open opposition to divine justice, he wishes a different fate for his teacher, that he might yet dwell among the living. Moreover, the poet of the *Commedia* recognizes that as long as he will live, Brunetto's words will live on in his own. Most famously and most poignantly, in Dante's last glimpse of Brunetto he depicts him receding into the distance as if he were the winner, and not the loser, of a footrace.

For readers alert to the ironies of context, however, these apparent gestures of sympathy shed further light on the nature of Brunetto's sin. While Dante the character professes reverence, Dante-as-poet places Brunetto and the other sodomites within a landscape that severely undermines that reverence. The sterility of the burning desert sands creates an ironic frame for Brunetto's attempt to reproduce himself through the mind of his student, offsetting his depictions of the disciple as a "sweet fig" (*Inf.* 15.66), "plant" (74), and "holy seed" (76). In a similar fashion, the endless, circular footrace of the sodomites stands in contrast with the "glorious port" (*Inf.* 15.56) awaiting Dante, with its implicit suggestion of eternal rest. Dante's character will eventually return to his celestial "home" (54), while the damned remain forever "banished" (81) outside the city walls. In light of this journey toward eternity, the sodomites' concern for immortal fame—through political actions and civic-minded writings— begins to appear more tragicomic than heroic.

Recent criticism on the relationship between Dante and Brunetto has demonstrated the extent to which the poet's irony undermines the protagonist's conflicted sympathy.[43] But why should Dante's character express special sympathy toward the sodomites and experience "non dispetto, ma doglia" (not scorn, but grief; *Inf.* 16.52) at their condition? Why are the judgments of poet and pilgrim at odds in this circle more than in any other?[44]

I would suggest that Dante emphasizes his character's flawed process of evaluation in this episode because of the long-standing associations in legal discourse between sodomy and social infamy. Dante uses his own inability to see what's in front of him to question the domineering force of *fama* in predetermining perceptions. He dramatizes his own misperceptions about Brunetto in order to illustrate how such fictions function more broadly across society—regardless of the "facts" before one's eyes. Exemplifying the enduring power of the social imaginary,[45] Dante's character succeeds in discerning "la cara e buona imagine paterna" (dear, kind paternal image; *Inf.* 15.83) underneath Brunetto's burnt visage. Even in Hell, he continues to enact the process of false estimation examined in *Convivio* 1, relying on a biased, inflated "image" of his friend. Yet the brutal details of the poet's realism prove the Pilgrim's vision to be naive, a state of psychological denial undermined by the objective circumstances surrounding him. Like the stink of the siren's belly, the "piaghe" (lesions; *Inf.* 16.10) of the sodomites are meant to awaken readers from their unconscious projections of how the world should be.

Dante's powerful commentary notwithstanding, an element of ambiguity persists in these cantos. This ambiguity depends less on Dante's judgment of Brunetto as an individual and more on the ideology his teacher espouses: that of worldly immortality. On the one hand, Brunetto's eternal damnation discredits his commitment to "living on" in cultural memory through his words and deeds. When viewed through the perspective of celestial glory, Brunetto's negative example exposes the false promise of temporal acclaim (a point Dante will reiterate in the discussion about artists' shifting reputations in *Purgatorio* 11). His attempt to transcend the life cycle of the species by extending the memory of his individual identity— summarily represented in his attachment to his full name—is met with a punishment that highlights the mortal biological self, leaving him naked, exposed, and a slave to necessity.[46]

Yet Brunetto's dedication to the polis distinguishes him from the anonymous seriality of those among the damned who, like autumn leaves, fall ceaselessly into the Acheron. Brunetto represents for Dante an ideal of civic humanism and collective sacrifice that resists facile moralization. Indeed, his former master serves as a model for an enduring, revisionist *fama* (*fama* in its various acceptations, not just in our diminished notion of celebrity) that itself overshadows the ephemeral opinions of the crowd. In Brunetto's *Rettorica*, a partial translation and commentary of Cicero's *De inventione*, the exiled Florentine statesman draws inspiration from the unjustly exiled Roman orator.[47] In *Inferno* 15, Brunetto's pupil now inhabits the role of the Roman Cicero against the Fiesolan Catilines. His sacrifice for the common good will bring short-lived disgrace, but will also secure glory in posterity.

Indeed, the paternal Brunetto, who indicates for the Pilgrim only those fellow damned "di gran fama" (of great fame; *Inf.* 15.107), introduces many of the lessons about *fama/infamia* that the ancestral Cacciaguida (whom he also addresses with the respectful "voi" form) will elaborate in *Paradiso* 15–17. Most notably, Brunetto's prophecy of Dante's exile—that the Florentine populace will turn against him because of his "ben far" (just actions; *Inf.* 15.64)—will be explained and expanded upon by Cacciaguida in *Paradiso* 17. In both cases, these figures promise Dante future "honor" (*Inf.* 15.70; *Par.* 17.135) as a palliative for his earthly bad fortune: his work, his voice, will bring him enduring literary glory. Dante's *infamia*, begotten by exile, will be transformed into *fama* by his defamation of others.

Of course, in the case of Brunetto, the prediction of Dante's literary greatness is simultaneously ironic, since one of the pupil's most effective defamatory portraits will target the teacher himself. The richness and ambiguity of this canto hence depends on two parallel, but temporally distinct, instances of defamation with regards to Brunetto. During his life on earth he bore the stains of infamy because he was sentenced to exile, foreshadowing Dante's unmerited punishment and enhancing the emotional camaraderie with him. In death, however, Dante-the-poet will deprive Brunetto of positive *fama* by exposing him as a sodomite. The wounds incurred by the poet's pen will prove to be more indelible than those instituted by official justice.

Infamia ex genere poenae: How to Do Things with Wounds

Mohammed and Bertran de Born

Of the three subcategories of legal infamy, the ambiguous nature of infamy *ex genere poenae* posed a special problem for medieval jurists, who struggled to formulate an adequate definition for it. There was, for instance, the difficulty of deciding whether *infamia* was a cause or an effect of punishment. Exile, exclusion from public office, whipping, and forced labor defamed a culprit, but they were also penalties arising from the conviction of an infamous act. As a result, jurists disagreed about whether a penalty could defame on its own, or only when accompanied by a sentence of infamy. Those who distinguished infamy by sentence from infamy by punishment argued that the former was permanent while the latter would expire as soon as the punishment had been fulfilled (as in the case of temporary exile). Those jurists who saw infamy by sentence and infamy by punishment as inextricably linked, however, conceived of such punishments as the expression and application of the defaming sentence.[48] In this view, the sentence was the content of infamy, and the punishment was the form. Both had to exist in order to defame an individual.[49]

At its foundation, the source of the ambiguity around infamy by punishment was its performative aspect, its ability to effect what it said. Infamy *ipso iure* described someone who was already viewed as socially infamous, fitting word to world; infamy *per sententiam* ordered that the culprit be rendered infamous, fitting world to word. Infamy *ex genere poenae* went in both directions: it simultaneously enacted what it described, pronouncing the condemned infamous and then making it so. What was at stake was nothing less than the creative force of the law, its capacity to bring things to life simply by showing them to be the case.

Dante explores the speech act of defamation through his presentation of the *contrapasso* (countersuffering), a form of retributive justice through which the punishment is conceived to fit the crime. Dante renders this "fit" aesthetically, by turning the punishment of the souls into an ironic emblem of their sins. The punishments mark the souls' bodies with their faults and announce their crimes to all who behold them. As we have already seen, Dante had special insight into what it meant to have the "wounds" of one's punishment (exile, poverty) on display for everyone to see and judge, and in the *Commedia* he asks readers to contemplate the circumstances under which such a wound can be made to signify. This performative aspect of defamation, its ability to "blame the wound on the wounded," is explored in detail in the depictions of the lacerated bodies in *Inferno* 28.

The term *contrapasso* derives from Aristotle's *Nicomachean Ethics*; it denotes a conception of justice in which every harmful action is reciprocated by a corresponding "passion" or suffering. Aquinas further associates its symmetry with Old Testament justice, the so-called *lex talionis*.[50] In his own treatment of the *contrapasso*, Dante probes the *aesthetic* basis of retaliatory, eye-for-an-eye justice. What are the stakes in founding a concept of punishment on principles of decorum? What is the role of poetry in poetic justice?

Dante waits until canto 28 of *Inferno* to explicitly define the *contrapasso*, and he places the definition in the mouth of a fellow poet, the troubadour Bertran de Born. We will examine Bertran's statement shortly, but first it is necessary to place it within the context of this highly self-reflexive canto, with special attention to the connection it establishes between poetry and violence. The damned in this valley of Malebolge are condemned as "sowers of scandal and schism" (*Inf.* 28.35) for their instigation of civil and religious strife. In one of the most violent episodes of the poem, a sword-wielding demon ritually mutilates these sinners, making a series of purposeful and geometric cuts each time they pass by in their eternal circling. Just as they split the corporate bodies of church and state, their own bodies are now cut open and split.

The first soul we encounter, Mohammed, or rather, a cruel and demeaning caricature of the Islamic prophet, is split open from his chin to his genitals, "dove si trulla" (where one farts; *Inf.* 28.24). According to Dante's medieval sources, Mohammed was originally a Nestorian Christian who in founding Islam had perverted Christian doctrine and hence misled former believers of the true Church.[51] For removing a section of the faithful, he is now missing a section of flesh, exposing his vital organs like a barrel missing a stave. His cousin and successor Alì, cleft from chin to forelock, follows him. The next sinners—Pier della Medicina, Curio, and Mosca—suffer forms of amputation as retribution for having advocated actions leading to civil war. The devil subtracts from each soul the member or appendage that corresponds to his crime (including a nose, ear, forearms, and tongue). Bertran is part of this procession, having divided Prince Henry II from his father King Louis VII—the figurehead of the kingdom. In one of the most memorable and frequently illustrated images of the poem, Bertran accordingly carries his own severed head in his hand. This clean horizontal cut balances the vertical cuts made to Mohammed and Alì, turning the perpendicular slashes into the form of a cross.

Yet perhaps the most chilling element of the schismatics' punishment results from a conceit rather than from a violent image. Directly after the avenging devil has carved up the sinner, his wounds begin to heal so he can be cut open again after completing the circle. Albeit sardonically, the sinners' mended wounds anticipate the penitential P's that a sword-yielding angel carves on Dante's forehead as he prepares to enter Purgatory. As an emblem of the restorative structure of *Purgatorio*, one of these seven "piaghe" (wounds; *Purg.* 9.114) is erased or "cleansed" each time Dante's character leaves a cornice in his ascent. In contrast, the ceaseless opening and closing of the wounds of the damned—a Promethean punishment—makes a mockery of rehabilitative justice and the possibility of a "cure."

The aestheticization of violence in this canto permeates its literary form as well. Here Dante creates a "poetics of schism" through an expansive employment of hyperbaton and parenthesis.[52] On a narratological plane, the mimetic presentation of the characters and their speeches is unexpectedly broken or split at several points. For example, the retrospective backdrop provided for Mohammed's warning to Fra Dolcino, mysteriously uttered while the speaker was still in mid-step, both describes a suspension and enacts one within the diegetic flow of events (as does the post factum narration of Virgil's sighting of Geri del Bello). With respect to syntax, phrases and grammatical clusters are interrupted with conspicuous artifice. When Dante introduces the lurid "mode" of the *bolgia*, "il modo de la nona bolgia sozzo" (the wretched mode of the ninth pocket; *Inf.* 28.21), the distance between the noun "modo" and its modifier "sozzo" creates a gap in the verbal texture like the one the poet will soon describe in Mohammed's body. Similarly, when Bertran concludes the canto by describing how he "partito porto il mio cerebro, lasso! / dal suo principio" (I carry my brain divided, alas from its origin; *Inf.* 28.140–41), the separation of "partito" and "cerebro" and the interjection of "lasso" between "cerebro" and its complement "dal suo principio" forms a double hiatus mirroring the separation of brain and body. Finally, Dante's rare usage of a *rima franta* or broken rhyme

("Oh me"; *Inf.* 28.123)—a technique that reproduces Bertran's use of broken rhymes in his own poetry—attests to Dante's ambitious goal that the "word may not be different from the fact" (*Inf.* 32.12).

Dante first calls attention to the parallels between the mode of punishment represented in the canto and his mode of representation in the extended simile that opens the canto. He announces the futility of encompassing the carnage he has witnessed within the boundaries of poetry, as the vision of blood and wounds exceeds the capacity of the mind, much less the capacity of language. Then the poet asks readers to perform a thought experiment: imagine all the bleeding bodies, perforated limbs, amputated members, and gathered bones that were ever wrought by the wars on the Apulian territory, from the time of the Trojan colonizers to the contemporary wars between Church and Empire, Guelph and Ghibelline. Even this ghastly exercise of *compilatio* would not equal the "manner" of violence achieved in the ninth *bolgia*.

As critics have long noticed, the inexpressibility topos of this exordium draws on Virgilian models, while the inventory of dismembered bodies imitates the battle-inspired lyrics of Bertran himself.[53] Through the allusions to such literary precedents in this depiction of carnage, Dante situates the mantle of the martial poet within the parallel histories of real and literary violence.[54] In fact, in *De vulgari eloquentia* 2.2.8, Dante identified Bertran as a poet of arms, a genre no Italian poet had yet undertaken. In *Inferno* 28, Dante now fashions himself as a crusading knight armed with a pen (his first victim, the Prophet himself), a role that Cacciaguida will sanctify in the Heaven of Mars. At the same time, by choosing a poet who sought to incite armed combat as the spokesperson for the repercussions of the *contrapasso*, Dante homes in on the ethical dilemma of using words as deeds. This dilemma includes the matter of wounding with speech, of course, but it extends also to speaking through wounds.[55]

Throughout this canto, the damned display their wounds and then gloss their meaning. The consequences of their sins are thus constantly visible before the eyes of readers. Bertran, for instance, concludes his story by describing his punishment and using it to exemplify the general rule of punishment in the poem: "Così s'osserva in me lo contrapasso" (Thus it is observed in me the countersuffering; *Inf.* 28.142). Bertran's use of the impersonal passive construction ("s'osserva") underscores the idea that legibility is the defining characteristic of his countersuffering. Mohammed also comments on these punishments, explaining that the rationale behind them is expressed with "mathematical clarity."[56] Since ("però"; *Inf.* 28.36) the sinners were schismatics, they are now split open; Bertran carries his severed head in his hand because ("perch'"; *Inf.* 28.139) he divided the formerly joined father and son. While readers have long admired Dante's artistry in creating real, fleshed-out characters out of the infernal souls, the sowers of discord come close in their exemplarity to mere personifications.

Through the "fearful symmetry" of the language and images in this canto, Dante celebrates the transparency of the law as it is stamped on the souls' bodies. By making the penalties signify the crimes, he provides a prime instance of how infamy by punishment expresses the "content" of a sentence. The punishments of the otherworld identify the souls as gluttons, thieves, suicides, and traitors. To borrow the language of the jurists: it is the "cause" of their punishment, not the punishment itself, which defames. From this perspective, the countersuffering appears to call attention to the underlying significance of the penalty, not its application. It seems to foreground the semantics of law, not its performative force.

The *contrapasso* is thus meant to be interpreted by its emblematic nature. Yet at the very moment it is finally defined, illustrated with the clearest possible examples, a hermeneutic breakdown occurs between the Pilgrim and the desecrated bodies that are paraded before him. Dante does not interpret Mohammed's wounds; he only gapes at them, stunned into a state of suspension. His eyes become "drunk" with the vision of violence in the canto, and Virgil reprimands him as he continues to stare at the mutilated bodies. Dante is literally blocked ("impedito"; *Inf.* 29.28) by the imagery of the sowers of discord, just as the damned are momentarily frozen in awe when they discover that he is still alive. Although the *contrapasso* is presented as a generalized rule of the otherworld, there remains something exceptional about the punishments of canto 28. Dante's character struggles to fit them into the system he has experienced so far, and Virgil notes that Dante has not been mesmerized in this manner by any of the other punishments.

When Dante's character observes the injuries of Mohammed and Bertran, he is overwhelmed by more than their message. In these passages, he marvels not at how the punishment fits the crime, but at the terrible manifestation of force he sees applied to these mangled bodies. What disgraces Mohammed is not just the revelation of his divisive nature by way of his divided body, but the dehumanizing shame that results from having to walk around with his intestines and inner organs hanging between his legs, including his stomach, "that wretched bag that makes shit" (*Inf.* 28.26–27). What is the "meaning" of these ghastly details, except that the performative force of law always exceeds its semiotic container? As we have seen, Dante indicates in the introduction to the canto that the violent spectacle he has witnessed overflows the limits of language and mind, "c'hanno a tanto comprender poco seno" (which have little capacity to comprehend so much"; *Inf.* 28.6). The episode closes in the same vein, with Virgil telling Dante that it is futile to try and count the wounds of the damned, since the space he would need to survey (the valley is twenty-two miles in circumference) is too vast for the time allotted for the journey.

The tension between equivalence and excess in the canto is especially striking when we consider the arithmetical conception of justice in Aristotle's *Ethics*.[57] In Aristotle's theory of commutative justice, his emphasis is on compensation and the necessity to reestablish the equality that existed before the unjust act was committed. Thus, whatever was subtracted from the injured party—whether material or immaterial—must be repaid to the victim and taken from the culprit who profited from it. Aristotle realized, however, that reciprocal justice was ill-adapted for many real-life situations. Namely, it failed to take into consideration questions of proportion and social rank. If a citizen struck a magistrate, for example, he should be not only struck back but additionally punished. In his gloss to this passage, Aquinas reimagines the question within a contemporary political-juridical context: "Clearly, worse damage is done when someone strikes a ruler than a private person, by reason of the fact that injury is done not only to the person of the ruler but also the whole commonwealth. In such cases, reciprocation (*contrapassum*) simply taken is not suited for justice."[58]

Beginning in Dante's time, the governments of Italian city-states started demanding reparations for criminal offenses in excess of those paid to victims. Local statutes increasingly required judges to mete out large, onerous fines and corporal punishments for any offense that threatened the security and sanctity of the commonwealth. According to jurists such as Dinus de Mugello and Gandinus, the victim of public disorder was ultimately the state itself: "Omnis delinquens offendit rem publicam civitatis" (Every perpetrator of a crime offends the commonweal of the city). The state, therefore, should demand satisfaction as one of the injured parties.[59]

What Dante witnesses in canto 28 is this very surplus that public authorities demanded from citizens who had violated the symbolic body of the state. When Bertran, echoing Lamentations, asks Dante if he has ever witnessed a punishment as great as his ("vedi s'alcuna è grande come questa"; *Inf.* 28.132), he reminds readers that in legal terms his crime would have been classified as *enorme*. Medieval jurists developed the concept of *enormitas* to deal with heinous crimes they saw as attacking the foundations of order. At first this extended to crimes such as heresy and *lèse majesté*, but it eventually described more common crimes as well. An *enorme* offense was considered irregular both with respect to its scale—it exceeded measure—and because it fell outside the purview of standard norms of sentencing: *e-normis*.[60] Since irregular crimes could not be assimilated within the preexisting economy of regulations and penalties, it was left to the discretion of judges to select an appropriately "enormous" punishment.

As offenders to the *persona* of kingdom and church,[61] Bertran and Mohammed are made to endure a new form of spectacular punishment, one that cannot be reduced to a system of reparative equivalencies. We see then in *Inferno* 28 a demonstration of how the exclusive right of God and his earthly representatives to exceed all measure could be reestablished. Only a transcendent authority has the right to produce the theological miracle of "due in uno e uno in due" (two in one and one in two; *Inf.* 28.125). The surplus of force inscribing the bodies of the damned with the *contrapasso* expresses not only what they did, but also what public authority can do.

Dante's critical awe in the face of these new methods of public justice comes into focus when we compare it with his portrayal of private vengeance in the same episode. At the beginning of canto 29, when Virgil reprimands him for staring at the wounds of the damned, Dante excuses himself by explaining that he was searching for one of his relatives. This relative, Geri del Bello, a cousin of Dante's father, passed by unnoticed while Dante was observing Bertran so intently. Virgil tells Dante that, before departing from view, he saw Geri make a threatening hand gesture at him from under the bridge. Dante realizes that Geri is offended because his violent death is still unavenged by his family, by anyone who "shares the shame of his death" (*Inf.* 29.33). The Pilgrim's acknowledgement of this unfulfilled vendetta renders him more compassionate toward Geri.

Critics often associate the private vengeance Dante's character invokes in canto 29 with the vengeance visited upon the souls in canto 28, highlighting the problematic ethical relationship between the two.[62] Yet the customary, private, and decentralized nature of the vendetta—although often regulated by local statutes—had little in common with the new techniques of public justice. The differences in the forms of justice personified by Geri del Bello and the sword-wielding devil are made clear in the differing narrative styles with which Dante represents them. The episode with Geri is personal, elegiac, and, most importantly, peripheral to the main action of the canto, both temporally and spatially. It is presented as an addendum to the primary narrative, and is not represented in the foreground but recounted indirectly. The punishments of canto 28 are, on the contrary, spectacular, centralized, and rationalized. All the souls must pass by the devil who, as a representative of the infernal bureaucracy, administers the unavoidable punishments. The vulnerability of the damned is further underscored by the fact that the devil is the only character in *Inferno* who carries a weapon. He alone has the right to bear arms—a terrifying symbol of the state's monopoly of violence and its sinister ability to extract the extra "debt" owed to it.[63]

Staging the destruction of human bodies in canto 28, Dante acknowledges, in ways the jurists could not, how infamy by punishment both relied on and reinforced institutional authority. The message conveyed by this type of punishment is irrational, self-reflexive, and self-perpetuating—independent of the criminal sentence it decries. For this reason, the efficacy of the violence performed in this canto is enhanced, not damaged, by its gratuitousness. It is this surplus of force that allows public authorities to enact infamy on the bodies of the culprits, instead of simply describing it or ordering that it should be done.

Manfred

Dante returns to this sacramental power in *Purgatorio* 3, explicitly attacking church authorities for desecrating the body of King Manfred of Sicily in an attempt to create "things" through wounds. Dante encounters Manfred among the excommunicants in one of the most memorable episodes of *Purgatorio*. The defeated prince wears the marks of his disgrace on his body for all to see. His heroic visage is maimed by a sword's gruesome blow: "Biondo era e bello e di gentile aspetto / ma l'un de' cigli un colpo avea diviso" (Blond he was and beautiful and of noble appearance, but a blow had divided one of his eyebrows; *Purg.* 3.107–8). When Dante fails to recognize him, he points to a wound at the top of his chest and then eerily smiles and declares: "I am Manfred" (*Purg.* 3.112)

The natural son of Emperor Frederick II and the last hope of the Hohenstaufen dynasty after the death of his legitimate brother Conrad, Manfred was instrumental in defeating the anti-imperial forces at Monteperti. His death on the battlefield at Benevento (1266) in many ways signaled the end of imperial rule in Italy. Considered an enemy of the Church for refusing to cede the kingdom of Sicily and Naples, he was excommunicated in 1262 by Pope Urban IV. According to canon law, Manfred would have been considered automatically infamous as the result of his excommunication. For our purposes, it is revealing that this infamy is externalized in the canto and rendered visually.

As various critics have noted, by beckoning Dante to behold his wounds, Manfred reproduces Mohammed's gesture. Moreover, as with the countersuffering of the sowers of discord, his lacerated body can be seen as a fitting punishment for having rebelled against the mystical body of the Church. In fact, Manfred's mutilation is foreshadowed in the preamble to *Inferno* 28, where Dante compares the punishment of the schismatics to the defaced corpses and amputated body parts produced by the wars between Church and Empire in southern Italy, including the battle in which Manfred received his mortal wounds.[64] The Church viewed the struggles against the Hohenstaufen regime for control of Sicily and Naples as crusades. The forces of Charles of Anjou (brother to King Louis IX of France) defeated Manfred in a "crusade" issued against him by Pope Clement IV. After Manfred's death, Guelph propaganda continued to portray him as an apostate, numbered among the damned.

Given these precedents, readers could expect Manfred's wounds to identify him as being marked by infernal infamy, just as Mohammed's had. Instead, they provide proof of his salvation, resembling the wounds that Christ showed to Thomas as evidence of his resurrection. Although Dante is on firm theological ground in saving Manfred despite his excommunication, the placement of this notorious sinner at the beginning of *Purgatorio* is clearly polemical.

John Freccero has famously interpreted Manfred's wounds as a metaphor for Dante's poetics.[65] A representational anomaly incompatible with the souls' "airy bodies," these cuts into unreal flesh mark the poet's imposition of his vision within the fiction of the otherworld—a jarring image of the authorial signature. Breaking through any purely realistic account of events, moreover, they are meant to be read as "self-consciously symbolic." The promise of redemption, together with the drama of male identity—including the poet's Oedipal struggle with Virgil—lie hidden beneath the seemingly realistic details of Manfred's violated face and body. Freccero draws a special contrast between Auerbach's concept of mimesis and this symbolic and allegorical mode of representation. According to Freccero, Auerbach's famous account of the discovery of Ulysses's scar cannot do justice to the polyvalence of Manfred's wounds.[66]

Whether intentionally or not, Freccero misrepresents Auerbach's theory of mimesis, which is anything but simply "putting a mirror up to nature." It is thanks to Auerbach's studies of medieval typology, after all, that we are able to understand how Manfred could be both a *figura* of the resurrected Christ and still maintain his historical existence.[67] For Auerbach, Dante's realism is a reflection not of nature but of God's way of writing meaning into history. In this view, Dante's Hell is a higher, intensified reality—fulfilling but not negating the reality of events on earth, which are never emptied of their original significance. This insistence on the reality of the otherworld is crucial for understanding Manfred's initial gesture toward Dante.

If we restore the context of judgment to the story of Manfred's fate, we can see how his wounds actually undercut a symbolic representation of reality. Manfred's gashes, like Ulysses's scar or even Christ's wounds, are not symbols, but proof. Their phenomenal presence defies conventional cultural myths. The idealized portrait of Manfred as a beautiful heroic warrior is deflated by the materiality of his disfigurement. The adversative "ma" preceding the description of his cleft eyebrow introduces the violence of historical fact into his stylized depiction. Manfred's surreal smile likewise prevents any facile interpretation of his wounds. As Freccero elegantly puts it, "His smile is a revisionist smile, belying the official versions of his fate."[68] But this revision is accomplished not through symbol or allegory but through realism—the realism of estrangement. Manfred smiles because his wounds are proof of his salvation, "the truth if anyone says otherwise" (*Purg.* 3.117), and their real presence in purgatory undermines the belief that his defeat and mutilation were signs of disgrace. Unlike Palinurus and Deiphobus and the other sorrowful shades Aeneas encounters in the otherworld, Manfred's improper burial and disfigured corpse do not preclude an illustrious place within collective memory—at least not within a Christian narrative of martyrdom.[69]

With the description of Manfred, Dante suggests that the pope does not have the authority to defame by punishment alone. He cannot transform a wound into a mark. This is precisely what the bishop of Cosenza misunderstands when, at the order of Pope Clement, he disinters Manfred's body and scatters his bones outside of the realm in a ceremony of anathema. As Manfred himself makes clear, the bishop misreads his "face" (*Purg.* 3.126) when he interprets his wounds to mean anything beyond the expression of a relationship of force. He sees Manfred as doomed because of his punishment, the result of having the papal sentence inscribed on his body. But Dante removes the performative effects of this punishment and makes it just one statement among other possible representations of reality; the pope and the bishop may treat Manfred's body as damned, but that does not make it so. In this way Dante places the Church's officially sanctioned violence on par with Dante's defaming poetics. Both are fallible verbal constructs for assigning disgrace.

The fallibility in this case, Dante suggests, surrounds the difference between Manfred and Mohammed: the pope fails to properly distinguish between an enemy and an adversary, treating Manfred, an internal opponent, as an external threat by characterizing him as a menace to the system itself.[70] In Dante's view, Manfred's "horrible" (121) crimes could have been addressed adequately through ordinary justice, including provisional excommunication. The crusade waged against him, and the desecration of his corpse, were ill-founded attempts at placing him beneath the law, both human and divine. The extraordinary justice inflicted upon Mohammed, on the other hand, is justified, as he was intent on subverting the laws of Christendom, not just on attacking its individual representatives.

Dante limits the extreme measures of the *contrapasso* to culprits who have incurred what medieval lawyers referred to as *summa infamia*. Even among the damned, he distinguishes between those whose status is diminished and those who are no longer even human in legal terms. Yet by announcing the law of the countersuffering through its limit case, Dante seems to suggest that, even in ordinary justice, an excess of force lies behind the "fit" of retribution.

While drawing on the epic and lyric tradition, Dante recognizes that his artistic experimentation in this episode—and, indeed, throughout the poem—is ultimately without precedent. The creativity of his poetry participates in the "modern" creativity behind these new forms of punishment. This link between judicial activism and literary innovation will be the subject of the next chapter.

2

Beyond the Law
Arbitrium

This chapter analyzes the legal connotation of Dante's "libero arbitrio." In Dante's time, *arbitrium* referred to a judge's discretion or to a special grant of political power. Viewed by contemporaries as essentially rule-bound and normative, however, it is not to be confused with our modern concept of sovereignty. Scholars have mistakenly interpreted the freedom Dante's character achieves in Eden as a form of "negative liberty"—a private sphere of action not bound by traditional authorities. This line of thought has it that Dante frees himself from the jurisdictions of both Church and Empire by claiming the sovereign territory of the artist. I will argue instead that when the pilgrim is crowned a "lord of himself" in *Purgatorio* 27, the psychological freedom he achieves is modeled on judicial discretion rather than political sovereignty. The purgatorial journey, as a form of virtual government, creates this delegated freedom by conditioning the pilgrim's will through the law. Dante can judiciously adapt the norms of the system to meet the needs of specific cases only after he has so completely internalized these principles that they govern his way of thinking.

The question of what political and psychological freedom means for Dante has consequences for how we understand his poetics. We are accustomed to seeing Dante's relationship with his literary precursors as primarily agonistic. Especially in the case of Virgil, we are told, the modern poet struggles to free himself from the ancient poet's shadow in order to create an unheralded Christian epic. Yet Dante viewed the ancient and modern worlds as being governed by a continuous living law. In employing the concept of *arbitrium* to characterize his theory of literary innovation, then, Dante stakes out an aesthetic philosophy that differs starkly from our modern myth of artistic freedom. For him, poetic license is always rule-bound, case-specific, and an expression of the continuing relevance of tradition. Artistic innovation thus does not renounce the past, but helps to sustain it.

"Libero, dritto e sano è tuo arbitrio"

In a still provocative essay entitled "The Sovereignty of the Artist: A Note on Legal Maxims and Renaissance Theories of Art," Ernst Kantorowicz locates the origin of Renaissance artistic theory in medieval legal scholarship. Although he rehearses the commonplace that both art and law imitate nature, he focuses on claims that the legislator, like God, is able to make something out of nothing (*de nichilo facit aliquid ut Deus*). Kantorowicz asserts that this formula, found most often in canon law as an illustration of the pope's plenitude of power (*plenitudo potestatis*), contributed to a new artistic theory of creation wherein the artist could add something to nature rather than merely imitate it. The modern conception of the autonomous artist thus owes a debt to legal theories that enable the legislator to transform reality.[1]

Although for Kantorowicz these political and artistic theologies are fully manifested only in the burgeoning national monarchies and artistic rebirth of Renaissance Europe, he grants Dante a precocious role in the construction of artistic sovereignty. In particular, he cites as a defining moment the scene of investiture that takes place at the top of Mount Purgatory. As they enter Earthly Paradise, Virgil informs Dante that he is free to roam Eden on his own volition while waiting for Beatrice to arrive. He then crowns him lord over himself:

> Mentre che vegnan lieti li occhi belli
> che, lagrimando, a te venir mi fenno,
> seder ti puoi e puoi andar tra elli.
> Non aspettar mio dir più né mio cenno;
> libero, dritto e sano è tuo arbitrio,
> e fallo fora non fare a suo senno:
> per ch'io te sovra te corono e mitrio.

> (Until the lovely eyes arrive in their gladness which weeping made
> me come to you, you can sit and you can walk among them. No longer
> await any word or sign from me: free, upright, and whole is your will,
> and it would be a fault not to act according to its intent. Therefore
> you over yourself I crown and mitre; *Purg.* 27.136–42.)

In this passage, according to Kantorowicz, Dante claims for the office of poet the plenitude of power typically associated with the offices of emperor and pope. Like these rulers, Dante's will is free to create something out of nothing.[2]

This coronation scene is also crucial for Kantorowicz's epochal monograph, *The King's Two Bodies*, as an example of "man-centered kingship." In receiving the insignia of emperor and pope, crown and mitre, Dante's character acquires "sovereign status" as an individual who has "incorporated" the nature of man as a whole.[3] The poet becomes an example of "man's two bodies," independent from, and in some sense in competition with, the theologically founded authority of secular and ecclesiastical institutions.[4]

Kantorowicz's juxtaposition of artistic and legal theories of creation is profoundly insightful, but his analysis is skewed by an overriding interest in the foundations of the modern constitutionalist state.[5] In his effort to uncover the theological origins of secular power, Kantorowicz interprets those passages from medieval law allowing rulers to set aside specific legislation as permission for them to act absolutely, even unlawfully. In this view, the right of an ecclesiastical or secular monarch to enact, reform, or suspend laws depends wholly on his subjective political authority. From a post-Enlightenment standpoint, such discretionary power may seem directly related to, or even synonomous with, absolute power. But this was hardly the case for jurists working within the legal framework of late medieval Europe. For them, law could never be reduced to the legislation promulgated by a sovereign power (since no such stable centralized power existed), and no one, not even the pope or emperor, was above the law with regard to higher universal norms. Even the legal concept of plenitude of power was never as unfettered as Kantorowicz makes it appear. In the decades since the publication of *The King's Two Bodies*, legal historians have demonstrated that the invocation of *plenitudo potestatis* typically applied only to positive law, the canons in particular; these "full" powers remained bound by the parameters of natural and divine law.[6]

Despite these and other examples of presentism, Kantorowicz's treatment of the purgatorial coronation remains invaluable because it emphasizes the political and legal aspects of the passage instead of focusing solely on the philosophical question of "free will." Virgil's speech at the end of *Purgatorio* 27 is typically considered noteworthy because it is the culmination of this major philosophical theme. Kantorowicz usefully reminds us that the philosophical conclusion is embedded within a legal ceremony, and that the model of the psyche it offers is coexistent with Dante's understanding of political authority. The structure of the well-functioning mind is not solely a philosophical matter; it also represents the ideal organization of power within the state.

In a recent important treatment of the coronation scene, Albert Ascoli reexamines and expands upon the political/philosophical/artistic nexus identified by Kantorowicz.[7] Like Kantorowicz, Ascoli interprets this "graduation ceremony" (350) as marking the poet's accession to "an autonomous and sovereign subjectivity" (330). He also traces how Dante actively exploits the dual crisis of imperial and papal authority, the "intermediate space of the *aporia dantesca*" (337), to insert and assert his own innovative poetic authority. In this reading, Dante's investiture is a rhetorical stratagem aimed at constructing a vision of the "individual subject outside the grasp of Emperor, Philosopher, and/or Pope" (333). By becoming lord over himself, Dante fuses the authority of universal, transhistorical reason with the personal will.

Ascoli's interpretation of the coronation scene is significant because it places Dante's psychological and artistic claims in dialogue with contemporary institutional power, and my own indebted reading of the passage will complement his analysis at several points. Yet despite his insistence on situating the poet within a historicized intellectual context, Ascoli also describes Dante as "circumscribing papal and imperial authority" and "questioning the requirement that he submit to them" (337). Reading these phrases, one cannot help but feel that he has catapulted the "modern author" back into the Middle Ages in order to observe his heroics in striving to break free from the constraints of his time. In other words, while historicizing the context Dante had to negotiate, Ascoli neglects to historicize the concept of freedom itself. He still views Dante's liberty through the lens of a liberal "negative freedom,"[8] an area of noninterference in which a "buffered self" stakes out a claim against public authority.[9] From this post-Enlightenment vantage point, the moment at the top of Purgatory marks Dante's newfound "autonomous status," which he achieves by freeing himself from the authority of the pope and emperor.

In contrast with these protoliberal accounts of Dante's coronation, which share an interest in uncovering the origins of (early) modernity, I argue that the passage caps a longstanding concern in Dante's corpus: to imagine a *regulated* space beyond—but not in opposition to—the law. For Dante, the dilemma is not so much individual versus institution, but how the actions of both can be simultaneously freed from specific proscriptions yet still ruled by transcendent standards and collective norms. I propose that we take seriously Dante's definition of "perfect liberty" as the "willing," "joyful," and "free" observance of *ius commune* law (a stark contrast to Florentine claims for jurisdictional autonomy).[10] In fact, the overarching goal of the journey to Beatrice, I will argue, is to achieve this "yoke of liberty" (*iugum libertatis*) by experiencing Purgatory as a simulacrum of good government. In this light, the ascent of Purgatory does not exempt

Dante's character from being subject to institutional authority, but it demonstrates precisely how institutions should form subjects.

The difference here is more than one of degree or perspective. It speaks to the very ethical design of the poem. Ascoli is certainly correct to situate Dante's quest for a new vernacular authority within the crises in political and spiritual authority in late medieval Italy. But what is the purpose of acquiring such authority? To my mind, interpreting Dante's engagement with contemporary political catastrophes as, above all, one of self-authorization impoverishes what remains one of the most impressive examples of "radical hope" in all of Western literature.[11] I would propose instead that Dante offers his poem as a magisterial yet temporary measure aimed at ensuring the continuity of normative legal institutions. The *Commedia* sustains the laws the political authorities should be enforcing, and it serves as a supplement to, but not a substitute for, the paternal role of institutions in educating and disciplining their subjects. As does the ethical training embedded in the application of law, Dante's emergency poetics instills in the individual a disposition to obey longstanding collective norms.[12] The coronation scene, in short, celebrates not the emergence of the sovereign will, but the successful implementation of a dependent *arbitrium*.

A key feature behind the critical misunderstanding of this episode stems from a mistranslation of *libero arbitrio* as "free will" rather than "free choice." For the majority of theologians and especially for those considered "voluntarists," *liberum arbitrium* resides in the will's *dominium*, its capacity to rule, even if this means rejecting what the intellect judges as good. Here is not the place to rehearse the complex debate among medieval philosophers over the nature of free choice and its source in the psyche.[13] For our purposes, it is enough to note that Dante's view of *liberum arbitrium* diverges from that of the majority; as previous scholarship has demonstrated, his view is a decisively intellectualist one,[14] and he locates free choice in the governance of the will by reason. As he explains in *Monarchia* 1.12.4, when judgment dominates desire and is in no way captive to it, then one's choice is truly free.[15] This is freedom *from* disorienting appetite, rather than freedom *to* will something.

In this chapter I focus on the largely neglected legal conception of *arbitrium*. In the medieval period, philosophical approaches to discretion were entwined with legal ones much more than we realize. Medieval scholars drew heavily on notions of judicial discretion and political freedom in order to convey the mechanisms of judgment at work in man's *forum internum* (inner court). Albertus Magnus, for example, depicted the faculty of *liberum arbitrium* as an *arbiter* whose responsibility was to settle conflicts between the litigants of reason and will.[16] In Dante's figuration of the psyche as an ideal "state" in *Monarchia* 1.12, instead of representing the will as a sovereign possessing dominion over the soul, he conceives of *arbitrium* as a judge who willingly obeys dictates of reason; the power of "free choice" is jurisdictional rather than proprietary. Moreover, just as the impartiality of the universal Monarch depends on his status *super partes*, the free individual's power of discernment—fostered by the Monarch's execution of just laws—stands "above" the passions.

In its legal acceptation, *arbitrium* denoted a delegated and rule-bound authority beyond the ordinary application of the law.[17] *Arbitrium* was always considered circumscribed in its application, even at its most extensive, when it was *liberum*. In this respect, it represented the exact opposite of the concept of sovereignty delineated by Bodin and Hobbes. As I show in the next section, that distinction is crucial for understanding Dante's conception of political and artistic freedom: in contrast to Kantorowicz's projection of monarchic absolutism onto the investiture scene in *Purgatorio*, Dante would have imagined the freedom his character received on top of the mountain as politically, psychologically, and poetically bound.

Arbitrary Power and Legal *Arbitrium* on Top of Purgatory

Though ultimately untranslatable, *arbitrium* as a legal term comes closest to our concept of judicial discretion. *Arbitrium* referred to a sanctioned leeway in both private and public transactions, to be exercised within a specified jurisdiction. In public law it often took the form of an emergency power—a special liberty granted to officials so that they could investigate and punish crime in response to a perceived threat to the social order. Despite this leeway in judging cases and prosecuting crimes, legal *arbitrium* was always understood to be regulated, at least to some extent. Jurists described *arbitrium* as being "ruled like a horse by its bridle or a ship by its helm."[18] It was an oriented or justified will, a will held in check by reason.[19]

In Dante's time, a new legal use for *arbitrium* emerged that is especially relevant for his character's coronation. In handing over governmental jurisdiction to a single individual, the urban communes would bestow upon the new *signore* of the territory "liberum et generalem arbitrium," or wide jurisdictional and legislative powers.[20] The shift of power from elected representatives and assemblies to individual *signore* would become truly widespread later in the fourteenth century, but even in the later thirteenth the transmission of *arbitrium* from city to lord was already common in the northern centers where Dante spent most of his exile.[21] It was the method, for example, by which the Dante's patrons, the Scaligeri family, assumed power in Verona and in neighboring towns.[22] This legal ceremony typically involved delivering the rod or staff of the city to the signore, and conceding him the *arbitrium* to oversee its laws and protect the public good as he deemed fit. Given the increasing visibility of such scenes in northern Italy, the investiture of Dante's character in *Purgatorio* 27, where Virgil proclaims that his "arbitrio" is "libero," would have likely recalled for readers a similarly formalized delegation of power.

Local statutes were careful, however, to limit the reach and duration of their grants of *arbitrium*. Officials were allowed to exercise their discretion in dispensing justice only for a certain period, in certain circumstances, and with certain types of subjects (such as foreigners, traitors, and notorious thieves).[23] Jurists often classified this delegated power as *arbitrium regulatum*, specifying that it was ruled "clara et recta ratione" (by clear and right reason) and beholden to the principles of the *ius commune*. Even in its most unrestricted form, when *arbitrium liberum* permitted the lord of a city or its highest assembly to suspend, revise, and invent municipal regulations, jurists confined this extraordinary use to positive law and legislation.[24] The signori and their officials were still expected to be bound by higher norms and to justify their discretionary measures by providing a *ratio* (reason or underlying principle) or by explaining their contribution to the *utilitas publica* (public good).[25]

It is almost never mentioned that Dante's newly acquired freedom at the top of Purgatory is similarly restricted, both temporally and spatially.[26] He is free to roam Eden at his desire *until* Beatrice arrives, who will once again rule over him with her "commandments" (*Purg.* 32.107). Indeed, even before her arrival, his wanderings through Earthly Paradise are suddenly obstructed by the river of Lethe: "ed ecco più andar mi tolse un rio" (and behold, walking further was denied me by a stream; *Purg.* 28.25). The Pilgrim's discretionary powers are thus bracketed between the guides of secular and divine law (Virgil and Beatrice) and contained, in practice, within twenty-five verses of a single canto.

Dante's freedom of movement provides a rather weak illustration of individual sovereignty. If we consider *arbitrium* as an extension of the legal system rather than a circumscription of it, however, this targeted edenic promenade assumes a richer symbolic function. For instance, the reason given for allowing Dante free rein to make decisions is that Virgil, as an embodiment of empire and law, has reached a place beyond which he can no longer discern ("per me più oltre non discerno"; *Purg.* 27.129). This schema was a familiar one for medieval lawyers, who regularly acknowledged that there were regions of human existence not covered by positive law, and phenomena which, because of contingencies of time and place, legislators could not fully anticipate. These situations were left to the discretion of the judge, not in violation of the legal system but ideally as a means for updating and promoting it, to fill in its natural gaps—and the spaces intentionally left blank. The judge's *arbitrium* thus guaranteed a continuity between norm and reality, universal and particular, tradition and history.

Within this conceptual framework, it is perfectly natural for Virgil to entrust the jurisdiction of Earthly Paradise to Dante's discretion, since it would be classified as an "emergent case." From a post-Enlightenment standpoint, Dante's freedom is *from* the law. For late medieval readers and jurists, however, this discretionary space would have been a demonstration of the adaptability of law, and consequentially of its universal reach.

For this dialectic between "going beyond" and "returning" to the law to function properly, however, the subjective moment of discretion must be something besides pure voluntary decisional-ism. It must be in dialogue with the objective demands of the legal system—its fundamental principles, if not with specific legislation. Otherwise, *arbitrium* expresses only the caprice of power, or what the legal reformers of the Enlightenment perceived in the king's "ar-bitrary" exercise of his will. This semantic shift in the term *arbitrium*, from denoting discernment to denoting whim, encapsulates the dif-ferences between a medieval and modern perspective on the place of discretion in the public sphere.[27]

This is not to say that a conception of sovereign self-governance was unimaginable in the Middle Ages, and jurists were beginning to legitimate territorial-based political power in which *rex in regno suo imperator est* (a king is emperor in his own kingdom).[28] But for what Dante might have thought of this development, we need to turn from the legal delegation in *Purgatorio* 27–28 to the apocalyptic vision of the tyrannical giant in *Purgatorio* 32. Seated in the chariot of the Church, the giant viciously beats his lover, the whore of Bab-ylon—an allegorical representation of the corrupted papacy—for having dared to look in Dante's direction. Critics have long identified the giant with the French king Philip the Fair (1268–1314). The rule of the emergent French monarchy is thus equated with the paranoia of a possessive lover. Ignoring jurisdictional limits, the giant-king exercises his power as a proprietary right, treating the papal office itself as one of the earthly goods that, as explained by Virgil in *Pur-gatorio* 15, causes strife because it cannot be shared. This willful do-minion, founded on suspicion and brute force, surpasses even the pope's plenitude of power, whose law-based authority now seems outmatched by the new political reality. As the giant drags the harlot and the unnatural hybrid chariot into the no-man's-land of the for-est (symbolizing the removal of the Church to Avignon), Dante gives us a vivid glimpse of what he considered the unnatural "art" of creat-ing something out of nothing.

Operating within the limitrophe territory of Eden's forest, both Dante's character and the monstrous giant enjoy a freedom of action that, at least in some sense, is beyond the law. To distinguish his employment of juridical discretion from the giant's sovereign will, then, Dante needs to posit a normative space in which individual decisions, while not formally adhering to preexisting regulations, nonetheless remain faithful to their essential spirit (their *mens* or *ratio*). In light of this imperative, we must remember that Dante's coronation culminates a *process*; it is the result of a carefully guided reeducation program that allows the Pilgrim finally, upon "graduation," to exercise a form of regulated improvisation. At the threshold of Eden he has internalized the legal and ethical attitudes of his community so thoroughly that his power of choice is at once free, "libero," and properly oriented, "dritto e sano."

In his efforts to define this paradoxical concept of regulated liberty, Dante moves fluidly between politics and poetics. Indeed, his entire postexilic corpus, from the *De vulgari* to the *Commedia* to the *Monarchia*, can be seen as an attempt to construct a legitimate space for political and artistic discretion by reconciling the demands of autonomy and heteronomy. In particular, he conceives of literary innovation as a form of legal *arbitrium*: a case-specific and delimited zone of autonomy necessitated and justified by unforeseen phenomena. In order to shed light on Dante's theory of artistic innovation, it is necessary to first explore his treatise on the eloquence of the vernacular language, *De vulgari eloquentia*. Despite its technical nature, *De vulgari* is the work of Dante's in which he makes his most explicit statement about the relationship between judicial discretion and artistic license, and in which he details the fundamental role of practice for both.

Arbitrium and Poetic License in *De vulgari eloquentia*

De vulgari eloquentia was composed between 1303 and 1305, during the first years of Dante's exile. Although he initially joined forces with a group of exiled white Guelphs, by 1305 he had already separated from them, leaving Tuscany to spend the rest of his life under the patronage of various northern Italian lords. His last official act as a representative of the Florentine white party was to write a letter (in the spring of 1304) to Cardinal Niccolò da Prato, whom Pope Benedict XI had enlisted to arbitrate a peace between the exiles and the black Guelphs currently holding power.

The epistle to the cardinal is a valuable record of Dante's mindset when he was composing *De vulgari*. Dante justifies the rebellion of the exiles as a defense of the Florentine populace against the Black Guelphs, "who have maimed civil laws through their brazen desire" (*qui civilia iura temeraria voluptate truncaverant*).[29] In particular, Dante asserts that the Whites waged a civil war (*civile bellum*) against the Blacks to compel them to submit "to the yoke of sacred law" (*iugo pie legis*); their use of force was aimed at restoring the peace. In this way, Dante contrasts two violent and "exceptional" acts, depicting one as a tyrannical expression of unchecked will and the other as paradoxically necessary to maintain the reign of law. Dante's characterization is unquestionably partial, and needs to be understood rhetorically in the context of his political situation. Yet the question of legitimate and illegitimate actions "beyond the law" continues to concern him in the less explicitly political *De vulgari*. Throughout the work, Dante explores the conditions under which one may or may not set aside existing norms.

The treatise itself opens with a mythic example of violence against natural and divine law. Dante traces the loss of a single sacred language and the origins of multiple vernacular tongues back to the construction of the Tower of Babel. Nimrod and his followers dared to build a tower unto the heavens in an attempt to surpass not just nature but the Creator himself: "Presumpsit ergo in corde suo incurabilis homo, sub persuasione gigantis Nembroth, arte sua non solum superare naturam, sed etiam ipsum naturantem, qui Deus est" (Incorrigible humanity, therefore, led astray by the Giant Nimrod, presumed in its heart to outdo with its art not only nature but the source of its own nature, who is God; 1.7.4).[30] God punishes Nimrod and his followers for this unprecedented and impious act by inaugurating the modern era of linguistic multiplicity and confusion. From this point on, instead of communicating in a universal tongue, mankind will be divided irreversibly by linguistic difference.

In *De vulgari*, Dante elaborates on this biblical legend by adding an important sociological detail. After Babel, he writes, the languages were dispersed according to the labor and craft involved in the tower's construction; those with the highest occupation now speak the lowest idiom. Dante thus resituates the building of the tower within a contemporary municipal landscape, which features such identifying markers as a guild-based structure, economic expansiveness, and social mobility. Yet Dante does not reject the *civitas* per se, as is often claimed.[31] His specific objection fits well within the ethos of the medieval communes: he condemns the perpetuators of Babel for disregarding public law for private gain and thwarting the common good.

That distinction is especially apparent when we compare the building of the tower to the construction of Dido's Carthage in the *Aeneid* (1.418–44), long considered the literary source for Dante's description. While the Carthaginians work together to institute laws, elect judges, and build gates, roads, and other symbols of public civic life, the Shinarians build a private, self-referential tower.[32] The tower, moreover, was the archetypal symbol of aristocratic privilege in medieval Italy. Finally, in canon law, Nimrod was regarded as the originator of private property, the first to violate natural law by expropriating for himself what had formerly belonged to all.[33] Like the unchecked will of the giant-monarch of *Purgatorio*, Nimrod's presumptive art is founded on proprietary dominion rather than jurisdiction.

In his retelling of biblical events, Dante ascribes the excesses of Babel to man's fallen nature, which is perpetually prone to sin, "nequitatrix" (1.7.2; a neologism contrasting human instinct to the principle of equity). His description of the emergence of the first vernacular languages is similarly influenced by this pessimistic and Augustinian view of human nature. After Babel, human beings formed new words and syntax according to their whim (*ad placitum*; 1.1.3) and pleasure (*beneplacitum*; 1.9.6 and 1.9.10).[34] The relationship between sign and signifier in these natural languages was thus an arbitrary one. Because they depended solely on man's unstable and variable appetite, the vernacular tongues continued to change and divide across time and space in the same fashion as other customs based on usage and imitation. As a result, differences in speech could be found within the same city, the same neighborhood, and even the same family.

In order to stem this descent into multiplicity, the regulated grammar of Latin was created. According to Dante, the "inventors of Latin" decreed by common consensus the new laws of grammar, creating a fixed artificial language as opposed to the natural ones.

(Dante did not view the modern European languages as having derived from Latin, as we do today.) In this way, writes Dante, those "inventors" ensured the survival of the words and deeds of the ancients across time and space:

> This was the point from which the inventors of the art of grammar began; for their *gramatica* is nothing less than a certain immutable identity of language in different times and places. Its rules having been formulated with the common consent of many peoples, it can be subject to no individual will (*singulari arbitrio*); and, as a result, it cannot change. So those who devised this language did so lest, through changes in language dependent on the arbitrary judgment of individuals (*arbitrio singularium*), we should become either unable, or, at best, only partially able, to enter into contact with the deeds and authoritative writings of the ancients, or of those whose difference of location makes them different from us (1.9.11).[35]

The rules of grammar are thus seen as a check on individual *arbitrium*, which assumes in this context a pejorative connotation very near our modern conception of whim or caprice.

At this point in the treatise, Dante has established a clear contrast between artificial Latin and natural vernacular. It is notable that he articulates those differences in primarily legal terms. Latin is the product of collective decision-making and consensus—an example of lawmaking by popular sovereignty. Its rule-based and normative nature is made possible by setting aside individual desires in order to preserve the greater good (in this case, a shared classical heritage). The vernacular languages, on the other hand, are entirely without rules ("sine omni regula"; 1.1.2). Their formation depends on the *arbitrium* and *beneplacitum* of singular individuals whose speech is unrestricted by a formalized grammar. Within the Neoplatonic perspective of this section of *De vulgari*,[36] the natural languages represent the fragmentation and multiplicity of fallen human nature. In order to counter this arbitrariness, individual linguistic choice needs to be disciplined by the laws of Latin.

As the treatise progresses, however, the confines between rule-bound Latin and free vernacular are gradually eroded. When, toward the end of Book One, Dante takes up his hunt for a noble Italian vernacular that transcends local dialects, the gap between the two has already begun to close. In 1.16.3, for example, the illustrious vernacular is compared to the law, as both are standards of measurements for interregional populaces (imperial citizens, residents of Italy).[37] Yet the real shift takes place in Book Two, in which Dante turns his attention to poetic craft in an effort to instruct modern poets to compose *regulariter* (2.6.2; 2.8.6) and not solely *casualiter* (at random; 2.4.1). While in Book One Latin alone is "artificial," in Book Two Dante refers to the "art" of the *canzone* (2.3.8) and to "regulated" syntax structure (2.6.2) in describing his poetry and that of his peers. Moreover, he explicitly contrasts poetic forms that are "inlegitimos" (lawless) and "inregulares" (unregulated) to metrical genres such as the *canzone*, *ballata*, and sonnet, which are ruled by customary norms (2.3.2). Given the scholastic commonplace deriving *lex* (law) from the verb *ligare* (to bind), Dante's conception of poetic space as an arrangement of "bound" bundles also seems purposeful. In fact, the entire book is concerned with demonstrating that modern poets are as constrained by specific laws as the Latin poets were, even if their conventions have yet to be codified.

The Latinization of the vernacular that occupies Book Two is by now well known. Little attention, however, has been paid to the shift in how Dante depicts *arbitrium*. While in Book One he portrays individual liberty as problematic and destabilizing, in Book Two he celebrates it in the form of artistic freedom and poetic license. For example, when it comes to how, and even whether, the verses in a stanza are to rhyme, he writes: "Almost all poets grant themselves a considerable degree of license (*amplissimam licentiam*) in this matter" so that they may "achieve the sweetness of overall harmony" (2.13.4). With rhyme scheme as well, Dante recommends that "as much liberty as desired should be conceded" (*omnis optata licentia concedenda*; 2.13.8). Ultimately, the exercise of artistic freedom is what transforms a vernacular poet into an authoritative *auctor*:

> So you can see, reader, how much license [*quanta licentia*] has been given to those who write *canzoni*, and you should consider why poetic practice [*usus*]) has bestowed such extensive discretionary powers

[*largum arbitrium*] on itself. If reason has guided you along the right path, you will see that what I describe has only come about in recognition of the stature of authoritative models" (2.10.5).[38]

Extensive *arbitrium* is evidently no longer a pathological threat to the system, but has instead become a defining and foundational element of it.

The reasons behind such a transformation come into clearer focus when we consider Dante's first exploration of poetic license, the excursus on figurative language in the *Vita nova*. In this excursus, Dante seeks to justify his personification of love, which, deviating from current philosophical teaching, he has portrayed in the sonnet "Io mi senti' svegliar dentr'a lo core" as walking and talking, as if he were a separate "substance" instead of merely an "accident" (*VN* 16.1).[39] He draws on two important precedents to support his apology. First, he recalls the dramatic move on the part of the first vernacular poets to compose in a language other than Latin. They did so, according to Dante, in order to communicate with women, their beloveds. Yet since this innovation was primarily formal, he argues that there remains a substantial continuity between Latin ("composing in verses") and vernacular poetry ("composing in rhyme"). For this reason, he also limits the possible thematic scope of the latter to the topic of love, since the precedent offered by earlier experiments of writing poetry in the vernacular was motivated by case-specific necessity.

For his second example, Dante invokes the "maggiore licenza" (greater license; *VN* 16.7) afforded to poets, both ancient and modern, in employing metaphors. His description of love as a separate substance thus falls within the accepted parameters of poetic language. It does not follow, however, that a poet can arbitrarily use figures of speech as he pleases. He should be able to "undress" a given metaphor and explain its intended meaning, its "ragionamento," in prose; there must always be an underlying rationale, "ragione," for the use of tropic language (*VN* 16.10). Dante here pits the "reasonable" free use of poetic language against the boldness, "baldanza" (*VN* 16.10), of those boorish poets who use it in a haphazard manner without any connection to objective meaning.

In both these instances, Dante underscores his belief that true artistic freedom is not arbitrary but justified. The decision to write poetry in Italian was caused by new historical circumstances, namely the *utilitas publica* of communicating with women. This innovation is bound by the requirement of providing what lawyers referred to as a *iusta causa* (just cause), an internal motivation based on legal principles.[40] In such a historiographical narrative, instead of signaling a rupture with the old system, the vernacular poets promote it by updating the laws of versification to encompass unforeseen circumstances. Similarly, the troping of signifiers from their proper meaning has to be based on the higher norm of an underlying message. Just as a judge's discretion was nonetheless subject to the *ratio* of the normative legal order, so too was the poet's when diverging from ordinary linguistic usage.

Dante's proposed limits on artistic freedom remain idiosyncratic (does he really believe that poetry can only be written about love?) and no doubt they are influenced, as is often pointed out, by a personal agenda (whose target is primarily the moralizing poet Guittone). At the same time, from the perspective of legal theory they are absolutely coherent. In fact, Dante's excursus about personification is also an elegant exemplification of legal *arbitrium*, the employment of which needs to be predicated on objective reason and validated by a just cause.

Dante calls on legal terminology as well in the *Convivio*, where he uses it to defend his decision to compose a prose commentary in the vernacular. To explain the extended length of the proem, for instance, he quotes Ulpian from *Digest* 1. 4. 2: "Ne lo statuire le nuove cose evidente ragione dee essere quella che partire ne faccia da quello che lungamente è usato" (In legislating new things the reason that makes us depart from what has long been in use must be evident; 1.10.3).[41] In declaring new laws (whether legal or poetic), some evident advantage must be identified in order to justify the departure from longstanding tradition. By selecting Ulpian's justifying cause for the introduction of new laws to characterize his own innovative poetics, Dante clearly asserts that *both* artistic and political authority must provide an *evidens utilitas* or "evidente ragione" in order to sanction their actions.

In *De vulgari*, Dante expounds at length on the contrast between artistic license and mere caprice. On the one hand, he celebrates the free play allowed in choosing among vast combinations of metrical divisions, verse lengths, and rhyme schemes. Yet he also dismisses poems composed "more by chance than by art" (2.4.1), and takes specific aim at the "presumption" of would-be poets who write without art or science, daring to emulate the star-seeking eagle (2.4.11). These crude poets share in the presumptive art practiced by Nimrod and his followers. Dante ridicules them for not understanding the rules of the game, and for confusing freedom *from* specific technical conventions with freedom *to* express their will in any fashion whatsoever. Even though he grants vernacular poets "wide discretion," Dante clearly envisions them as working within a normative system.

But how does a poet come to internalize that normative system? How does he achieve the *discretio* that Dante claims it is the aim of his work to illustrate?[42] By the end of the treatise, it is clear that the key to acquiring this second nature—one is tempted to translate it simply as "taste"—stems largely from practice (*usus*). While not following codified precepts, "noble" poets who have mastered the art of the canzone know when something sounds right, and their poetic ear will not fail them even when they veer from ordinary usage, as Dante did when he created the double sestina "Amor, tu vedi ben che questa donna."[43] They are able to correctly judge under which circumstances and in what manner it is justified to diverge from the norm, because the fundamental principles of their craft have been thoroughly ingrained in them. The artist's professional discretion is in this view free from both legislated rules and the whims of individual desire; it is grounded in custom.[44]

Where the inventors of grammar came together and issued sovereign laws, Dante's approach to authority in *De vulgari* is more jurisprudential. In lieu of the legislative precepts of grammar, he seeks to formalize established practice. To this end he enshrines existing poetic techniques of versification, sentence structure, rhyme scheme, and diction arising spontaneously "from below" as part of a collective art. This jurisprudential model is especially appropriate given the Italian political context, which, as Dante points out, lacks a single monarch and tribunal (unlike in the kingdom of Germany). Because of their prolonged exceptional situation, the Italian poetic *doctores*—like their juristic counterparts—were forced to innovate and adapt. In the absence of a central political-cultural authority (such as that found in the Sicilian School under the "illustrious heroes" Frederick II and his son Manfred [1.12.4]), custom reigns. The members of the dispersed Italian court remain united by a transregional natural law as dictated by the "gracious light of reason" (1.1.8.5).[45] Having assimilated a corpus of classical and vernacular precedents as *iura* rather than *leges*, these poets remain open to justified exceptions and their norms arise from tacit consent.[46] This is a living law.

Discretionary Justice, Confession, and Torture in *Inferno*

Dante's focus on training, habit, and practice in *De vulgari eloquentia* as a means for transforming the "bad" *arbitrium* of Book One into the "good" *arbitrium* of Book Two already provides us with some insight into how his character becomes a "master" in the craft of judgment through his otherworldly journey. Echoing the trajectory of *De vulgari*, the healthy exercise of discretion in *Purgatorio* follows more unsettling instances of judgment in *Inferno*. Before we return to the peak of Purgatory to analyze the significance of Dante's crowning for his relationship with literary tradition, we must survey the negative examples of judicial discretion that emerge from his character's interaction with the damned. In two of the most emotionally charged of these encounters—with Pier della Vigna in *Inferno* 13 and Bocca degli Abati in *Inferno* 32—Dante investigates the problematic connection between judicial discretion and torture. What brings these two phenomena together, however, is the fundamental role of confession in medieval justice. Questions about the means involved in guaranteeing these confessions are first raised in the presentation of the monstrous confessor Minos.

Minos and Troubling Confessions

The unchanging universal laws of Hell are manifest in its geography, where all sins have their proper place. Yet this infallible system does not release Dante from the responsibility of individually evaluating sinners as he travels through the otherworld. Throughout *Inferno*, Dante shows the Pilgrim employing judicial discretion in his encounters with the souls, interacting with them in a space normally reserved for divine retribution. In fact, much of the drama of the *Commedia* lies in the tension that Dante's character—and by proxy, his readers—must navigate between the universal demands of the system and the personal circumstances of each sinner's case, between the map of Hell and its animation as narrative.

Of course, the Pilgrim's exercise of discretion is limited by the fact that the damned have already been definitively judged by God and sentenced by his magistrate Minos, who "essamina le colpe ne l'intrata; / giudica e manda secondo ch'avvinghia" (examines the souls' guilt at the entrance; he judges and passes sentence by how he wraps; *Inf.* 5.5–6). Minos's sentences are final, and the punishments he imposes cannot be appealed or modified. Critics have long noted the legal language and imagery used to describe Minos's function, including the summary trial he oversees before judging and dispatching the souls. Like Virgil's Minos in *Aeneid* 6, who presides over a silent jury trial before assigning the shades their allotted *sedes* (seats; *Aeneid* 6.431), he rigorously assigns the damned to their particular circle of Hell. Mapping the souls onto their place in Hell with his spiraling tail, Minos reminds us of Dante-the-poet, who created Hell's spiraling geography as a normative system.[47]

But Minos has another less obvious judicial role as well. He is described as an expert ("conoscitor"; *Inf.* 5.9) for his ability to probe and uncover the sins of those who come before him. If Minos's role in assigning the damned their lots recalls his namesake in the Virgilian underworld, his role as inquisitor points to the harsh judge of Tartarus, Minos's brother Rhadamanthus: "Gnosius haec Rhadamanthus habet durissima regna / castigatque auditque dolos subigitque fateri" (Gnosian Rhadamanthus holds here his iron sway; he chastises, and hears the tale of guilt, exacting confession of crimes; *Aeneid* 6.566–567). But Dante's Minos differs from Virgil's Rhadamanthus in one key respect. Rhadamanthus uses force to extract a confession from the shades, while the damned confess of their own free will to Minos (just as they were "desirous" to cross the river Acheron). If we compare the triad *essamina/giudica/manda* with *castigat/audit/subigit*, we can see how Dante has removed the spectre of violence from the juridical ritual. Or so it would appear. Dante also transforms his Virgilian sources by turning Minos into a hybrid beast, an anthropomorphic monster who greets the souls with a menacing snarl and signifies with his tail. While the comic brutishness of his rage seems darkly appropriate for the punishment of judged souls (including when he bites his tail before sentencing Guido da Montefeltro), can the same be said for the discovery phase of their trial? What are we to make of this confluence of bureaucratic rationality and animalistic passion?

Dante follows his initial description of Minos with a parenthetical explanation: "Dico che quando l'anima mal nata / li vien dinanzi, tutta si confessa" (I say that when the ill-born soul comes before him, it confesses all; *Inf.* 5.78). Readers since Boccaccio have viewed this curious recapitulation as a means of expanding on the concise initial sketch of Minos's office.[48] But what provokes this clarification? I would argue that Dante feels compelled to elaborate because he recognizes the dissonance between the automatism he has just described and the difficulty actual judges face when trying to discover the truth about crimes. Unlike in the utopian scenario imagined for Minos, contemporary judges could rarely rely on the "full proof" of a confession, at least not without resorting to rhadamanthine measures. In Dante's "dico," he is allaying readers' uncertainty about the outcomes of judicial examinations, especially when they involve "troubling confessions."[49]

If in his capacity as infernal administrator Minos evokes the totalizing vision of Dante-the-poet, his inquisitorial duties, which are never directly represented, seem instead to be displaced onto Dante's character, whose mission is to interrogate the souls and relay the truth of their sins to the living. In this sense, as a "connoisseur of sin," Dante truly is a judge, continually investigating and at times even provoking the statements of the damned. Moreover, Dante still needs to contend with the unreliable narrations of the damned and ascertain the *fides* of their testimony.[50] In order to perform this task, Dante uses all the interrogatory methods at his disposal—from simple courtesy and offers of compensation to deception, threats, and outright violence. Contemporary judges were similarly granted a great deal of procedural flexibility when it came to interviewing witnesses during the interrogatory phases of a trial.[51] In *Inferno*, Dante illustrates what happened when these liberties were abused, and when *arbitrium* became the expression of lower passions rather than of higher norms.

The use of torture in obtaining a confession from the accused provides a limit case for the discretion granted to judges during the inquisitorial portion of a trial, and it plays a key role in Dante's penal colony as well.[52] Despite widespread ordinances prohibiting its use against citizens, torture was a recognized instrument of medieval justice, especially if the accused was deemed infamous.[53] The discretionary use of torture often increased during situations of civic unrest, particularly insofar as it helped secure guilty verdicts. For example, in the so-called *Litterae arbitrariae* (Arbitrary Letters), King Robert of Naples delegated wide discretionary powers to local magistrates, allowing them to arrest, torture, and condemn well-known criminals without the conventional procedural guarantees, so as to counter a sudden rise in banditry and interpersonal violence.[54] These officials were to administer justice according to their *arbitrium*, regardless of procedural law, "keeping nonetheless God and justice before their eyes."[55]

At the same time, many jurists feared that such practices risked undermining the legitimacy of the trial process (*ordo iuris*). As a result, they regulated and restricted the use of torture, and often considered inadmissible the confessions and testimony extracted with its use, citing Ulpian to the effect that torture was a "fickle and dangerous business that ill serves the cause of truth" (*Digest* 48.18.23). Keeping justice before their eyes meant not violating certain fundamental rights of the accused.[56]

Pier della Vigna

Contemporary anxieties about the ethical and epistemological stakes of torture inform the episode of Pier della Vigna in *Inferno* 13. Dante encounters Piero in the seventh circle of Hell among those who have committed violence against themselves: the suicides. Since the suicides tore apart the subtle and sacred knot uniting the human with the divine, thus commanding the body to rebel against the soul, they are punished by having their faculties fragmented and reassembled in a new monstrous hybrid form—a plant that speaks and feels. After death, the severed souls are randomly planted as seeds in the soil of the seventh circle, where, in a parody of reproduction and generation, they grow a plant body. The Harpies—themselves a hybrid of girlish faces and foul bird bodies—feed on the new plant bodies, tormenting them and, paradoxically, giving the damned their only outlet for speech, through their wounds: "Fanno dolore e al dolor fenestra" (They cause pain and a window for that pain; *Inf.* 13.102). Even at the Last Judgment, when the other shades will be reunited with their bodies, the disrespected bodies of the suicides will hang from their branches in eternity—an ironic image of suicidal death by hanging.

But Dante's character only learns these details gradually, as the conversation with Piero unfolds. His initial confusion about his surroundings plays an important role within the action of the episode. At the beginning of the canto, the pilgrim finds himself in the midst of a sterile forest of gnarled trees and thorn bushes, apparently populated only by the Harpies. At this point he is ignorant of the source of the screams heard emanating from the forest. In order to prove that these come from the trees themselves (when they are bitten by the Harpies), and not from persons hiding behind the trees, Virgil prompts Dante to tear off a nearby branch. The branch Dante chooses turns out to be one of Piero's metamorphosized limbs. Piero cries out twice in pain at the violation he sustains at Dante's hands: "Perché mi schiante?" (Why do you split me?; *Inf.* 13.33) and "Perché mi scerpi?" (Why do you pluck me?; 35).

Virgil is forced to resort to this extreme gesture because he suspects Dante would not have otherwise believed the "incredible" (*Inf.* 13.50) truth. In particular, Virgil doubts whether Dante would have been able to simply trust his speech, his "sermone" (21), or the description of a similar phenomenon found in his poem, "la mia rima" (my verses; 48). In mentioning his "rima," Virgil is calling attention to the episode in *Aeneid* 3.39–48 in which Aeneas, while plucking shrubs to sacrifice on the Thracian shore, unwittingly draws blood from a myrtle bush covering the grave of murdered Polydorus. At this violation, Priam's youngest son cries out from beneath the ground in words that Piero echoes here. Yet despite the close parallel between what Dante has read and what he sees and hears before him—plants that feel pain, and speak—he needs to be convinced by another of his senses, touch. Unable to heed Virgilian precedent, the observer Dante uncharacteristically becomes an active participant in the infernal theater of justice. Indeed, an atmosphere of sustained interpretive doubt permeates the canto. Even Virgil's telepathy is temporarily blocked, as teacher and pupil cannot seem to read each others' intentions (i.e., "I believed that he believed that I must have believed . . . "; *Inf.* 13.25). In order to cut through this semiotic impasse, Virgil suggests a violent solution. If neither written evidence (*rima*) nor testimony (*sermone*) will suffice, then Piero's body can be made to speak through physical harm. In order to discover the truth, a dehumanized body is manipulated and forced to speak. Dante emphasizes this dehumanization by objectifying Piero's speech; he compares it to a green log which, when lit on one end, drips sap and sputters air out of the other. While the poet conceives of human speech in terms of a fusion between divine reason and corporeal voice—a figure of the Incarnation—the speech of suicides who have renounced that union is reduced to pure materiality.[57] The terrifying uncanniness of this creaturely speech, emanating from the plant flesh as bodily discharge, is disturbing precisely because it reminds us of the non-human elements of our embodied lives, a plane of existence that the technology of torture deliberately seeks to access.

Yet despite the monstrous imagery and language pervading the episode, Piero pleads for mercy by appealing to the common humanity he shares with his tormentor:

Uomini fummo, e or siam fatti sterpi:
ben dovrebb'esser la tua man più pia
se state fossimo anime di serpi

(We were men, and now we have become plants; truly your hand should be more merciful had we been the souls of serpents; *Inf.* 13.37–39.)

No longer a citizen, the author of the Constitutions of Melfi now seeks to ground his protections in a more comprehensive order: "We were men."

In a canto distinguished by its rhetorical inventiveness, this simple declaration gains poignancy when we recognize the similarities between Piero's and Dante's fates.[58] In an elegant speech, Piero testifies to his innocence and explains the circumstances behind his suicide. Although he had once been Frederick II's closest confidant, the envy of the court resulted in his being falsely accused—the same sort of political envy and false accusations that Dante the poet also suffered. It was this disgrace, Piero tells Dante and Virgil, that he had hoped to escape by taking his own life.

In an impenetrable forest not unlike the one in which he found himself at the onset of the poem, Dante's character encounters a Boethian figure whose dehumanizing punishment, at once tragic and just, could well have been his own were it not for the intervening grace of Beatrice and the consolation of the journey. Moreover, echoing Dante's concerns in Book One of *Convivio*, Piero seems especially sensitive to his loss of credibility; he insists in his speech on his own trustworthiness, his "fede" (*Inf.* 13.62, 74), and beseeches Dante to restore his memory. When he swears by his "new roots" (73) that he never broke faith with Frederick, he asks his interlocutors to perform a counterintuitive and extraordinary act of judgment: to recognize his *fides* despite his degeneration of status.

In this realm extant beyond the normal course of law, at the limits of the human, Dante's character (and vicariously his readers) are thus faced with a dilemma. Can this damned soul, "imprisoned" (*Inf.* 13.87) within a tree body, be believed? Moreover, does he still deserve certain fundamental rights? Virgil appears to think so, and is quick to point out that the violence he urged against Piero (Dante's splitting and plucking) was only a last resort. It personally pains him to have recommended it, he adds. Virgil also seems to agree that Piero has been treated unlawfully, referring to him in legal language as "lesa" (injured; 47) and one deserving of reparations in the form of a restored "fama" (53). In a similar vein, when Dante first harms Piero, Piero assails him for lacking all pity ("pietade alcuno"; 36), yet by the time the suicide has finished his story, Dante's character is so overcome by pity that he cannot continue the interview.

But according to recent criticism on the canto, pity for Piero is exactly what Dante wants to discourage in readers. Canto 13 has become a test case for those Dante scholars who see in the ironic and self-deceptive confessions of the damned a manifestation of God's—and the poet's—"fearful justice."[59] In this view, Piero is to be dismissed as a Judas, a traitor, and probably an avaricious embezzler as well.

To my mind, this liquidation of the Pilgrim's pity as simply misplaced seriously underestimates the challenge of the poem. What distinguishes the episode of Piero from that of Polydorus is the way in which Dante problematizes the role of pity for the two protagonists.[60] When Polydorus cries out to Aeneas, he warns him not to unwittingly tarnish his *already* pious hands by defiling his grave. Despite his initial fear, the Trojan hero is never in doubt about what the appropriate action in these circumstances should be: to provide Polydorus with a proper burial and tomb. In Dante's reimagining of the Virgilian episode, however, it is a truly open question whether his character should act piously toward Piero. The poet situates the episode, moreover, within an evidentiary framework in which the pilgrim needs to evaluate the "fede" of both Virgil and Piero. Dante critics who view Piero's speech as mere deceptive rhetoric ignore the vital role that autonomous judgment plays in the narrative journey. In a sense, they want to return the Pilgrim to the transparency of epic justice, but in reverse: just as Aeneas need always be pious, Dante's character needs to rid himself entirely of pity. Yet a crucial element of the drama in this canto is the ethical tension created between the demands of Dante's mission and the "rights" of individual souls. Further, while Polydorus belongs to the same race and clan as Aeneas, Piero confronts Dante with a figure of extreme otherness, forcing him to navigate within an ethical space to some extent beyond the law—or at least beyond its explicit precepts.

We must account for the undeniable fact that at some level Dante's character regrets having used the license afforded him as a means for discovery, recognizing it as wrong despite Piero's guilt and deserved punishment. The violation of the borders of Piero's ghastly body provokes a prolonged discomfort in readers, a sense of taboo, which cannot be easily dismissed as naive interpretation. When Dante gathers the leaves for the anonymous suicide at the beginning of canto 14, an exceptional and unique moment in which he alleviates the physical torment of one of the damned, this discretionary gesture emerges out of a conscience stricken by having faultily administered the power that had been delegated to him.[61] Unlike Minos, he is troubled by the charge of his office.

Bocca degli Abati

Dante shows no such squeamishness further down in the journey, when he encounters the traitors condemned to Cocytus. In *Inferno* 32, while traversing the frozen lake in which the damned are imprisoned, he inadvertently kicks the head of the political traitor Bocca degli Abati. Like Piero, Bocca twice objects to this inadvertent offense, a repetition that links the two episodes: "Perché mi peste?" (Why do you pound me?; *Inf.* 32.79) and "Perché mi moleste?" (Why do you bother me?; 81). Bocca complains in particular that the treatment is excessive, "troppo" (too much; 90)—a supplemental punishment beyond what has been divinely decreed.

Yet instead of provoking pity, Bocca's outbursts only inflame the Pilgrim. In this instance, Dante takes the initiative in assuming the role of inquisitorial judge, asking Virgil for license to interrogate Bocca: "Maestro mio, or qui m'aspetta, / sì ch'io esca d'un dubbio per costui; / poi mi farai, quantunque vorrai, fretta" (My master, now wait for me here, so that I can be freed from a doubt by him; then you can hurry me as much as you will; *Inf.* 32.82–84). After Dante promises Virgil that he will make up for lost time after the interview, Virgil gives him leave to move and act on his own—one of the rare occurrences in *Inferno* in which Dante's character is without a guide. Dante then makes Bocca (whose identity is still unknown at this point) his standard offer of "fama" (*Inf.* 32.92). When this diplomatic gesture fails, however, he grabs the shade by the scalp and begins pulling out clumps of hair in an attempt to force him to reveal his name. This brutal method for eliciting information from the damned appears to be sanctioned within the chronotope of the poem by a form of *arbitrium*, a delegated power granted outside the normal course and time of the journey.

The primary reason why Dante's character treats Bocca differently from Piero is that Bocca is a traitor. The traitors of Cocytus belong to an entirely different category of sinners; instead of violating a specific law, they reject the entire system on which individual norms are based. Since they are unconcerned with the shared values of human society, it is also impossible to negotiate with them. (Dante learns this when Bocca, unlike Piero, rejects his conciliatory offer of fame.) These damned are beyond the pale.

Dante elaborates on this outsider status when he breaks his pact with another traitor, Brother Alberigo, refusing to remove the ice from his eyes after having promised to do so in exchange for the damned shade's testimony. Effectively casting Alberigo beyond the reach of the law, Dante justifies his mistreatment by explaining that "cortesia fu lui esser villano" (it was courteous to deal rudely with him; *Inf.* 33.150). With its paradoxical language, this terse formula resembles the popular legal maxim: "In these cases it is the order of law not to observe the order of law."[62] Lawyers in favor of strengthening the public authorities' ability to prosecute crime (such as the judge Gandinus) invoke this adage to justify deviating from normal procedural guarantees (including protections against torture) when dealing with notorious criminals; these "repeat offenders," like the souls of Cocytus, have themselves already rejected the "order."

Dante is at first confused to find Brother Alberigo among the damned because as far as he knows the friar is still alive. Both scenarios turn out to be true: Alberigo reveals to him that the damned who inhabit Ptolomea, the subregion of Cocytus in which traitors against guests are punished, have committed sins so abominable that their living bodies have been possessed by devils while their dead souls are vanquished to the underworld (one of the damned mentioned in this region, Branca Doria, died in 1325, outliving Dante). This uncanny depiction of demonic possession has long piqued critics' interest for its potential heterodoxy. Yet to my knowledge no one has remarked upon the ethical questions it foregrounds regarding the nexus of real and representational violence. Dante suggests that there are some among us who no longer deserve to be considered fully human, who speak and act and breathe like living mortal flesh, but whose souls are irredeemable. The basic human "courtesy" his character withholds from the damned souls in these last cantos—in contrast, for example, with the *cortesia* still afforded the sodomites—enacts a specific conception of emergency justice, one that authorizes denying the *ordo iuris* to those who pose an existential threat to it.

Yet even in the depths of Hell, where Dante seems to endorse the proactive torment of traitors, something is amiss. Despite its brutality, the torture of Bocca turns out to be ineffectual. Bocca defiantly refuses to say his name and claims he will not do so even if Dante were to fall upon him a thousand times (another of the damned eventually informs on him). The nature of Bocca's resistance is lucidly explained by Ulpian in his oft-cited criticism of torture. According to the Roman jurist, torture is frequently an unreliable interrogatory method because some culprits are so hardened by it that "the truth can be in no way squeezed out of them," while others, out of sheer terror, "tell any kind of lie rather than suffer torture" so that they "confess in various ways, incriminating not only themselves but others also" (*Digest* 48.18.23). Bocca clearly exemplifies the obstinate defendant under torture.[63]

Considering these negative examples of torture as a means for discovering truth, it is difficult to read the superfluous violence in Cocytus as an unproblematic expression of Dante's righteous anger, as modern critics often do. More likely, rather than assuming the perspective of the divine judge at this point, the Pilgrim is temporarily participating in the vindictiveness of the damned, and hence blurring the line between state-supported and criminal violence. One of the traitors suggests as much when he accuses Dante of "mirroring" himself in them: "Perché cotanto in noi ti specchi?" (Why do you mirror yourself so much in us? *Inf.* 32.54).[64] Even worse, by abusing the *arbitrium* which he has been granted, Dante's character risks placing himself on the same level as the rogue squadron of demons who patrol the Malebolge and torture their captured prisoners (see, in particular, their treatment of Ciampolo in *Inferno* 22). While in the scheme of things the demons still may be unwittingly performing God's will, their actions are motivated by pure sadism rather than by a regulated discretion; they require no "just cause" or "public good" to harm the souls in their jurisdiction. For a moment in *Inferno* 32, Dante similarly experiences what it means to rule by unbound power. When Buoso da Duera, the soul who betrays Bocca, cries out to him "Qual diavol ti tocca?" (What devil is tickling you?; *Inf.* 32.108), the literal meaning of this proverbial expression may be more apt than would first appear.

Literary Tradition, Political Crisis, and the Disappearance of Virgil

Dante's discretionary punishments at the end of *Inferno* in many ways parallel the liberty granted him at the top of Mount Purgatory: in both scenes the Pilgrim is temporarily without a guide, and thus free to make his own choices. The unfettered and problematic application of *arbitrium* observed in *Inferno* 32 is answered by the self-regulated movement of *Purgatorio* 27, where Dante's decision-making is similarly unbound by specific laws, yet at the same time is "upright" and "whole." As in *De vulgari*, Dante thus sets up a contrast between two types of discretion or license: one an antinomial no-man's-land, the other still responsive to higher norms.

The distance between these two forms of autonomy is the distance from Cocytus to Eden. Dante's otherworldly journey, and the purgatorial ascent in particular, exemplifies the process by which private whim is transformed into regulated discretion. In particular, the Pilgrim's voyage is undertaken in order to reeducate and discipline his inclinations, which jurists referred to as the *motus* of the judge. By the time he arrives at Earthly Paradise, his "motion" can be given free rein because he has succeeded in internalizing the correct orientation of his guide.

Outside of Purgatory, the development of a full-fledged *conscientia* from the general inclinations of *synderesis* depends on positive law. In contrast with Augustine's conception of political authority, Dante views the injunctions and prohibitions—the "guida" (guide) and "fren" (rein; *Purg.* 16.93)—of the law not as repressing fallen human desire, but as directing it. The emperor habituates his subjects toward proper ends and spontaneous good judgment through the enforcement of the law. The natural law universally implanted in human minds is thus fully realizable only through the historical implementation of the *ius commune*.

In Dante's diagnosis of contemporary society, mankind has been led astray by the lack of a proper authority to enforce the laws: "Le leggi son, ma chi pon man ad esse?" (The laws are there, but who lays hand to them?; *Purg.* 16.97)—hence the need for the Pilgrim's exceptional journey. But the poet's solution to this power vacuum is not to insist upon the freedom of the individual or the autonomy of the artist. Art does play a vital role in Dante's political philosophy, but it does so by enshrining a collective tradition rather than urging individual expression. The Pilgrim's rehabilitation in *Purgatorio*, for instance, would be impossible without the exemplars of virtue and vice encountered on each cornice of Purgatory. These texts mimic the public authorities by "whipping" the souls toward the good and "reining" them in from its opposite.[65] By deploying the same equestrian metaphors to describe the emperor's rule in ordinary conditions and the exemplars in these extraordinary ones, Dante suggests that artistic phenomena can at least temporarily fulfill the emperor's function as ethical "pilot."[66]

Dante's *Purgatorio* thus makes a remarkable case for art as a positive form of social conditioning. Nor does the poet shy away from the embodied aspect of this phenomenon: Dante's character does not simply interpret the exemplars he sees and hears; he is engrossed by them, and his reaction to them is profoundly physical. That relation between art and bodily *hexis* is most fully set forth on the first terrace of pride, where Dante's character must bow his head in humility in order to observe the bas-reliefs of pride punished. He must stay bowed to speak with the miniaturist Oderisi, who is bent over from having to carry a heavy rock—the punishment for all of the prideful. When the pilgrim tells Sapia on the terrace of the envious that the burden of the prideful already "weighs" on him (*Purg.* 13.138), he makes explicit the fact that one of the main instruments of purgatorial reeducation is the "bodily knowledge" that comes from these automatic, unconscious gestures such as posture and gait.[67] Reversing a millennium-long prejudice against mimetic representation due to its dangerous influence over the lower passions, Dante seizes on the potential of lifelike art to make the body understand before the mind is ready to do so.

But does this bold new ethical role for artistic representation amount to the same familiar claim: that against the backdrop of the twin crises of Church and Empire, Dante stages the emergence of the modern individual artist? It could appear so, if not for a crucial distinction. The texts Dante selects to illustrate the role of art in the re-education of the souls, the pilgrim, and, vicariously, readers, belong to a collective tradition: a world of schoolroom exercises, sermons, and church frescoes (the "Bible of the Unlettered"). This shared inheritance preceded Dante, and through his poem it will be sustained. By protecting the "public domain" in this way, Dante avoids the proprietary claims behind the presumption of artists such as Nimrod. Instead, just as David transferred the Ark of the Covenant from the northern kingdom into Jerusalem—one of the first "whips" depicted in the poem—his office is to shepherd the remnants of tradition through the interregnum.

These exemplary texts extend rather than counter the conservative, heteronomous qualities of the law by calling readers to order. Though seldom remarked on, one of the most important aspects of the "visibile parlare" (visible speech; *Purg.* 10.95) Dante describes on the terrace of pride is its interactive nature.[68] Despite their quasi-magical capacity to confound the senses, the bas-reliefs depicting examples of humility require viewers in order for them to "speak." Dante hears in his mind the archangel Gabriel's greeting, "Ave," and the Virgin's response, "Ecce ancilla Dei" (*Purg.* 10.40, 44) not only because of the realistic nature of the engraving but also because this text is already ingrained in his memory. The scene of the emperor Trajan and the widow calls to mind an entire dialogue, an exchange found in similar form in other contemporary vernacular texts. The oft-told tales found in the *Purgatorio* in fragmentary form serve as prompts, triggering recollections of the collective and interiorized narratives that not only Dante and the souls but readers as well were no doubt expected to supply. Dante's response to the political vacuum of his day was thus to provide for posterity an encyclopedic archive of verbal and visual cues capable of summoning forth the authoritative yet dormant scripts of social behavior. Like the effigies of dead loved ones engraved on the top of tombs, these triggers "prick" the memory and "spur" (*Purg.* 12.20–21) the conscience, almost as a bodily reflex.

The main representative of cultural survival amidst political catastrophe is of course Virgil himself. In *Inferno* 30, Dante makes explicit Virgil's role in transmitting the communal values of tradition to his character, despite the sociopolitical degeneration that surrounds them. Near the end of the canto, Virgil chides the Pilgrim for allowing himself to be captivated by the verbal skirmish between archsinners Master Adam and Sinon. Stung by this reprimand for having participated in the debased and "modern" spectacle between the two perjurers—a vituperative, comic *tenzone*—Dante feels shame, "vergogna" (*Inf.* 30.134), and views himself suddenly from the outside and through the eyes of his authoritative ancestors, his *maiores*. Virgil immediately pardons Dante, but not before cautioning him, should he ever find himself in similar circumstances, to always keep him (Virgil) by his side: "E fa ragion ch'io ti sia sempre allato" (*Inf.* 30.145). Dante's otherworldly journey aims to do just that.

The pilgrimage is meant to transform the traditional norms embodied by the Roman author into an internalized guide for the vernacular poet, an inner compass that will never abandon him. The process by which Dante incorporates this public conscience frames the entire purgatorial journey.[69] At the onset of the ascent of Purgatory, Dante directly apostrophizes Virgil's conscience: "O dignitosa coscïenza e netta" (O worthy clear conscience; *Purg.* 3.8), realizing how much he depends on his guide to scale the mountain. Psychological and physical movement fuse at this moment; Dante still needs to be directed in both.

At the other end of the journey, Dante again explicitly associates Virgil with externalized conscience. Before entering Earthly Paradise, Dante's character must traverse the purgatorial fire, yet despite Virgil's prodding and encouragement, he hesitates, frozen in terror: "E io pur fermo e contra coscïenza" (And I being still fixed and against conscience; *Purg.* 27.33). For the very last time before being granted "libero arbitrio," Dante acts against Virgil and against conscience. When his character willingly submits to the punishment of the fire—which reminds him of real punishments he has already witnessed, "umani corpi già veduti accesi" (human bodies already seen burning; *Purg.* 27.18)—the final hindrance between the demands of the system and personal autonomy is overcome. Dante is free to roam in Eden, but he is not freed from the memory of what happened to him at the beginning of the canto, the experience of a measureless— literally meterless ("senza metro"; *Purg.* 27.51)—pain.

Dante is granted a circumscribed liberty in his coronation to adapt what he has absorbed—not to distinguish himself from it or to create it *ex nihilo*. This distinction between judicial *arbitrium* and sovereign will is meaningful for literary critics as well as for scholars focusing on Dante's political thought, for the poet's views about psychological and juridical freedom are intimately linked with his conception of artistic innovation. While there is a long tradition in Dante studies celebrating Dante's rewriting of canonical texts as an agonistic act against his precursors, Dante himself conceives of his innovations as a means to conserve and revive literary tradition—a tradition he conceived of as a living law. Nowhere is this more pronounced than in the baton-passing from classical to Christian poet staged in the last cantos of *Purgatorio*, where Virgil grants Dante liberty shortly before disappearing and leaving him with a new guide in Beatrice. While most modern critics view Virgil's disappearance as symbolizing Dante's artistic liberation from his literary father, in reality it signals the successful interiorization of Virgil's vision. Dante is free to innovate the poetic system represented by Virgil at this point only because he has become inseparable from it.

The Oedipal reading of the relationship between Dante and Virgil finds its most fertile testing ground in the dizzying series of Virgilian allusions that accompany the advent of Beatrice in *Purgatorio* 30.[70] First, while enclosing Beatrice in a floral nimbus, the angels sing "Manibus, oh date lilïa plenis" (Oh, give lilies with full hands; *Purg.* 30.21), a direct citation of *Aeneid* 6.883, the dramatic climax of Anchises's lament for the premature death of Augustus's heir, Marcellus. Second, Dante translates *Aeneid* 4.23, in which Dido confesses to her sister that the passion she felt for her deceased husband has been reawakened by Aeneas, to convey his commotion at once again beholding Beatrice: "Conosco i segni de l'antica fiamma!" (I recognize the signs of the ancient flame!; 48). Finally, after Dante's character discovers that Virgil has disappeared, the poet cries out to him, naming him three times within a single tercet (49, 50, 51), an allusion to Orpheus's dying calls to Eurydice in the fourth *Georgic*.

In John Freccero's powerful reading of this episode, he interprets the progression from direct citation to translation to mere allusion of Virgil's text as an "effacement" of the sign of the father.[71] Yet in light of Virgil's role throughout the ascent as Dante's *coscïenza*, I would argue that, rather than an effacement of the master signifier, these allusions are meant to indicate the degree to which Virgil's texts have fused with Dante's poetic superego. The resulting intertextuality does not come at Virgil's expense, turning Virgil's texts against him. Instead, it is evidence that the initiate has been successfully interpellated within the symbolic order. Virgil's perspective and values are now so profoundly a part of the Pilgrim's apprehension of the world around him as to be reflexive, an automatic response beneath the level of consciousness to the world around him. Dante now spontaneously thinks and speaks in Virgilian, and the Latin poet can finally vanish, because he will now truly always be by Dante's side.

Of course, Dante needs to reformulate the Virgilian models to meet the radically altered conditions brought about by Christian revelation. Beatrice's victory over death is imagined in purposeful contrast to the doomed passion of Dido, the tragic sacrifice of Marcellus, and the irreconcilable loss of Eurydice; Christian redemption supercedes classical fatalism. Yet to see this reworking of classical sources as willful misreading, or indeed as a betrayal or even violence, is to perpetuate our own bourgeois myths about artistic creativity. No one would deny Dante's almost unprecedented literary ambition and the rhetorical maneuvering he undertakes to assure himself a place in the canon. However, if we focus primarily on the all-too-familiar metanarrative of individualistic artistic striving, assuming the revisions to Virgil's texts are meant primarily to undercut him, we miss much of the poignancy of the Dante-Virgil relationship. What we witness atop Mount Purgatory is not a heroic overcoming of tradition but a heroic recuperation of it, the culmination of Dante's attempts at salvaging the authoritative narratives of Western culture in the face of personal and political catastrophe. Virgil's faint voice, almost imperceptible because of neglect when the Pilgrim first encounters him in *Inferno* 1, is made to speak again in *Purgatorio* 30 with renewed relevance. Dante employs a newly delegated *arbitrium* to guarantee the continued vitality of a collective and transgenerational enterprise. Transforming pagan tragedy into Christian comedy, he acts beyond the law to fulfill it.

3

Above the Law
Privilegium

Introduction

The most fundamental exception of the *Commedia* is the journey itself: Dante's character is allowed to travel unharmed through the otherworld while still alive. His singular access to this restricted territory is justified by his mission to ensure the salvation of himself and his readers. But that mission is in direct violation of the laws of the afterlife, as Cato registers when he marvels that Virgil and Dante have escaped, in defiance of the divine edicts, from the "eternal prison" (*Purg.* 1.41). In fact, many guardians of the infernal city call into question Dante's exemption from local jurisdiction and the authority of his writ of safe passage.

In this chapter, I argue that Dante treats the extraordinary grace of the Pilgrim's journey as if it were a legal privilege, much like an imperial rescript or a papal dispensation. At several key moments in the narrative, this special provision brings to the fore questions that were much discussed by contemporary legal thinkers. The two central issues raised by Dante's privilege are (1) the relationship of the ruler to his laws and (2) the potential inequalities created by laws aimed at specific persons. The first three sections of the chapter will focus on the relationship between the ruler and his laws. Each time the infernal guardians test Dante's writ, they call into question the source of the authority underwriting his privilege. Does it reside in the constituted order or in the sovereign's absolute decree—in God's capacity or in his justice? How can we reconcile, moreover, the universality of God's power with the jurisdictional conflict at the gates of Hell? Most importantly, can the violence of history, as experienced firsthand by Cato, ever be incorporated within a stable and lawful conception of providence?

The last two sections of the chapter will confront the inequalities created by privileges and immunities. Dante's specific privilege is contrasted to the general privileges of the clergy and the nobility, the categories of persons who most benefited from privileges in medieval Italy. In his encounters with the Jovial Friars in *Inferno*, Dante questions the legal practice of exempting individuals from the collective burdens of a community. In his meeting with his noble ancestor Cacciaguida in *Paradiso*, not only does he discover the higher norm regulating his journey, but he ultimately seeks to refound the authority of privileges on obligations rather than rights.

Two of Dante's interlocutors identify his fated journey specifically as a "privilege," emphasizing the technical term each time in rhyme position. In *Inferno* 23, Catalano dei Malvolti wonders "per qual privilegio" (by which privilege; 89) Dante and Virgil are exempt from wearing the heavy leaden cloaks that weigh down the rest of the hypocrites. In *Purgatorio* 26, the poet Guido Guinizzelli recognizes Dante's "ampio privilegio" (great privilege; 127) of visiting God while still alive. Between these two statements, the fundamental elements of Dante's privilege are set forth. Above all, it is a writ of safe passage, valid until he reaches his ultimate destination (which coincides with the granting authority). As a corollary, he is released from the normal obligations and burdens imposed by the local jurisdictions he traverses. The collective rule that punishes the souls he encounters and restrains their movement does not apply to him.

These characteristics are perfectly in line with the standard juris-prudential thinking about privileges in Dante's time. For the most part, legal theories about privileges in the Middle Ages coalesce around two traditional definitions.[1] The first definition derived from Isidore of Seville's *Etymologies* V.18 and was disseminated in Gratian's *Decretum*: "Privilegia autem sunt leges privatorum, quasi privatae leges, nam privilegium inde dictum quod in privato feratur" (Privileges are moreover laws of individuals; they are, so to speak, private laws. For, the privilege is so called because it is applied in pri-vate use; *Dist.* 3 c. 3). Medieval commentators glossing this defini-tion focused on the beneficial conditions *privilegia* afforded specific individual recipients (*privus* is here synonymous with *singulus* and opposed to *communis*). Although jurists occasionally used this attes-tation of privilege to refer to any advantageous condition protected by the law, in its strict technical sense a privilege was an ad hoc pro-vision expressly benefiting a specified individual or entity, and was valid only for the case at hand. Dante's permission to travel through the otherworld clearly belongs to this more restricted usage.

By Dante's time, another definition of *privilegium* had become increasingly influential in Italian legal circles. In this definition, the etymology of *priv-* in *privilegium* derives not from the substan-tive *privatus* but from its related verb *privare* (to deprive or release): "Privilegium est quod aliquem a iure communi privat vel immunem facit" (Privilegium is that which frees someone from the *ius commune* or renders him immune).[2] While the first definition had defined *priv-ilegium* positively, emphasizing its effects on specific individuals, this definition described it negatively, as a release from the obligations of the *ius commune*. This second definition also foregrounded the essen-tial relationship between privilege and immunity in medieval legal thought. Jurists often treated the terms *privilegium* and *immunitas* as near synonyms—especially in canon law, where privileges formed the legal foundation for the Church's autonomy. By exempting the recipient from what touched all, a privilege released its holder from the common *munus*—from the duties, burdens, and obligations that bound others in the community. Viewed through the lens of immu-nity, privileges limited the general validity of norms, depriving the *ius commune* of its universal reach.

Although jurists always treated privileges as an exception to the rule, this deviation was not in itself deemed unlawful. Rather than *contra ius* (against the law), privileges were classified as *praeter* and *extra ius* (beyond and outside of the law). While contradicting the tenor of certain positive laws, they did not violate the fundamental principles of the legal order. On the contrary, privileges ensured that these principles were applied to concrete reality by allowing rulers to suspend on occasion the general law or to declare its inapplicability for a specific individual or case.

Medieval jurists nonetheless remained concerned by two potential sources of injustice inherent in such exceptions. First, the right of rulers to issue privileges exposed a tension between the ordinary course of positive law and a ruler's decree. More than any other juridical phenomenon, privileges presented legal theorists with the possibility of a norm rendered valid solely by the will of the ruler, without reference to an objective rationale or long-standing tradition. In investigating the source of a privilege's authority, as well as potential limits to its application and interpretation, jurists navigated the conflicting claims of subjective and objective visions of the law.[3] Under what conditions could a ruler issue privileges that were at odds with reigning laws?

The second issue stemmed from the inequalities created by privileges. Individual privileges violated a fundamental precept of the *Corpus iuris civilis*, expressed in Ulpian's dictum that "laws are created generally and not for singular persons" (*Dig.* 1.3.8).[4] In his gloss of this passage, Accursius underscored how the general applicability of a law guaranteed its fairness: "Laws are not enacted so that one law holds for one person, another for another . . . but generally for all persons."[5] Privileges, on the other hand, were seen by their nature to "deprive" (*privare*) the law of its general reach: "Privilege is the name for that through which the laws are deprived of their general applicability."[6] Although in theory they functioned outside of the law and were thus not in conflict with the *ius communis*, these exceptional decrees remained troubling for jurists whose reputations and livelihoods depended on upholding the rule of law. Indeed, at least since Cicero's critique of *privilegia* (the likely source of Isidore's definition), a long-standing school of legal thought had questioned the legitimacy of provisions aimed at benefiting (or harming) select individuals.[7]

In order to ensure that these special administrative provisions remained within their purview and did not undermine their legal order, jurists demanded justification for them in higher norms. The guarantee of a privilege's validity depended on its containing an explicit or implicit "just cause" in line with the fundamental principles of the system or a "common benefit" (*utilitas communis*) for the community. Dante constructs his journey through the otherworld as a way of arriving at and probing the source of these matters.

The Dual Authority of Dante's Writ of Safe Passage: "Perché venirvi" versus "Chi 'l concede"

Dante first questions the reasons behind his journey in *Inferno* 2. The canto begins with the Pilgrim having lost his resolve before the "war" (4) that awaits him on the other side of Hell's gates. In comparison with the providential voyages of Aeneas and Paul, he finds his own journey wanting.

Aeneas and Paul undertook their otherworldly missions as part of the establishment of Church and Empire, so each is justified by a distinctly public purpose. God granted Aeneas the courtesy of descending into Hades while still alive, "pensando l'alto effetto / ch'uscir dovea di lui" (considering the high effect that was to come forth from him; *Inf.* 2.17–18). The durative participle *pensando* and the enjambment of the line unfold like God's counsel in the world, underlining the conformity of this extraordinary and punctual decision—the election of the hero to found Rome—with the greater providential order. Paul's journey requires even less explanation (a single *terzina*). The apostle was elected in order to succor the faith of believers: "per recarne conforto a quella fede / ch'è principio a la via di salvazione" (to bring thence confirmation of that faith which is the beginning of the way of salvation; 29–30). If Dante provides a "just cause" for Aeneas's journey, for Paul's he invokes a "common benefit."

In contrast with these clearly providential missions, Dante wonders aloud at why he, as a private citizen, should be chosen for a similar journey:

Ma io, perché venirvi? o chi 'l concede?
Io non Enëa, io non Paolo sono;
me degno a ciò né io né altri 'l crede.

(But I, why should I come there? or who grants it? I am not Aeneas,
I am not Paul; neither I nor others believe me worthy of that; *Inf.*
2.31–33).

Although it is easy to gloss over the parallel expressions *perché ve-
nirvi?* and *chi 'l concede?* as nearly synonymous, in reality they rep-
resent two opposing perspectives. From a legal standpoint, Dante
seeks to understand both the objective, rational cause behind his
privilege and the subjective source of its authority. As we will see,
Virgil provides only a partial response to his inquiry, focusing on the
source of Dante's writ of safe passage (on the *chi* rather than the
perché).

Virgil seeks to restore Dante's courage by explaining why he has
come to the Pilgrim's aid. While residing in Limbo, the pagan poet
was visited by a messenger from heaven, Beatrice, who beseeched
him to save Dante's character from the forest of despair and the
flood of sin. In her speech, Beatrice further traces the hierarchical
origin of her request back to St. Lucy and the Blessed Virgin.

Donna è gentil nel ciel che si compiange
di questo 'impedimento ov'io ti mando,
sì che duro giudicio là sù frange.
Questa chiese Lucia in suo dimando
e disse:—Or ha bisogno il tuo fedele
di te, e io a te lo raccomando
Lucia, nimica di ciascun crudele
si mosse, e venne al loco dov' i' era,
che mi sedea con l'antica Rachele.

(There is a noble lady in Heaven who grieves for this impediment to
which I send you, so that she breaks harsh judgment there on high.
She called Lucia in her request and said:—Now your faithful one
has need of you, and I put him in your hands.—Lucia, enemy of all

cruelty, moved and came to the place where I was sitting with the ancient Rachel; *Inf.* 2.94–102).

In her depiction of how the Blessed Virgin's extraordinary mercy for the Pilgrim has overridden the ordinary course of "harsh judgment," Beatrice emphasizes who authorized the decision and whence it came. Its origin resides "in heaven" and "on high," in that same court he will have the privilege of visiting while still alive.[8] Virgil concludes the digression by asking Dante why he still hesitates, since "three such blessed ladies have a care for you in the court of heaven" (*Inf.* 2.124–25). The power backing Dante's writ of safe passage is thus clearly set out.

Critics now generally interpret Dante's initial declaration that he is neither Aeneas nor Paul as a sly rhetorical move aimed at positing himself as *both* a new Aeneas and a new Paul, the author of the first Christian epic. Yet by refusing to accept this statement at face value, we paper over one of the major difficulties addressed in the poem. While Aeneas's and Paul's journeys are explained by their future contribution to Roman and Christian civilization, at this point Dante discovers only who authorized his journey, not why. Virgil and Beatrice illustrate the subjective aspect of Dante's privilege, the power deriving from its authoritative source. But they do not refer to any grounding in objective reason. Indeed, the social causes and collective purpose of his mission will not be revealed until Dante meets with Cacciaguida in *Paradiso* 15–17.

Dante's journey tells the story of a subjectively sanctioned privilege seeking an objectively just cause. While in the traditional epic the encounter with supernatural forces situates the hero's mission within a providential narrative, the revelation of *Inferno* 2 provides an incomplete picture of the divine plan. Virgil's speech explains who is behind the Pilgrim's privilege and identifies Dante's endangered soul as its immediate catalyst. But why in the modern era Dante alone has been chosen for such a singular journey remains unanswered. The repeal of God's "duro giudicio" (*Inf.* 2.96), instigated by the three ladies in Paradise, appears gratuitous, unmerited, and detached from the constituted system of punishments and rewards that Dante's character is about to explore—a form of prevenient grace.[9]

Rather than externally justifying Dante's extraordinary journey as fated and foreseen, Virgil's response actually elides its ultimate foundation in the public good, an absence for which the narrative must itself compensate.

Dante investigates the nature of his poetic vocation by figuring it as a diplomatic immunity under threat. Unlike Beatrice's heavenly ambassadorship, which is recognized in legal terms as *sancta*,[10] inviolable—"la vostra miseria non mi tange" (your misery does not touch me; *Inf.* 2.92)—Dante's right to descend *ad inferos* is continually put to the test. Such challenges were also common in Dante's Italy, where multiple jurisdictions over a single territory meant that border crossings were spaces charged through with potential conflict.[11] Dante capitalizes on the legal commonplace associating *limes* (border) with *lites* (disputes) by having his character traverse one boundary after another:[12] the Pilgrim is continually crossing over or through rivers, doors, gates, bridges, and mountain passes—all recognized by medieval jurists as "natural" borders. Each one of these crossings is a possible site of contention, bringing to the fore tensions between individual privileges and general laws, local autonomy and universal jurisdiction, de jure authority and de facto power. Yet for the most part Dante scholars have been preoccupied with what occurs *within* the various confines dividing up the journey, (i.e., within the circles of Hell or the cornices of Purgatory). In the next sections I investigate the liminal spaces of the poem: the frontiers dividing the actual geography of the otherworld, as well as the narrative transitions linking the metrical units of the cantos.

"Vuolsi così colà dove si puote ciò che si vuole": Absolute and Ordained Power

In the first border crossing of the poem, Virgil and Dante are met by Charon, the ferryman of the underworld. This encounter establishes a pattern to be repeated with variations throughout *Inferno*. When Charon refuses to carry Dante, as a living soul, across the river Acheron into Hell, Virgil admonishes him for his futile defiance, telling him, "Vuolsi così colà dove si puote / ciò che si vuole e più non dimandare" (This is willed there where what is willed can be done, so ask no more; *Inf.* 3.95–96). A few cantos later, Virgil repeats these exact words to Minos when he threatens to block Dante's passageway; he repeats the phrasing once more, in a slightly modified form, when Plutus threatens the Pilgrim at the beginning of canto 7. The effects of Virgil's words are always the same: the infernal guardian is rendered powerless and is compelled to allow Dante to pass (or even to facilitate his safe conduct).

The specific phrase Virgil uses to pacify Charon, Minos, and Plutus has been criticized as overly "schematic" and "mechanistic"— part of a narrative ploy abandoned by the poet as his style grew more assured.[13] But the repetitive aspect of Virgil's pronouncements is actually crucial for establishing the legal nature of Dante's writ of safe conduct. When Virgil announces that Dante is in possession of a divine concession, his listeners submit to the efficacy of his *verbum* in part because it is expressed as a juridical formula, a ritualized command with the quasi-magical qualities of a password. There is something uncanny, in fact, about the relationship between Virgil's words and what they do, between the semantic and performative aspects of his utterance. On one level, the guardians of Hell respond to the content of the expression: the threat of God's power and the reach of his will. But on another, it is their recognition of the authoritative source of the decree (*colà dove*) that ensures their obedience. In other words, God's supremacy is both the message of the formula and the guarantee of its enforcement.

Critics have for the most part reduced Virgil's repeated disarming of the demonic guardians to mere reminders of God's omnipotence. But the conceptualization of divine power that Dante explores through these interactions is more complex. To begin with, medieval theologians were hardly unanimous in their definitions of God's omnipotence, and they disagreed especially about its possible limitations. The core problem lay in the difficulty of reconciling God's absolute freedom with the dependability of his ordained system of rewards and punishments. One of the most discussed theological questions of the Middle Ages, for example, was whether God could ever act against the laws of his own creation. Could he have chosen, say, to damn Peter and save Judas? Dante's insistence on dramatizing the exceptionality of his voyage indicates that the relationship between divine intervention and the established order of creation was still an unsettled—and unsettling—topic for his public.

The language Virgil uses to describe divine authority is also more significant than is generally recognized. He divides God's power into what he wills ("si vuole") and what he is able to do ("si puote"). This definition turns on the modal verbs *potere* and *volere*, and recalls the language used in theological debates regarding the relationship between God's capacity and his volition.[14] Some early theologians argued that God's omnipotence should be defined by his power to do as he wished. By the later Middle Ages, however, most thinkers agreed that God was *able* to act other than he wished, but refrained because of his justice. In other words, his capacity exceeded his volition. The standard formula for this point of view was drawn from Augustine's concise response to the question of whether it was within God's power to have prevented Judas's betrayal: "Potuit sed noluit" (He was able to, but he did not wish to).[15] Once we recognize the contours of this century-long debate about the nature of divine omnipotence, we can better understand the significant variations in how Virgil employs his right-of-way formula with Charon, Minos, and Plutus.

Early medieval scholars drew a distinction between God's absolute and ordained powers (*potentia absoluta* and *potentia ordinata*). Yet in this classical conception, *potentia absoluta* and *potentia ordinata* were simply two perspectives on the same divine power: the first considered that power in the abstract, while the second interpreted its application from a human vantage point. (In abstract absolute terms, that is, God's power exceeded his volition. But from the perspective of the preordained creation he had willed into being, his capacity and his volition were coextensive.) By Dante's time, however, a new vision of the relationship between God's absolute and ordained powers had emerged. Instead of understanding them as different perspectives on the same power, this new view saw each as a distinct form of *action*. Drawing on the political realm to illustrate this new understanding, theologians likened God's capacity to act outside of the preordained order of nature and grace—that is, miraculously—to a ruler loosed from the laws. In its most extreme formulation, as posited by the Franciscan Duns Scotus (d. 1308), a monarchic God operated either according to his ordained power, de jure, or according to his absolute power, de facto—that is, outside the laws of his own creation.[16]

No doubt there had long been cross-fertilization between theologians writing about divine omnipotence and jurists developing the concept of absolute power. The shared use of the term *absolutus* suggests as much. Yet the canon lawyer Hostiensis (d. 1271) was the first to put this political-theological connection to explicit use. In response to the question of whether the pope could release a monk from his vow of poverty, Hostiensis drew a direct analogy between God's *potentia absoluta* and the pope's *plenitudo potestatis*. Previous canonists, whose solutions Hostiensis reviewed before proffering his own, had argued that the pope could not release this vow because it belonged to the substantial state of being a monk. At most, he could restore a monk to secular life.[17] Hostiensis instead believed that, in an emergency situation, the pope could by his fullness of powers act outside of the law to relax even substantial vows, such as those of poverty and chastity. Provided that it were for the greater good of the Church, he could in specific instances change the nature of the monastic state, "not through his ordained but through his absolute power" (*non de potestate ordinata, sed de absoluta*).[18]

Hostiensis's formulation played a vital role in the controversy between seculars and mendicants in Paris at the end of the thirteenth century.[19] At issue was the interpretation of the the privileges granted in the papal bull *Ad fructus uberes* (1281)—specifically, whether or not it allowed mendicants to effectively stand in for parish priests in the administration of confession.[20] For the secular clergy, such an expansive interpretation of mendicant privileges threatened to encroach on their jurisdiction and relegate their position to an ancillary one. In their eyes, such changes would pervert the immutable hierarchical structure of the Church.

At its core, the debate surrounding *Ad fructus uberes* pivoted on the relationship between privileges and established law.[21] The prime spokesman for the seculars was the Paris master and theologian Henry of Ghent (d. 1293), who expressed his fundamentally "constitutionalist" perspective on papal power in terms of the contrast between absolute and ordained powers.[22] According to Henry's interpretation, absolute power might be formally valid but was nonetheless sinful. In open contrast with the canonist position first voiced by Hostiensis, Henry argued that God never operated absolutely; because he was unable to do anything unjust, his capacity was wholly contained within his ordained power. On the other hand, accepting the canonist alignment of the pope's *plenitudo potestatis* with *potentia absoluta*, he allowed that the supreme pontiff might legally, albeit inordinately or even immorally, employ an absolute power outside of the law. Henry thus cast a dark shadow over the pope's fullness of powers, calling into serious doubt his absolute right to issue privileges that perverted the traditional laws and hierarchy of the Church (such as a grant to hear confessions at odds with conciliar protocols).

The friars who benefited from papal privileges naturally saw matters differently, and sought to justify those sovereign papal decrees even when they broke with tradition and existing laws. Theologians of this ilk often pointed out how the needs of the faithful differed across stages of history, making a significant distinction between the present order, *ordo ut nunc*, and the ordained order that governed the entire course of sacred history. From this perspective, historical change (such as the supplanting of circumcision with baptism) did not alter God's eternal law, but rather fulfilled it by realizing a higher purpose. The Franciscan theologian Richard of Middleton (d. 1302), Henry's main opponent in the controversy over *Ad fructus uberes*, viewed the pope as the means through which—via privileges and dispensations—God could alter present law and bring it into conformity with his general, providential plan.

Dante's privilege to roam through the otherworld, exempt from local jurisdiction as he seeks out the confessions of the damned, recapitulates the controversy between seculars and mendicants. With that comparison, I do not mean to suggest that Dante should be regarded as a mendicant and the infernal guardians as parish priests. But he did deliberately place his protagonist in situations of conflict which raise questions similar to those raised in contemporary debates over privileges: What is the relationship between the ruler and the existing order? How should long-standing tradition be weighted against historical contingency? What was the relationship between the subjective and objective grounding of the law, between the sovereign's will and intrinsic reason?

The legal-historical resonance notwithstanding, we should not read these similarities as equivalencies. Dante's privilege derives from God's authority, not from the emperor's or the pope's. But in representing this divine authority as if it were a continuously tested legal privilege, Dante inevitably draws on contemporary legal phenomena and experience. Dante's imaginative journey unfolds within an otherworldly but normative space in which theology provides a model for secular rule, and where legal practices inform theological principles. With these stakes in mind, it is important to take another look at the formula Virgil uses to defy the infernal guardians, and to analyze the subtle distinctions he makes in its various deployments.

In the first jurisdictional conflict with an infernal guardian, the encounter with Charon, the authority of Dante's writ appears to derive from the force of its issuing agent. Charon yields in the face of Virgil's formula "vuolsi così colà . . ." without conditions or context. His wooly jowls fall silent at the recognition of God's capacity to act absolutely, as he wishes. Virgil offers no further justification for Dante's privileged voyage.

The entire exchange between Virgil and Charon is modeled closely on the exchange between Charon and the Sybil in *Aeneid* 6—so closely that the elements of the Virgilian text that Dante elides, transposes, and displaces are blatant. Dante condenses the exchange in order to highlight the subjective authority of his writ irrespective of any objective cause. In the Virgilian model, Charon initially rebukes the Trojan hero and refuses him crossing because it is against sacred laws (*nefas*) and because of the punishments he (Charon) had suffered for allowing Hercules, Theseus, and Pirithoüs to violate Hades's borders. The ensuing reply of the high priestess can be divided into three parts. First, she assures Charon that Aeneas's weapons are not meant for battle, and promises that they will leave the residents of the underworld unharmed as they traverse its territory. Second, she explains the reason for the voyage, emphasizing Aeneas's piety and desire to visit his father. Third, she commands Charon to behold the golden bough, carried as a gift for Proserpina.

Of these three elements, Dante preserves only the final one in his rewriting of the episode. Virgil's formula functions like the sacred bough. It stupefies and silences not because of what it means, but by its illocutionary strength alone. It is, in other words, a synecdoche for the *force* of law, not its underlying rationale. That said, the other two parts of the Sybil's response, while temporarily deferred, are not entirely absent: the specter of violence associated with Hercules, Theseus, and Pirithoüs will reemerge in the conflict with the demons at the Gates of Dis (*Inf.* 8–9), and the revelation of the final cause of Dante's *descensus ad inferos* will occur only when the Pilgrim meets his father figure Cacciaguida in *Paradiso* 15–17, an episode based on Aeneas's meeting with Anchises.

In the first instance of Virgil's formula, Dante chooses to emphasize the absolutist nature of God's intervention in his own created order of justice. In the second instance, however, he tempers this purely subjective perspective. When confronted by Minos, Virgil warns him, "Non impedir lo suo fatale andare" (Do not impede his fated journey; *Inf.* 5.22) before restating the formula "vuolsi così colà . . ." In doing so, he seems to reinforce the sentiment of the latter, implying that the unquestionable authority behind Dante's privilege needs no justification: "so ask no more" (*Inf.* 5.24). Yet by first qualifying his right of way as *fatale*—"fated" or "decreed"—Virgil hints that Dante's writ may be backed by an ordained rather than an absolute power. The distinction is especially crucial at this point in the journey because Dante's privilege is here explicitly contrasted to ordinary justice. The Pilgrim's license to roam the underworld at will is at odds with its regular administration as overseen by Minos, whose primary duty is to assign individuals to their "place in Hell" (*Inf.* 5.10). Indeed, in his freedom of movement, his usurpation of Minos's job as confessor and judge, and his providential mission, Dante's character could be seen as playing the role of mendicant friar to Minos's bishop. Perhaps due to the topicality of this jurisdictional conflict, Minos's reaction to the divine decree is not represented, and the relationship between the two potentially competing figures is left implicit.

By the time Virgil repeats the formula a third time, in his words to Plutus, it is clear that Dante is using these utterances to explore the relationship of God's capacity to his justice (not simply to reiterate his omnipotence). Virgil's third iteration strongly suggests that the concession allowing the Pilgrim to travel unscathed through Hell emanates from an ordained, rather than an absolute, exercise of power:

> Non è sanza cagion l'andare al cupo:
> vuolsi ne l'alto, là dove Michele
> fé la vendetta del superbo strupo.

> (Not without cause is the descent to the depths: it is willed on high, there where Michael avenged the arrogant rape; *Inf.* 7.10–12)

The modal *potere*, representing God's capacity, has been substituted in this version of the formula with an allusion to the banishment of the rebel angels, a synecdoche for God's justice and the reason for which Hell itself was originally created. This allusion firmly places Dante's exceptional voyage within an order based on reliable rewards and punishments. In *Paradiso* 20, Dante affirms that the rebel angels merited their damnation; here too they are depicted as "raping" heaven's territory. The authorizing "there where" of the formula is no longer simply the source of an unconditioned power, but the place in which the reign of law is enforced. Capacity and justice have become coextensive, syntactically interchangeable. While Virgil's circumlocution of God's omnipotence still functions as a threat, the threat is now underwritten by the ordained order; its violence is legitimized as self-defense.

In disarming Plutus, Virgil frames Dante's grant of safe passage within a providential plan, introducing a theme that will occupy the rest of the canto. Dante's *privilegium* may temporarily and for a specific person suspend the laws of Hell, hence neutralizing the infernal police force, yet it is not without cause ("non è sanza cagion"). The subjective authority of God's grace is ultimately grounded in an objective higher norm (although the exact nature of this *cagione* remains to be fully revealed).

At the same time, the encounter with Plutus introduces a dangerous complication to the portrayal of Dante's grace as an imperial privilege: the problem of disobedience. Although Virgil assures Dante that Plutus cannot prevent them from descending into the next circle of Hell, he nevertheless raises the specter of imperial and divine limitations, a much discussed legal and theological question.[23] God's *volere* is pitted in this passage against Plutus's *potere*, hinting at a possible gap between the law's intention and its enforcement. But the real challenge to the legislative authority behind Dante's privilege will not come until cantos 8–9, where despite Virgil's intervention, the devils will refuse Dante entry through the Gates of Dis.

The Standoff at the Gates of Dis: Messianism and Narrative Suspense

In *Inferno* 8, having crossed the river Styx, Dante and Virgil arrive at the innermost gates of Hell, the walls protecting the infernal city of Dis. As at previous border crossings, the administrators of this realm attempt to block the travelers' way. Thousands of demon guardians threaten Dante from atop the city's ramparts, snarling, "Chi è costui che sanza morte / va per lo regno de la morta gente?" (Who is he there, that without death goes through the kingdom of the dead?; *Inf.* 8.84–85). The fallen angels will speak only with the shade Virgil, and they taunt Dante by daring him to retrace his steps through Hell without a guide. Dante intensifies the menace behind the devils' threats by directly addressing readers for the first time in the poem:

> Pensa, lettor, se io mi sconfortai
> nel suon de le parole maladette,
> ché non credetti ritornarci mai.

> (Think, reader, if I became weak at the sound of those cursed words,
> for I did not believe I would ever return here; *Inf.* 8.94–95)

From the start of this episode, then, readers are called upon to vicariously experience the Pilgrim's anxiety.

Dante heightens that anxiety by breaking the established pattern. Instead of handily defeating the infernal guardians with a simple formula, Virgil goes off to speak with the devils alone. Although he assures Dante that he will not abandon him in the underworld and advises him to feed his spirit with "good hope" (*Inf.* 8.107), Virgil leaves the Pilgrim in a state of radical doubt: "with yes and no arguing in my head" (111). In fact, the diplomatic relations with the devils quickly fall apart, and Virgil returns angered and rebuffed. The devils swing the gates shut, reenter the city, and prepare for a siege. Whatever else Virgil has said to them during their secret meeting, we can assume that his invocation of Dante's special grace was ineffectual.

Virgil assures Dante's character that they will nonetheless overcome the impending "prova" (test; *Inf.* 8.122) with their adversaries. He has already encountered their delusional hubris, "tracotanza" (124), at another battle, when they futilely attempted to defend the lower gates of Hell—an obvious reference to Christ's victorious conquest at the Harrowing. In a replay of that *descensus*, the travelers now await the arrival of a Christ-like legate: "tal che per lui ne fia la terra aperta" (such a one that by him the city will be opened to us; 130).[24] The canto closes on this note of anticipation, ending atypically without resolution.

As modern readers of these cantos aided by centuries of commentary and criticism, we know from the outset that the devil's refusal is only a temporary setback, serving to illustrate, among other things, the limits of Virgilian reason when unaccompanied by grace. In other words, we are already aware of and focused on the solution culminating in the arrival of the angelic messenger. Without a contemporaneous reader's investment in the suspense of the episode, we tend to examine synchronic elements—allegorical figures, for example—at the expense of the poem's moment-by-moment action.[25]

But that action, along with the sense of apprehension it encourages, is vital to Dante's project. The juxtaposition of the quick victories over the pagan monsters—the "seven times" (*Inf.* 8.97–98) Virgil has come to Dante's aid—with the standoff with the Christian devils is purposely designed to create suspense, and the drama spans two cantos (8–9) and 150 verses. The break between cantos and the interlude of Medusa and the Furies—irrespective of their ultimate allegorical significance—also delays resolution, further embroiling readers in the fear and doubt of the Pilgrim and his guide. Readers share with Dante's character the messianic longing for a heavenly savior—"Oh quanto tarda a me ch'altri qui giunga!" (Oh how long it seems to me until someone arrives; *Inf*. 9.9)—and must similarly negotiate the gap between faith in the precedent of the Harrowing and hope for imminent deliverance.

Indeed, the entire episode can be read as an interpretive "prova" for the Pilgrim and readers alike in navigating the hiatus between present perfect and future Advents, between Revelation and Judgment.[26] We can observe *in nuce* the challenge created by this historical limbo in Virgil's incompletely expressed doubt at the beginning of canto 9: "'Pur a noi converrà vincer la punga,'/ cominciò el, 'se non . . . Tal ne s'offerse.'" ('Still, we must win the fight,' he began, 'unless . . . Such a one was offered to us'; *Inf*, 9.7–8). In his attempt to assure Dante that they will defeat the demons, Virgil momentarily wavers, contemplating a different outcome: "se non." He quickly corrects himself, however, changing subject mid-sentence and reminding the Pilgrim of the "Tal" who has been promised to save them. This rare anacoluthon frightens Dante's character above all for what it doesn't say. He fills the gap of this "parola tronca" (truncated phrase; *Inf*. 9.14) with his own pessimistic fantasy, most likely understanding a worse meaning ("peggior sentenza"; 15) than Virgil intended.

In his inability to make the "leap" of faith from one end of Virgil's sentence to the other, Dante anticipates a similar hermeneutical failing in the next canto, that of Cavalcante dei Cavalcanti.[27] Cavalcanti notices that the Pilgrim uses the past tense *ebbe* (had) when speaking about his son—who is also Dante's "first friend," the poet Guido Cavalcanti—and anxiously asks whether his son is still alive. When Dante's character hesitates before answering, Cavalcanti assumes the worst (incorrectly, as it turns out), and collapses back into his tomb. Predisposed to skepticism, the heretical Epicurean transforms a simple vocal pause into a blank canvas onto which he projects his metaphysical despair.

If Dante and his readers are to avoid such a spiral of hopelessness, they need to experience the gap from the perspective of the eschaton, to live *as if* the messiah were already here, even if all they can see on the horizon are the concealing fogs of Styx. This is the point of the anticlimax at the resolution of the episode: when he does arrive, the heavenly messenger opens the gates effortlessly, dispatching any hint of Manichaeism with the mere touch of a wand. He upbraids the devils for their continued "oltracotanza" (*Inf.* 9.93)—picking up Virgil's allusion to their "tracotanza" at the Harrowing—and returns whence he came, apparently annoyed at this petty task: "Fé sembiante / d'omo cui altra cura stringa e morda" (he had the look of a man whom other cares urge and gnaw; *Inf.* 9.101–2). The brevity of the angel's intervention, conveyed through his terse reproach of the devils and the parataxis describing his actions, puts into perspective the seemingly endless wait for his arrival.

In retrospect, the entire drama at the Gates is revealed to be nothing more than an impotent "acting out." The devils' rebellion is reduced to a nuisance, a simulacrum of power without any actual foundation.[28] Most importantly, the angel affirms the unbroken reach of the divine will: "Perché recalcitrate a quella voglia / a cui non puote fin mai esser mozzo?" (Why do you kick back against the will whose ends can never be cut short?; *Inf.* 9.94–95). Reuniting divine capacity and will, "puote" and "voglia," the messenger reinstates the basis for Dante's right of safe passage. Virgil's word may be temporarily "tronca," but God's authority is never "mozzo."

From a theological standpoint, then, the crisis at the Gates of Dis is one of skewed vision and perspective internal to Dante's character rather than a crisis of fact. This is, after all, a comedy: we know it will end well. Yet this very theological and generic certainty, I would argue, creates a safe space to explore a much more fraught *political* reality: namely, the potential inability of the Holy Roman Emperor to enforce his own laws. Dante's fear—that God has turned away his just eyes (*Purg.* 6.120) and become a *rex inutilis* who reigns but does not rule[29]—is shown to be misguided. But its political analog, that the prince has abandoned his law, remains a real possibility: "Le leggi son, ma chi pon mano ad esse?" (The laws are there, but who lays hand to them?; *Purg.* 16.97). While God's command remains operative even during the suspenseful wait for the angel, for much of Dante's life the seat of empire was in fact left vacant—constituting a real gap in effective rule.

Indeed, as the oversight of roads and the protections of travelers was the prerogative of imperial authority, it is no coincidence that the devils' disregard of universal law comes in the form of a challenge to a writ of safe passage. The emperor issued specific guarantees of safe passage (*litterae securitatis*) to foreigners, diplomats, and scholars, especially when these individuals were en route to the imperial court. Border crossings were thus sites in which the emperor's valid power was made visible and effective. But they could also occasion a challenge to that power, bringing to light the discrepancy between de facto power and de jure authority.[30] The emperor himself was a victim of the gap between theoretical and actual jurisdiction whenever rebellious cities blocked his passage through their territories or refused entry to his legates.[31]

The denial of a right-of-way is so destabilizing because a *privilegium* foregrounds, more than any other aspect of law, the external authority backing a legal system.[32] In terms of the poem, then, the devils' defiance of this authority threatens to reveal the fiction of law's universality. In theory, that reach was guaranteed by the emperor, whose jurisdiction was "circumscribed by no limits" and coincided with the territory bounded by the rising and setting sun.[33] Without a belief in this transcendent, limitless "tal" the overriding principles of any "common law" risk becoming a dead letter and the action of the law is reduced to the enforceable legislation of particular territories. For the historical Dante, who never returned home from his ambassadorship to Rome, the loss of a genuinely universal law would have condemned him to a permanent state of insecurity. Deprived of the privileges of municipal law, he relied especially on the protections of the *ius commune*.[34]

Ultimately, a loss of faith in the enigmatic "tal" endangers not only the salvation of Dante's individual soul but also the survival of the political community. Although modern critics of these cantos generally identify the "such a one" that Dante and Virgil anxiously expect as a religious figure—an angel, a Christ-type, or a Christianized version of Hermes (messenger of the Olympian gods), over the centuries commentators have occasionally proposed an alternative "political" reading of the *messo*, identifying him, for instance, as Caesar or Henry VII.[35] Yet in many ways this contrast is a false one. When considered from a political-theological perspective, the exact identity of the messianic figure is far less important than the messianism itself. Dante repeatedly uses the indefinite pronoun to describe the anticipated savior for this reason. Even when the authority who guarantees them is difficult to envision, he implies, it is imperative to believe in the transcendence of laws. The interregnum is an important case of this imperative: for the sake of the law, Christian citizens needed to live *as if* the emperor were already crowned and reigning universally.

For the most part, the doubts raised by the devils' refusal at the gates are quickly dissipated when the angel arrives in canto 9. Nevertheless, several questions raised by the actions in this episode remain unanswered. Given God's omnipotence, why does Virgil's formula function with other infernal guardians but not with the devils? Why is the intercession of the angel necessary now—or why was it unnecessary before? How, in this regard, are we to understand the status of the miracle represented by the angelic messenger? Are his actions already included in the natural, created universe and providential order, or do they represent a direct intervention, after the fact, on God's part? Are they examples of ordained or of absolute power?

The words of the angelic messenger would seem to situate his extraordinary intervention within an ordained order. He berates the devils for their continued defiance and for tempting to "buck the fates" ("ne le fata dar di cozzo"; *Inf.* 9.97), and he reminds them that their recalcitrance has time and again only increased their suffering: "v'ha cresciuta doglia" (96). His own infernal descent is placed alongside Hercules's chaining of Cerberus, one more case of a necessitated providential punishment. Most importantly, he apostrophizes the demons with a telling epithet: "O cacciati del ciel, gente dispetta" (O driven forth from Heaven, despised race; *Inf.* 9.91). By invoking a primordial violation of Heaven that preceded even the creation of Hell, the angel depicts the demons as always already punishable. As a consequence, rather than an act of aggression, his opening of the gates for the travelers' entry remains within a law-bound conception of justice—an act of retribution, not conquest.

This providential, ordained interpretation of the angel's intrusions into the created order does not, however, shy away from the role of force necessary to resolve the conflict. The travelers' entry into the gates "sanz'alcuna guerra" (without any battle; *Inf.* 9.106) belies the threat of violence necessary to overcome the impasse of competing jurisdictional claims. As Virgil realizes after his diplomatic relations with the devils have deteriorated, there can be no solution without a "fight" (*Inf.* 9.7) or "without wrath" (*Inf.* 9.33). In the end, setting aside for a moment the allegorical significance of Medusa and the divine intercessor, what we witness in cantos 8 and 9 is the violation of a city's territorial and normative autonomy by a superior external power. The municipal statutes engraved on the lower entrance to Hell are rendered inoperative, "scritta morta" (dead writing; *Inf.* 8.127), when Dante as a living soul is permitted to enter (and escape from) the land of the dead.

The female Furies underscore that sense of violation when they allude to the invasion of Dis by Theseus and Pirithoüs, whose abduction of Persephone is still experienced as a threat to boundaries: "Mal non vengiammo in Tesëo l'assalto" (We did ill in not avenging the assault of Theseus; *Inf.* 9.54). The invocation of Medusa as "reinforcement," who was herself transformed into a monster after being ravished by Poseidon in the Temple of Athena, can be seen as a reaction to this domination of vulnerable female spaces. In this respect, the violence effected in cantos 8 and 9 is structurally similar to the violation of nuns' cloisters recounted in *Paradiso* 3. However, this forced entry is viewed as a "legitimate" sexualized violence, avenging the "rape" (*Inf.* 7.12) of heaven by the rebellious angels.[36]

Finally, as we are continuously reminded throughout the siege of Dis, Dante and Virgil were not the first to have violently trespassed the infernal boundaries. The final labor of Hercules, the failed abduction of Persephone, and the descent of the angel are all figures of Christ's Harrowing of Hell, in which a triumphant Christ breaks through the infernal gates, rescues the Old Testament prophets from Limbo, and carries them off to Heaven. In that dramatic instance, Christ opened the "roads" (*Par.* 23.38) between heaven and earth. (That effect is rendered in literal terms for Dante's character, as the crucifixion created a landslide that he ascends and descends as he makes his way through Hell.) In legal terms, the intervention of Christ in history is experienced as a destabilizing executive order, a new imperial "decree" (*Purg.* 10.34) at odds with previous norms. Yet the new dispensation cannot take effect without an act of founding mythic violence, a duel between the Savior and the devils. As in Book Two of *Monarchia*, where Dante argues that the conquest of the Roman Empire was achieved lawfully because it was the outcome of a trial by combat,[37] Christ's victory, although wrought with might, is simultaneously a judgment. As a reenactment of the Harrowing, the violence caused by Dante's *privilegium* paradoxically reveals its lawfulness.

Privilegium and Violence: Cato

That Dante views his character's *privilegium* as a lawful violation comes into relief when we compare the episode at the Gates of Dis with his encounter with Cato the Younger in the first cantos of *Purgatorio*. Cato is both a suicide and a Stoic figure deeply associated with justice (he took his own life so that he would not have to submit to Caesar and witness the destruction of republican liberty). Dante and Virgil encounter him on the shores of Purgatory immediately after seeing four blazing stars (symbolizing the four cardinal virtues of justice) in the dawn sky, which no one has seen since Adam and Eve were banished from Eden and mankind was deprived of original justice. The overwhelming brightness of these stars shine on the face of Cato, who suddenly appears before Dante as a venerable old man, with a long white beard and his white hair parted into two strands.[38] Cato is the first otherworldly guardian Virgil and Dante meet in their voyage who is also a saved soul, so his reception of Dante's writ of safe passage is an important test case.

At first, Cato reacts to Dante and Virgil's appearance in a manner similar to that of his infernal counterparts; he interprets their trespass as a violation of the laws of the afterlife and demands to know who authorized their escape:

Chi v'ha guidati, o che vi fu lucerna,
uscendo fuor de la profonda notte

che sempre nera fa la valle inferna?

Son le leggi d'abisso così rotte?

o è mutato in ciel novo consiglio,

che, dannati, venite a le mie grotte?

(Who has guided you, or what has been your lantern, coming forth
from the deep night that makes the valley of Hell forever black? Can
the laws of the abyss be broken, then? Or has some new counsel been
adopted in Heaven, that although damned you come to my cliffs?;
Purg. 1.43–48)

Virgil, as usual, responds in Dante's stead, explaining that their voy-
age is guided by a "lady descended from heaven" (i.e., Beatrice; *Purg.*
1.53) and is aided by "a virtue from above" (*Purg.* 1.68). After assur-
ing Cato that they have not broken any laws, he proceeds to request
safe conduct for Dante, associating the Pilgrim's quest for freedom
from sin with Cato's self-sacrifice for political freedom: "Or ti piac-
cia gradir la sua venuta: / libertà va cercando, ch'è sì cara, / come sa
chi per lei vita rifiuta" (Now may it please you to favor his coming:
he seeks freedom, which is precious, as one knows who rejects life
for her sake; *Purg.* 1.70–72).[39] As an additional enticement, Virgil
promises to take Cato's greetings to his former beloved, Marcia, who
also resides in Limbo.

Rejecting Virgil's *captatio benevolentiae*, Cato dismisses the influ-
ence of Marcia now that he is saved. He follows a new law: "Or che di
là dal mal fiume dimora, / più mover non mi può, per quella legge /
che fatta fu quando me n'usci' fora" (Now that she dwells beyond the
evil river, she can move me no longer, according to the law that was
made when I came forth from there; *Purg.* 1.88–90). That dismissal
notwithstanding, however, Cato does recognize the higher authority
backing Dante's special grant: "Ma se donna del ciel ti move e regge, /
come tu di', non c'è mestier lusinghe: / bastisi bene che per lei mi
richegge" (But if a lady from Heaven moves and governs you, as you
say, no flatteries are needed: let it be enough that you ask me for her
sake; *Purg.* 1.91–93).

Cato is himself an exception to the laws of the otherworld he
has been elected to oversee. He is saved despite being a pagan, a

suicide, and a fatefully staunch opponent of Julius Caesar (who, in Dante's view, was the first true emperor). Here is not the place to rehearse the many scholarly investigations into why Dante felt justified in saving Cato. Whatever the precedents for sparing Cato from condemnation,[40] Dante no doubt intended to surprise or even shock readers by installing the pagan suicide as the guardian of Purgatory. By attempting to reabsorb this anomalous case back within an immutable set of laws, then, we miss Dante's larger commentary on the normative system itself. Above all, we miss the relationship between Cato's unprecedented salvation and Dante's unprecedented journey—two exceptions to the universal laws Dante clearly intends to place in conversation.

When Cato asks "Son le leggi d'abisso così rotte?" (Can the laws of the abyss be broken, then?; *Purg.* 1.46), he reveals his concern for the status of the laws and exposes his awareness of their fragility. If we consider how Cato is portrayed in Lucan's *Pharsalia*, this alarm seems entirely in character. As John Scott has observed,[41] the depiction of Cato by Lucan as a worshiper of justice stands in contrast with that of Caesar, "the hated tyrant"[42] who disdains the law. Cato offers his own blood to redeem the republic—an act already interpreted by Gelasius I as prefiguring Christ's redemption:

> Let this my blood preserve the people, let this my death atone for all the penalties deserved by Roman morals. Why should peoples ready for the yoke and willing to endure cruel tyranny perish? With your sword attack me, me alone, in vain the guardian of laws and empty rights [*leges et inania iura*] (2.312–16).

In contrast, Caesar relishes the violence of border violation: "He would rather smash the city-gates than enter them wide open" (2.443–44). Preparing to cross the Rubicon, he declares: "Here I abandon peace and the already desecrated laws [*temerataque iura*]" (1.225). When Dante and Virgil breach the boundary between the damned and the saved, moving against the flow of the "blind river" (*Purg.* 1.40), Cato is forced to relive for a moment the sacrilege of that other crossing.

Virgil the poet had already depicted Cato on Aeneas's shield as a "lawgiver" to the just in *Aeneid* 8.670. Perhaps with this image in mind, Virgil responds to Cato with a legalistic explanation for his and Dante's escape from Hell. According to his account, since Dante is still alive and he (Virgil) has been relegated to Limbo—and is therefore not confined by Minos—they have not broken any law in passing from one realm to the other: "Non son li editti etterni per noi guasti" (The eternal edicts have not been broken by us; *Purg.* 1.76).

As he polices his realm, Cato partly maintains the conservative moralism of his former life, insisting upon the impermeability of legal boundaries such as the infernal river Acheron. (On one side of that divide lie the damned, earthly love, and Marcia; on the other are the saved, spiritual love, and Beatrice.) Yet Cato's salvation has apparently altered his former rigidity. He disregards Virgil's attempts at grounding the privilege of the journey in the legality of reigning law and concerns himself only with the *voluntas* behind Dante's writ, assured that its legitimate authority derives from a "lady in heaven" (*Purg.* 1.91). In other words, he accepts with equanimity the possibility that universal laws can be modified by a rescript or privilege, a "novo consiglio" (*Purg.* 1.47). In contrast with Virgil's standard legalist position on Dante's writ, Cato's attitude toward this privilege is decidedly more expansive. Perhaps as a result of his forcible rescue from Limbo, he now acknowledges that the violations of borders can inaugurate a new law: "the law that was made when I came forth from there" (*Purg.* 1.88–89).

Having directly experienced the violence of exception in the Harrowing of Hell, Cato's perspective on justice has apparently moved beyond simple contrast (with the rule of law on one side and chaos on the other). He no longer views the suspension of the law as apocalyptic, seeing it instead as a necessary historical rupture. On the other side of that rupture, he has learned, one may find a new dispensation (Christianity/Empire) rather than an abyss.[43] More than any other figure in the poem, Cato recognizes the unqualified right of the ruler to issue privileges at odds with the ordinary course of positive law. In this respect and in his own transitional position, the republican martyr ironically embodies the potential continuity of a higher constitutional law—even in the face of regime change.

Despite acknowledging the validity of Dante's exception, Cato never relinquishes his role as overseer of Purgatory's communal laws. In canto 1 he requires Dante's character to undergo a ritual of purification before entering Purgatory, and in canto 2 he suddenly reappears to reprimand the souls for indulging in Casella's performance of "Amor che ne la mente,"[44] chiding the captivated souls for suspending the journey and urging them to resume the penitential ascent. That appeal serves to reintegrate Dante within the penitential community, as the rebuke applies equally to the Pilgrim, his guide, and the newly arrived penitents. As this united group heeds Cato and departs to climb Purgatory, Dante compares them to an flock of doves and underlines that his and Virgil's obedience was no less rapid: "né la nostra partita fu men tosta" (nor was our own departure less sudden; *Purg.* 2.133).

While we have examined the lawfulness of forceful challenges to the presiding legal order (specifically the matter of supervening decrees), we turn next to a different problem raised by the existence of privileges: the relationship between individuals and their community. Dante's initial separation from and subsequent reintegration with the "flock" of sinners highlights the possible inequalities that privileges create among the law's subjects. He explores these legal and social problems by juxtaposing his "specific" privilege, issued in favor of an individual and restricted to a particular case, to what jurists classified as the "general" privileges enjoyed by abstract categories of persons such as the nobility and the clergy. Through the depiction of the hypocritical friars, Dante calls into question the right of the clergy in particular to shirk collective duties and claim immunity.

Communitas and Immunitas in Inferno 23

As we have seen, later medieval scholars commenting on Roman law often defined immunity negatively, as a release or exemption *from* the collective restraints of the *ius commune*: "Privilege is like a private law, that is, an honor or status of one person before others or an immunity from the *ius commune* regarding those things which instead weigh upon others."[45] In this respect, as Roberto Esposito has suggested, the privative *immunis* (*in-munus*) is also in tacit contrast to the community, or those obligated by a collective duty (*cum-munus*).[46] Dante explores this conflict between *communitas* and *immunitas* in *Inferno* 23, in which the hypocrites are punished.

The canto begins with a comparison of Dante and Virgil to two Franciscans walking along the road, one after the other, "taciti, soli, sanza compagnia" (silent, alone, without companions; *Inf.* 23.1). After a final chase scene in which the travelers narrowly escape the Malebranche, the rest of the canto resumes in the somber, cloistered tone of the opening simile, an effect that is bolstered by various references to religious institutions, practices, and garb. The hypocrites are themselves dressed as monks, punished by being forced to wear crippling leaden robes that are gilded on the outside. Two representative hypocrites are interviewed in the episode, the Jovial Friars Catalano dei Malavolti and Loderingo degli Andalò, who Dante believed used their influence as supposedly impartial religious figures to play party politics in Florence (working in favor of Pope Clement against the Ghibellines).

The friars expect Dante to be bound by the same punishment they are. After an envious sidelong glance, one of the first things they notice about him is that he is alive and/or exempt from such a punishment: "Costui par vivo a l'atto de la gola; / e s' e' son morti, per qual privilegio / vanno scoperti de la grave stola?" (That one seems alive, by the motion of his throat; but if they are dead, by what privilege are they exempt from the weighty stole?; *Inf.* 23.88–90). In contrast with their collective rule, the "collegio / de l'ipocriti tristi" (the college of the sad hypocrites; *Inf.* 23.91–92), Dante's grant of safe passage appears to them as a form of immunity. Alert to the social implications of such privileges, the friars worry that this special status will cause the Pilgrim to withhold his identity out of "dispregio" (disdain; *Inf.* 23.93). Indeed, Dante opts not to name himself, and refers to his birthplace only through circumlocution: "I was born and raised beside the lovely river Arno in the great city" (*Inf.* 23. 94–95).

As members of a religious order, Catalano and Loderingo would have been especially sensitive to the advantages of privileges. In Roman law, the Church's relation to secular power—and indeed its entire institutional nature—was theorized in terms of privileges.

Many of these were already recorded and elaborated upon in Justinian's *Codex*, and large sections of the *Decretum* are also dedicated to them. Canon lawyers were committed to protecting the various immunities of the Church, especially its jurisdictional autonomy and exemptions from fiscal imposts. In fact, the two terms *privilegium* and *immunitas* were often used synonymously when discussing clerical exemptions.[47]

Municipal governments honored religious privileges, but also struggled to ensure that they would not be defrauded by claims of laymen whose religious status was one of convenience.[48] For many of Dante's contemporaries, the Jovial Friars fell into this category.[49] Although the Knights of the Blessed Virgin Mary, as they were officially known, enjoyed jurisdictional immunity and fiscal exemptions, they were not obliged to renounce property, business dealings, or family ties. According to the chronicler Salimbene da Parma, the epithet "Jovial Friars" was originally coined by the populace to describe the individualistic, anti-civic nature of these aristocratic friar-knights who "do not want to share their goods with others, but keep everything for themselves."[50] Thus, when Catalano and Loderingo, representatives of two of the most powerful noble families of Bologna, view Dante's immunity as a personal advantage, they perpetuate this negative perception of their order.[51]

In the clash between the Pilgrim's special privilege and the friars' general privileges, Dante brings into relief the injustice of releasing individuals from the collective burdens of a community when these dispensations are not counterbalanced by onuses of equal weight. The poet vividly expresses such inequality in his depiction of the hypocrites' punishment, an aspect of their *contrapasso* that has long gone unrecognized.

Scholars have traditionally explicated the graven stoles that the hypocrites are forced to wear by way of a famous etymology by Uguccione of Pisa: "*Hypocrita* derives from *hyper*, above, and *crisis*, gold, as it were gilt over, for on the surface and externally he appears good, but within he is evil."[52] Just as a false "gilded" piety hid the friars' self-serving intentions in life, the explanation goes, the gold on the outside of their robes now conceals the heavy lead within. The ultimate source of this interpretation derives from Jesus's comparison of the hypocritical Pharisees with "whited sepulchers" (Mt. 23:27): beautiful on the outside, but on the inside full of putrefaction and death. In his depiction of the hypocrites' two-toned robes, Dante follows this long tradition.

Yet the poet adds a new layer to the traditional critique by emphasizing the antisocial nature of the friars.[53] The depiction of semiotic confusion figured in the inside-outside structure of the hypocrites' cloaks ultimately gives way to another dilemma: the tension between individual and collective figured symbolically as an equitably distributed leaden weight. Indeed, for most of the canto Dante focuses less on what the robes hide and more on their weight.[54] With each additional reference we come to see that the leaden stoles symbolize not only the sin of deceptive appearances but also that of shirked civic duty, of having evaded public duties and obligations, *onera* and *munera*. The hypocrites have not carried their fair share. Now stooped under the cumbrance of these literalized burdens, their crippled bodies are transformed into tipped scales ("bilance"), an arresting image of social justice as a counterweight.[55]

The tension between privilege and community explored in this canto comes to a head in the presentation of Caiaphas. Crucified by three stakes pinning him to the ground, the high priest of the Israelites lies in the path of the hypocrites and is forced to suffer their massive weight as each one trammels him. Because he recommended handing over Jesus to the Roman authorities for the sake of the *communitas*, proposing that "convenia / porre un uom per lo popolo a' martìri" (it was expedient to put one man to death for the people) (*Inf.* 23.116–17), he must suffer the entire weight of the common *munus*. The singularity of Caiaphas's counter-suffering is especially fitting because his lip service to the Israelite nation belied his special interest in maintaining the privileges of his priestly caste. Like the "peacemakers" Catalano and Loderingo, the high priest wrapped his partisan interests in the discourse of the common good.

The punishment of Caiaphas is also one of the most significant Christological references in *Inferno*, albeit in parodic form.[56] Caiaphas is crucified in a manner similar to that of Christ, nailed to the ground by three stakes. Just as Christ is the Way for Christians ("I am the way, the truth, and the life"; John 14:6), Caiaphas is literally *the way* for the hypocrites, who walk slowly over him in their eternal circling. Finally, Caiaphas feels the weight of all the hypocrites as Christ bore the weight of all men's sins in the Atonement.

As with the reenactment of the Harrowing in cantos 8 and 9, an anacoluthon rhetorically signals the rupture of the Christ event into the sentence of history. Dante interrupts his rebuke to the friars at the sight of Caiaphas: "Io cominciai: 'O frati i vostri mali' / ma più non dissi" (I began: "O friars, your evil . . ." but I said no more; *Inf.* 23.109–10). Virgil is also momentarily overcome, just as he was in cantos 8–9, and he stands dumbstruck before the sign of the cross. Yet whereas at the Gates of Dis Dante's privilege was associated with the Harrowing of Hell, in *Inferno* 23 it is linked to the Atonement and martyrdom. Christ's sacrifice for all mankind appears in this context as a theological model for the ultimate duty of the citizen: to die for one's country (*pro patria mori*).[57] Already in the Gospel of John, Christ's martyrdom for all nations is interpreted as prophetically fulfilling Caiaphas's pronouncement that Jesus died so that "the whole nation perish not" (11.50). Dante will expand on this association between legal privilege and civic sacrifice in the pointed encounter with Cacciaguida in *Paradiso* 15–17.

"Il buon tempo antico" and Citizenship *ex privilegio* in *Paradiso* 15–17

Dante's journey through Paradise brings him into contact with various "sources"—from the founders of the universal secular and religious institutions, to the origin of humankind in Adam, and even to the First Mover himself. In the central, autobiographical cantos of *Paradiso* 15–17, he encounters a more personal "source": the figure of his great-great-grandfather, Cacciaguida. From this "root" or "principle" (*Par.*15.89–90), he learns the truth about his imminent exile. Cacciaguida lays out in harsh, unsparing details the circumstances that await the Pilgrim soon after the fictional date of the journey, emphasizing their injustice and the suffering they will bring. At the same time he also reveals the divinely ordained purpose of the journey being undertaken: Dante has been escorted through the other-world and introduced to the famous souls among the dead in order to write a poem that will serve as bitter medicine for the living.

In canto 15, Cacciaguida teaches Dante about the origins of his family's noble lineage, tracing back the history of Dante's surname ("cognazione" [*Par.* 15.92]; "sopranome" [*Par.* 15.138]). Even more important, he describes being knighted for his good works by the emperor Corrado III and dying shortly thereafter as a martyr in the Second Crusade. After discovering the lofty, ancient origin of his family's noble status, Dante's character immediately shifts from the informal *tu* to the formal *voi* in addressing his ancestor—a mark of vanity he cannot suppress, even in Heaven. In the next canto, Cacciaguida responds to Dante's request and elaborates on his family's residence in the quarter of Porta San Piero—one of the oldest neighborhoods in Florence, and one historically associated with aristocratic and knightly households.

The origin of Dante's poetic mission and the origin of his family's nobility are connected by the essential fact that both confer distinctive privileges.[58] Cacciaguida characterizes Dante's providential destiny as "privileged" as soon as he encounters him, proclaiming:

> O sanguis meus, o superinfusa
> gratïa Dei! Sicut tibi cui
> bis unquam Celi ianüa reclusa?"

> (O my blood! O poured out from above
> grace of God! To whom as to you
> has the gate of Heaven ever been twice opened?; *Par.* 15.28–30)

Cacciaguida is struck by the singularity of the grace afforded to his great-great-grandson, which has allowed Dante to pass through the "gate of Heaven." That exclamation is also a reminder of his character's passage through the Gates of Dis, and a confirmation of his once-contested writ of safe conduct.

The solemn, unprecedented Latin opening of Cacciaguida's speech to Dante, with its multiple allusions to Aeneas's voyage through the otherworld, also reopens the question of the motivation behind Dante's safe passage. In *Inferno* 2, the Pilgrim asked why he had been chosen for the otherworldly journey, distinguishing himself from Paul and Aeneas and the superior justification for their voyages. Cacciaguida now definitively answers this question. Just as God had been "cortese" (courteous; *Inf.* 2.17) to the founder of Rome, he is "cortese" (*Par.* 15.48) to Dante because of the public utility that will ensue from his journey. As Anchises prepared Aeneas for his historic mission, then, Cacciaguida charges Dante with a duty to write the *Commedia* for his future readers.[59] In *Inferno*, Dante's journey is preliminarily justified by concern for his individual salvation. Cacciaguida now expands the "just cause" validating his mission to encompass the collective salvation his poem will effect.

When Cacciaguida reintroduces the theme of Dante's privilege to travel through the otherworld while still alive, he focuses on how this providential grant applies to him alone: "sicut tibi cui." Dante's destiny is painted as an individual matter, an exclusiveness that becomes pronounced when he turns from Cacciaguida to Beatrice and experiences in her smiling eyes "lo fondo / de la mia gloria e del mio paradiso" (the utmost depth of my glory and my paradise; *Par.* 15.35–36). This remarkably proprietary expression of Beatrice as Dante's own risks upsetting the delicate balance between the communal nature of the heavenly polity—given that "every *where* in Heaven is Paradise" (*Par.* 3.88–89)—and the unequal allocation of glory among the blessed. If Dante's destiny is already written in the stars, and his special grace is mediated by Beatrice, where is the equity in such disproportionate and unearned glory? How can the order of God's merit-based creation, where all are equal under the law, be reconciled with his distribution of privileges?

In *Paradiso* 15 and 16, Dante places his special privilege in dialogue with the general privileges dividing contemporary Italian society in order to probe the justice of both. While the journey through Hell and Purgatory dealt with the "miraculous" suspension of the law for a single man, thus addressing the conflict between singular and general laws, Dante's passage through the gates of Heaven confronts the broader social inequalities that privileges create. In these cantos, that is, he connects his *privilegium* to the political theology of hierarchy.

The episode is replete with references to such hierarchy. When the Pilgrim addresses Cacciaguida with the honorific plural *voi* form, for example, he emphasizes the lofty status of his ancestor and feels himself similarly elevated: "son più ch'io" (I am more than myself; *Par.* 16.18). Similarly, the grace of Dante's special providence is "*super*infusa,"—that is to say, both derived from a higher authority and in excess when compared to others. And when Cacciaguida uses the class-based language of the *popolo* to contrast between the "grandi" and "minori" among the blessed, he implicitly links their ordering to the distinctions he draws between noble, artisan, and peasant in historic Florence. In the other direction, Dante's interest in which citizens of old Florence were worthy of the "più alti scanni" (highest benches; *Par.* 16.27) prefigures the amphitheatrical structure of the heavenly court.

Critics are understandably divided on how to interpret Dante's statements about nobility in these cantos.[60] At least to some extent, Dante's exile from the guild-based republican government of Florence and his experiences as a guest in various northern Italian courts appears to have prompted a reevaluation of his views about noble families and the traditional elite. Umberto Carpi believes that this evolution in Dante's thought was absolute, amounting to an about-face from his earlier urban politics.[61] Pointing out that the noble families of Cacciaguida's *ubi sunt* were all condemned as magnates in the municipal registers of Dante's time, he argues that Dante, in his new role as imperial propagandist under the patronage of Lord Cangrande della Scala, now conspicuously sides with the enemies of the "popolo" government. For Carpi, the Cacciaguida episode represents nothing less than Dante's categorical rejection of the *popolo*—along with their mercantile values, social mobility, and new wealth—and an idealization of the ethos of their political and social rivals, the feudal aristocracy.

In contrast, John Najemy has argued that despite his imperial convictions, Dante demonstrates a "tenacious attachment" to popular discourse in the Cacciaguida episode,[62] especially its attack on the nobles' excessive consumption and their predilection for family, clan, and party over the city's common good. In fact, the immigrant families Cacciaguida singles out for derision are hardly representative of the rank-and-file guild members of the *popolo*. They are either nobles, such as the Buondelmonti; international bankers and traders, such as the Cerchi; or jurists, such as the stinking "peasants" Baldo d'Aguglione and Fazio dei Morubaldini of Signa.[63] Moreover, when Cacciaguida identifies the citizenship of old Florence as being pure until the last artisan, "pura vediesi ne l'ultimo artista" (*Par.* 16.51), his association between citizenship and craft belongs to the rhetoric of the guild-based *popolo*, not to the elitism of the magnates. It is also worth noting, as recent historical studies have confirmed,[64] that Cangrande della Scala—the imperial vicar and protector of Dante singled out for praise in *Paradiso* 17—had come from a wealthy family of wool merchants, and had risen to power through his leadership role in the guild corporation known as the *domus mercatorum* (house of merchants). Of the northern *signorie*, Verona was also the one that demonstrated the greatest continuity, legally and institutionally, with its communal roots.

Much of the confusion about Dante's views of nobility can be resolved if we view Cacciaguida's comments as engaging with legal questions regarding citizenship rather than as sociological critique. Citizenship was one of the most debated issues of public law in the later Middle Ages, and it was often the subject of professional legal opinions. As the work of Julius Kirsher has illustrated, many of these opinions treated the complexities of naturalization or *civilitas acquisita* (acquired citizenship).[65] Grants of citizenship were frequent in municipal legislation, and were used to attract wealthy residents and useful professionals such as judges, physicians, and teachers. New citizens were promised the protections of the municipal laws, and, to a lesser extent and with various additional restrictions, access to public office. From the perspective of potential residents, these privileges could be an important instrument of social mobility, protecting their business dealings in courts and transforming their wealth into cultural capital through public appointments.[66] Citizenship was thus closely tied to privileges. Indeed, in contemporary documents, the new citizen was often referred to as a *civis ex privilegio*.

While jurists concerned with protecting the lawmaking power of municipal governments insisted that the statutes—not the city walls—created citizenship, these same statutes always separated native-born citizens from newly made ones; the latter were *quasi*, *tamquam*, or *velut* citizens, and never simply *cives*.[67] Because of this distinction, the new citizen was always vulnerable to outbreaks of nativism, and his acquired privileges were occasionally revoked or disregarded by subsequent administrations—particularly in times of political crisis and financial need. One source of hostility toward the new citizens regarded the various immunities that the city promised them. Although citizens *ex privilegio* were normally required to build homes and reside within the city or its boroughs, pay local taxes, and provide the services required by the commune, officials could offer fiscal and personal immunities to attract the citizens they wanted.[68]

Cacciaguida expresses a nativist perspective on new citizens, and clearly believes that the city walls make citizens, not its statutes. He twice sums up Florence's problems in terms of its citizenry. In canto 15, he polemically evokes Florence's formerly trustworthy citizenship, "fida/cittadinanza" (*Par.* 15.131–32), and in canto 16 he contrasts the purity of old Florence with the mixed citizenship, "cittadinanza . . . mista" (*Par.* 16.49), of the present-day populace. He seems especially concerned with the process of urbanization, in which residents from the annexed Florentine countryside were absorbed into the city proper. In legal language, the primary targets of his attacks are the so-called *cives silvestres*.[69] These "wild" citizens were often the subject of legislation and legal opinions (*consilia*) because of the risk of abuse inherent in their status. Some of the wealthier and more powerful members of the countryside were able to exploit the benefits of citizenship awarded for urbanization, including immunity from their local jurisdictions, while de facto residing for extended periods of time outside of the city (during harvesting, for example) and evading municipal taxes.[70] In other words, they were granted *privilegia* but avoided *munera*.

Yet Cacciaguida's nativism is not pure xenophobia or mere snobbery; his attack on sylvan citizens is only incidentally concerned with their mercantile, upstart origins. Indeed, several of the new citizens he targets are in fact members of the old feudal nobility. Rather than a particular class, Cacciaguida is rejecting a political/juridical phenomenon in which citizenship is treated purely as a private contract, a title bought and sold like the property of Montemurlo. Within the city walls, he implies, nobles and artisans alike should be united by shared obligations and responsibilities. When citizenship in Florence was still founded on the common *munus*, the government was uncorrupt and the army victorious in battle: "glorïoso / e giusto il popol suo" (glorious and just her populace; *Par*. 16.151–52). The danger arises when the acquisition of citizenship becomes unnaturally corrupted by the marketplace, leading to the abuse of communal offices for gain (graft) and the shirking of public duties, military service in particular.

Cacciaguida conveys the demographic distinction between his and Dante's Florence by specifying the number of residents who had the right to bear arms, "poter arme" (*Par*. 16.47), in his day—a mere one-fifth of those so qualified in Dante's time. This reference to the adult males who could bear arms is more than a synecdoche for the population at large, as it is traditionally understood. Rather, it indicates that Cacciaguida conceives of the "cittidinanza" of Florence as specifically encompassing citizens born with or granted full legal capacity—a distinct minority of the populace—and not simply the residents within the city's walls. Contemporary jurists also honored the connection between citizenship and military service, and permitted city officials to strip new citizens of their acquired status if they did not perform military duty.[71] Of course, even more than for rank-and-file citizens, the privileges of the knightly class were intimately tied to their obligation to defend the city. In this respect, Cacciaguida's *ubi sunt*, pronounced in the heaven of the warriors, is actually an especially poignant criticism of the Florentine aristocracy, which had severed the historic ties between "milizia e privilegio" (military service and privilege; *Par*. 16.130).

The imperative to military sacrifice, whether as part of the elite cavalry of old knights or in the city's standing army, is the overriding theme of the Cacciaguida episode, tethering the parade of blessed warriors in Mars, the depiction of old Florence, and even the revelation of Dante's divine vocation. If the crusaders were willing to die for Christ by taking up the Cross, the old Florentine citizens were willing to die for the commonweal as they defended the "giglio" (lily; *Par*.16.152). Dante's sublimated new self is similarly presented as a warrior,[72] armed by foresight against the blows of fortune. He too is charged with a mission: to serve mankind by testifying to the truth he has witnessed, whatever the costs. He even undergoes a type of martyrdom in the form of exile in order to write the *Commedia*.[73]

By locating the source of Cacciaguida's "voi" and Dante's "gratïa" in the duty to sacrifice, Dante defines both special and general privileges in terms of obligation rather than immunity. Instead of exempting the Pilgrim from military service (*munere vacare*), his grant of safe passage through the otherworld is itself a preparation for battle. Even at the risk of impinging upon a soteriology based on just rewards, he associates the privileges of citizenship with a political theology based on martyrdom: *pro patria mori*. Anticipating Simone Weil's critique of human rights,[74] he classifies both heavenly and earthly *cives* not by what they are owed, but according to what they owe others (or the Other), including their biological or—in Dante's case—civic life. The hierarchy of legal and theological privileges in *Paradiso* is rooted in an economy of the *munus*, or reciprocal duties and obligations (especially the responsibility to reciprocate the gift of citizenship), rather than on claims, rights, and dominium. Only in this way can the citizenry ever be "trustworthy." The import of this faith between citizens as a precondition for the law will be treated in the next and final chapter.

4

Beside the Law
Pactum

Dante's progress in the *Commedia* is realized through a sequence of dialogues with the dead. To proceed through the otherworld, the Pilgrim must draw out the souls' stories through negotiation and deal-making: if they speak to him, he will do something for them. In other words, these dialogues form contracts. This chapter illuminates Dante's engagement with changing forms of medieval contract, particularly the breakdown of the traditional distinction in Roman law between a formal, actionable contract and a bare pact, or one left partially "uncovered" by the law (*pactum nudum*). Medieval jurists reconfigured that distinction as the difference between "dressed" versus "naked" pacts, but, as I show, determining what it took to "dress" a "naked" pact—in literary as well as legal terms— remained a crucial problematic in Dante's oeuvre.[1]

While Dante's transactions with the souls in *Purgatorio* and *Paradiso* blend seamlessly within the overriding divine juridical order (in the first case, integrated into a global penitential economy; in the second, as an extension of God's reign of charity), his negotiations with the damned in *Inferno* are more ambiguous. Incapable of altering, in any way, the eternal sentence of the damned, the Pilgrim's agreements with them occupy a parajuridical universe adjacent to the law. On the one hand, Dante and the damned are allowed a degree of autonomy and freedom to generate contracts based primarily on mutual consent. On the other, no superior political institution guarantees or enforces these informal contracts, which are detached from the punitive mechanisms of the otherworld and its corresponding policing apparatus.

As an extreme instance of social disintegration, the *Inferno* constitutes a limit case for the study of contracts. The absence of shared standards and models makes its setting shaky ground for forming binding agreements. Yet to survive and accomplish his providential mission, the Pilgrim must make deals with the populace inhabiting the underworld, with whom he shares no positive laws, fundamental principles, or even gods. Rather than enforced and endorsed contracts, the deals Dante makes in Hell belong to the legally murky world of "naked pacts."

Ultimately, Dante's aim in investigating the changing nature of contractual obligation is to constitute a new basis on which to found the contract between reader and author. For him, received literary genres, not unlike received contractual types, could no longer adequately accommodate vernacular literature outside its municipal, performative context. In a world increasingly dominated by bare pacts, what role remained for traditional literary conventions such as tragedy and comedy? The matter was especially pressing to Dante, as he had been removed, by exile, from direct control over the dissemination and publication of his work. In titling his masterpiece a "comedy," then, he forged a new and novel agreement with his audience that this chapter seeks to elucidate.

Medieval Contract Law and Genre Theory: Consensus versus Type

Any reevaluation of Dante's literary contract with readers needs to take into account the basic differences between modern and ancient theories of contract law.[2] In Roman law there was no general theory of the contract, and no single accepted method for creating a legal agreement between parties. Instead, Justinian's *Corpus iuris* described various types of discrete contracts. The validity of these contracts depended on a range of nonsystematic criteria. Some contracts produced legal obligations because they adhered to external, formal requirements in their performance, such as the prescribed question-and-answer formulas of the *stipulatio*. Others derived their validity from the underlying economic transaction itself. In "real" contracts, for example, the physical delivery of the item loaned (*res*) established the agreement as binding.

In each case, the institutionally recognized type of contract took precedence over individual will. The various contract types served as molds or preexisting channels that fixed, limited, and conditioned the autonomy of the parties desiring to create their own legal realities. In contrast to modern contract law, in which parties may freely determine the content of the contract provided it does not openly violate positive laws, in Roman law they needed to adapt their transaction to existing forms or models. As both Roman jurists and their medieval commentators explained, for an agreement to be treated as a viable contract it needed already to have a "name."[3]

In a system built around collectively determined stable types, rather than around the modern "triumph of consensus,"[4] legal contracts were necessarily distinguished from informal pacts. Contracts were ratified not through the expression of a sanctified individual will, but because they conformed to a recognized social function, a model of economic behavior established over time.[5] The unenforceable agreement or pact was instead relegated to the ethical realm; as far as the law was concerned, it remained unprotected, naked—and "a naked pact does not produce an obligation" (*nuda pactio obligationem non parit*), as Ulpian famously put it.[6]

One of the major contributions of medieval legal scholarship was to recast the distinction in Roman law between legal contracts and informal agreements as a contrast between naked and dressed pacts (*pacta nuda* and *vestita*).[7] The glossators of the *Corpus iuris*, for instance, reorganized all bilateral transactions under the single heading of "pacts," which they further subdivided between actionable pacts and those creating only a natural, not a legal, obligation.

Working within this new framework, jurists sought to identify that vivifying *quid* (something) capable of covering a pact and granting it full legal protection.[8] Much of the legal literature on pacts consisted of divergent views about when a given pact became binding, and debates over precisely what "clothed" it.[9]

For the most part, dressed pacts continued to be identified with the traditional "named" Roman contracts. However, various types of medieval economic practices—such as corporate investment, currency exchange, insurance, and large-scale lending at interest—were clearly not "named" by Roman law. Jurists operating in late medieval urban contexts invented new "garments" and adapted old ones in order to accommodate emergent economic phenomena.[10] Although these jurists demonstrated remarkable ingenuity in reabsorbing the explosion of new forms of contracts within the framework and modalities of Roman law, the slippage between a system based on a closed number of valid pacts and the actual fluidity of modern economic life inevitably created uncertainty.

The expanded role of the Church in regulating, enforcing, and punishing economic transactions (since they involved promises and oaths) similarly blurred the line between legal contracts and naked pacts. Indeed, most canon lawyers, beginning with Johannes Teutonicus's gloss on Gratian's *Decretum* in the early part of the thirteenth century, argued that naked pacts were actionable in ecclesiastical courts.[11] They justified broadening the purview of canon law out of concern for the state of the defendant's soul, the *ratio peccati*, rather than on the basis of a claimant's rights. From the standpoint of Christian morality, it did not matter whether a broken promise arose from a formal contract or a simple pact.

Legal historians agree for the most part that both the Church and commercial practice played crucial roles in establishing the consensualist principle in contract law beginning in the early modern period. Yet the degree to which individual consent was already the dominant aspect of legal agreements in the later Middle Ages is much less clear. When in their opinions jurists sought to identify the name of a contract—or more often simply its *causa*, its ground or purpose—were they merely appropriating the external trappings of an authoritative system, having already embraced, de facto, the universal freedom to contract?[12] Or did these names still hold sway in shaping accepted behavior, the collectively endorsed type still considered ontologically prior to the expression of individual will? This matter is clearly more than just a technical problem, as it speaks to the basis on which a given society ratifies the possible relationships among its members.

When we view the question in these general and abstract terms, it is only a small leap from the medieval conception of contract to that of literary genre. Late medieval scholars similarly had to conciliate an authoritative arsenal of literary terms and concepts inherited from antiquity with a range of literary practices that shared little with the original contexts of their classical precedents. Terms such as "tragedy" and "comedy," for instance, continued to enjoy wide circulation in medieval literary criticism even though the practice of ancient drama had long since vanished. What was the function of these venerable "names" when they were applied to medieval texts? Did they still serve a normative purpose?

Ever since Erich Auerbach's pioneering study of the *sermo humilis*,[13] Dante's masterpiece has been distinguished by its rejection of strict literary categories. With its hybrid mixture of generic conventions, the *Commedia* strikes a bold contrast to the conservatism of classical literature and its rigid hierarchy of styles. Inspired by the formal variety and social inclusiveness of the Bible, Dante dispenses with the classical conception of *genera dicendi* to create a modern, democratizing, and encyclopedic poetics. Comedy, in this view, is the name for a category that paradoxically escapes categorization.

Zygmunt Barański has developed Auerbach's thesis more extensively than any other recent critic.[14] For Barański, the *Commedia* represents a radical refutation of the Horatian tradition and the *genera dicendi* as they are laid out in Dante's more "retrograde" works, such as *De vulgari* and the Epistle to Cangrande. The poet's experimentalism frees his masterpiece from the dogmatism and restraints of a hierarchy of styles. In fact, Barański challenges the appropriateness of using genre at all as a means for understanding medieval literature. He argues that, given the competing systems of classification in the period and the plethora of definitorial categories, terms such as "comedy," "tragedy," and "elegy" never acquired fixed meanings (and "comedy" was the most flexible of all). As a result of this conceptual and terminological fluidity, medieval authors and readers were allowed considerable freedom in composing and interpreting texts. Indeed, Dante's poem, the "most original book that Western literature ever produced," would have been unthinkable within a more restrictive notion of literature.[15] When Dante decided to call his poem a "comedy," it follows, he did not have in mind a specific prescriptive model, but was purposely associating his work with a category of literature that had come to embrace "the same all-inclusive and free-wheeling viewpoint as that which characterized the *Commedia*'s form and content."[16]

Barański's work raises important and still largely unexplored questions about our modern conception of genre as it is applied to the literature and criticism of the Middle Ages. He insists upon the need to historicize the literary environment in which the poet was formed and with which he continuously engaged. Yet Barański stops short of historicizing Dante's (and our own) conceptions of freedom and the law. He repeatedly characterizes "individual expression" and "artistic freedom" as something that needs to be emancipated from the dogmas and constraints of literary convention, and depicts the prescriptive laws of genre as one of the greatest limitations on poetic freedom. We saw in chapter 2, however, how Dante viewed both political and poetic freedom as accomplished *through* the law. What sense could Barański's notion of artistic freedom hold for a medieval poet who conceived liberty as a "willing obedience to just laws"? Indeed, despite greatly furthering our understanding about Dante and medieval literary theory, Barański remains inadvertently attached to a liberal and Romantic vision of artistic production as an "undisciplined, occasionally anarchic world of literary creativeness."[17]

If Barański stands at one end of the individual/collective spectrum, the influential work on medieval genre by Hans Robert Jauss stands at the other.[18] Jauss defines genre in terms of the "rules of the game" and the "horizon of expectations" that are formed spontaneously in communities. These rules and expectations are not prescriptive, however: they arise organically from their "locus in life" to fulfill social needs.[19] In the case of medieval vernacular literature, generic conventions are inscribed within the immanent poetics of a work, not explicitly decreed as norms. Turning to the history of literary genres, Jauss proposes a dialectical model in which collective genre and individual artistic expression continuously influence each other. This dynamic vision of medieval genre, in which, in Kantian terms, each new concretization alters a never-finalized exemplar, has the advantage of reconciling long-standing, traditional cultural forms with historically necessitated innovation. But when Jauss turns from theory to practice, his categorization of narrative genres tends to neglect the tension generated between traditional schemata and individual works of art. His model-heavy analysis of medieval epic, romance, and novella ends up being as prescriptive as the structuralist accounts he criticizes.

Barański's and Jauss's work on genre exemplify two opposing methods for dealing with the middleness of medieval literature. On the one hand, Barański finds in medieval literary theory, and in Dante in particular, a point of origin for the modern view of artistic freedom and creativity. Although he is careful to distinguish between Dante's inventiveness and that of an avant-garde poet, he clearly views Dante as a precursor of the modern artist, whose pioneering creation cannot be constrained by traditional dogmas. For all his attempts at balancing individual work and collective exemplars, Jauss, on the other hand, concentrates on identifiable narrative and lyric types. While allowing for the greatest amount of innovation and adaptability possible—in contrast with the rigidity of the classical tradition—he nevertheless names the stable literary forms while the artists themselves remain, for the most part, nameless.

These contrasting historiographical accounts of the medieval literary genre resemble, to a striking degree, the contrasting historiographical accounts of medieval contract law.[20] Barański's view of medieval artistic freedom echoes the views of legal historians for whom medieval legal practice anticipates the modern freedom to contract. The agreement established between author and reader, like that between two or more contracting parties, is based primarily on consensus and individual wills. Jauss's views of genre are instead similar to those of historians who emphasize the continued role of collectively established, traditional types as mediating between individual and institution. From one perspective, the medieval period is a milestone on the way to modernity; from the other, it continues to reproduce ancient traditions but with a new and, for the most part, improved face.

Taken on their own terms, both of these approaches are equally convincing and equally plausible. Yet neither can account for what contemporaries must have experienced when confronted with changing epistemic systems in literature and law, both of which were in an undeniable state of flux. For this reason, Dante's *Commedia* is an invaluable artifact for historians of both literary genre and contract law—not because it bolsters one historiographical theory or another, but because, at a more global and abstract level, the text directly enacts the shifting relationship between individuals and institutions, a relationship that was increasingly in crisis. When Dante chooses to name his poem a "comedy," he does more than simply associate it with a low style instead of a high one. He questions the value itself of using preestablished models when those models have ceased to apply.

In subsequent sections I will explore the developments in Dante's contracts with readers, both before and after exile, that culminate in his naming of the poem in *Inferno*. Before discussing these implicit poetic agreements, it is necessary first to investigate Dante's more explicit treatment of pacts among characters in the poem, as the contract the poet establishes with readers in *Inferno* distinctly echoes the agreements he makes with the inhabitants of Hell. Only by examining in detail Dante's diagnosis of the contractual crisis of his time—a crisis he radicalizes in the hostile interactions of the underworld—can we move beyond the false opposition between presentist individualism and nostalgic collectivism.

Infernal Deals and Naked Pacts in *Inferno* 27

Although the back-and-forth negotiations between Dante and the damned dominate *Inferno*, scholars tend to ignore them. As one of the structural conventions established by the poem, they seem self-evident and thus not in need of commentary; modern critics have instead focused on interpreting the "public" justice of the *contrapasso*. The "private," autonomous settlements between Dante and individual souls that occur after God's final sentence have been largely consigned to the realm of irony.

To be sure, making a deal with Dante's character often has undesired results for the dealmaker. The immortal fame that the Pilgrim offers the sodomites is clearly offset by the notoriety he confers by bringing their fate to light. Similarly, while fulfilling Pier della Vigna's request to vindicate his memory—by reporting his unswerving loyalty to Frederick II—Dante simultaneously reveals that the illustrious rhetor, having "betrayed" his body, is now numbered among the damned as a suicide.

Yet these "unforeseen" outcomes do not disqualify the agreements between Dante and the souls. Up to a certain point, the Pilgrim and the damned still seem governed by a shared natural law, and are hence capable of intersubjective exchange and symbolic commerce. Exploring the limits of accord possible between peoples who can no longer swear to the truth of their statements by means of a common God, Dante and the damned rely heavily on rhetorical blandishments: their dealings are often initiated through the formalized use of conditional statements and the employment of the optative subjunctive (if/let/so may x happen, . . . do/tell me y). Linguistic etiquette and diplomatic courtesy thus constitute the tenuous connective tissue remaining between them.

That connective tissue may be tenuous, but without it there can be no agreements at all. For example, when Dante arrives in the lower depths of Cocytus, the damned reject his entreaties to restore their renown. Recognizing that the exchange of personal information for a promise of notoriety is a bad deal, these wickedest of sinners would rather remain in oblivion. Though their cynicism is not unfounded, their utter disinterest in the economy of *fama* and honor nonetheless signals that these subhuman creatures are finally beyond the pale. The fragile grounds for a pact dissolve when confronted with this unrecognizable, unassimilable Other. What kind of agreement is possible when one of the contracting parties no longer values reputation, a good name, or one's word?

Dante pushes this question to its limits when his own character violates a promise to Frate Alberigo in *Inferno* 33 by failing to remove the ice from his eyes. By this point in the downwardly spiraling journey, the infernal pacts have become doubly "bare." Not only are they legally unenforceable, they lack the critical *fides* (trust) necessary for any law or convention to function properly. As we have seen in chapter 2, Dante justifies his treatment of Alberigo by claiming that it was "courtesy" to act villainously toward him, since through his heinous sins the friar had already placed himself beyond the human fold. Yet the Pilgrim's actions also represent a dangerous erosion of the shared code of conduct that sustains all contracts, including those entered into with one's enemies. Dante's doublespeak reveals the limits of formal conventions when the ethical and cultural substrata supporting them no longer hold.

The encounter with Guido da Montefeltro in *Inferno* 27 and his tale of broken pacts brings these extreme cases back within the contemporary and quotidian context of Dante's Italy, dramatizing how the current political and institutional crises risk "stripping" even normally dressed pacts, including the covenant between God and the Church concerning the sacraments.

Guido is found in the eighth *bolgia* of Malebolge—the eighth circle of Hell in which various forms of fraud are punished. His particular sin is fraudulent counsel, and his narrative appears in a canto after that of a more famous fraudulent counselor, Ulysses. Like Ulysses, Guido is swathed in a tongue of flame for spreading lies: an ironic echo of the Pentecostal gift of tongues. A successful statesman and military strategist renowned for his shrewdness, he tells Dante that while he was still in the flesh his works were "di volpe" (foxlike) and that he was an expert in "li accorgimenti e le coperte vie" (schemes and covert ways; *Inf.* 27.75–76).

The exchange between Dante and Guido begins with Guido patriotically asking about the state of his homeland, Romagna—specifically whether it is in peace or at war. The Pilgrim responds that although Guido's Romagna is not engaged in any open war, it lives under the perpetual tyranny of its rulers, who are compared to various beasts. Having provided this account, Dante asks in exchange to know about the shade's identity, offering him continued worldly fame as an added incentive. Mistaking Dante for one of the damned, and thus for someone who will never return to the world, Guido concedes to tell his fateful tale "sanza tema d'infamia" (without fear of infamy; *Inf.* 27.66).

In that period of one's life in which one should "calar le vele e raccoglier le sarte (lower the sails and coil the ropes; *Inf.* 27.81),[21] Guido entered the Franciscan order having repented of his former misdeeds. Heedless of this recent conversion, Pope Boniface VIII approached him for advice about how to defeat his enemies, the Colonna family, whose members were holed up in their fortress in Palestrina (the Colonna cardinals had questioned the legality of Celestine V's abdication, and hence the legitimacy of the reigning pope). Although Guido wavers initially, the pope ultimately overcomes his hesitation with the promise of future absolution: "finor t'assolvo" (henceforth I absolve you; *Inf.* 27.101). The advice Guido provides is profoundly cynical: Offer the Colonna a general amnesty to draw them out of their defensive position, he suggests, and then attack: "lunga promessa con l'attender corto / ti farà trïunfar ne l'alto seggio" (a long promise with a short keeping will make you triumph on your high throne; *Inf.* 27.110–11). At this point the narrative jumps forward to Guido's death, where St. Francis and a black cherubim argue over who has dominion over the false counselor's soul. The demon prevails.

The encounter with Guido is constructed around three interlocking agreements. At the heart of the narrative is the pope's promise of absolution in exchange for military counsel. The "payment" of Guido's half of this arrangement functions as the basis for the treaty between the pope and the Colonna, the long promise with the short keeping. Guido then utilizes the narrative of both these pacts as his portion of the bargain with Dante's character, swapping information about his identity and fate for news about the present situation in Romagna. In none of these transactions does Guido indicate that he believes in a higher order or a set of overriding principles, the authority of which might channel or check one's actions; the scope of human relations appears limited for him to competition and naked conflict. Unable to transcend this claustrophobic perspective, Guido estimates the net outcome of his *fama* in his deal with Dante with the same self-interested calculation with which he had measured the grace he would acquire from his agreement with the pope (both erroneous calculations, as it turns out).

Of these three agreements, Boniface's violation of the treaty with the Colonna might seem most peripheral, as it is only alluded to, not staged. But that violation, in fact, produces the psychic anxiety at the core of these contiguous deals, bringing to the surface the fragility of unactionable pacts. Many of Dante's readers would already have known about Boniface's reneged promise of amnesty, including the fact that he razed the Colonna family compound at Palestrina once they had surrendered peaceably. In breaching this truce, Boniface profaned what jurists considered the most basic and fundamental variant of the pact, the peace treaty—thereby putting the entire social covenant at risk.[22] When the pope, the supreme figure in charge of ensuring that both simple and solemnized promises are bound by an underlying Christian ethos, disregards the most essential good-faith contract, all deals suddenly appear vulnerable.

In his treatment of the Colonna family (whom he had previously excommunicated), Boniface clearly considered himself above the law. As *princeps* of Christian souls, the pope was, like the emperor, "loosed from the law"—at least according to canonists since Hostiensis (d. 1271).[23] Indeed, claims of papal absolutism reached an apex under Boniface VIII, with his lawyers making ever more expansive claims for his *plenitudo potestatis*.

We have seen in previous chapters how medieval jurists tempered such expressions of monarchic supremacy by stipulating their circumscribed applicability and need for justification. Yet despite insisting that the *princeps* voluntarily obey the directive power of the law, even moderate positions on papal and imperial absolutism allowed that his actions were not enforceable by any coercive power.[24] Any agreement with the emperor or pope was therefore potentially "naked" due to his standing within (or, in a sense, without) the kingdom. In order to overcome the possible antinomy of a ruler at once loosed from and bound to the law, jurists employed the voluntary obedience of Christ—the King of Kings—and God's promise to honor the sacraments as political-theological models for the monarch's legal status, which amounted to a self-imposed adherence to the law.[25] God keeps his word with respect to his new covenant with the Church, the theologians proclaimed reassuringly.[26]

But what happens, asks Dante, when his vicar on earth does not? What is to stop him when, unlike the ideal sovereign in *Monarchia*, universal jurisdiction cannot satisfy his cupidity? In Boniface's interaction with Guido da Montefeltro, Dante explores the practical consequences of a *princeps* who not only ignores the duties of his position—what he *ought* to do—but also cynically flaunts his freedom from fundamental laws and traditional morality.

Guido decides to help Boniface against the Colonna, mainly because of the pope's not-so-veiled threats. These threats pertain to the pope's capacity to damn or save through the sacrament of absolution and the power of the apostolic keys: "Lo ciel poss'io serrare e diserrare / come tu sai; e però son due le chiavi / che 'l mio antecessor non ebbe care" (Heaven I can lock and unlock, as you know; for that reason the keys are two which my predecessor did not hold dear; *Inf.* 27.103–5). Guido appears to believe that the pope's authority to transform signs into deeds is absolute, regardless of their relation to a superior order of justice. Such a reductive focus on the thingness of the sacraments and their quasi-magical efficacy pales in comparison, however, with the pope's appropriation of them as symbolic capital. Boniface sardonically taunts his predecessor Celestine V, whom he pressured to abdicate, for his naiveté in failing to recognize and properly access the value of the two keys—for not holding them "dear."

The pope's cynicism regarding the sacraments leads to a crisis of investiture within the episode. Boniface's actions, undertaken as a private individual, risk soiling his immortal "second body." His "office" (*Inf.* 27.91), "sacred orders" (91), "keys" (104), and "throne" (111), instead of being metonymically related to his sublime person, seem free-floating and detached. As the embodied *lex animata*, the pope should serve as mediator between the positive law and its justification in a divine realm of righteousness, ensuring that the daily negotiations within the system are backed, "underwritten," from without. Instead, Boniface's depravity threatens to bring the sacramental pact down to the level of the other pacts glimpsed in the canto, turning the performative "finor t'assolvo" into nothing more than a "long promise with a short keeping."

Faced with the limits on actionability presented by both naked pacts and treaties made with a technically unaccountable sovereign, Dante imagines an external court circumscribing even the pope's fullness of powers. At the moment of Guido's death, St. Francis comes to retrieve his soul, only to be intercepted by a demon who accuses the saint of committing a misdeed, a "torto" (*Inf.* 27.114), in taking possession of what rightfully belongs to his dominion. The demonic lawyer wins his claim by arguing that the pope's absolution was void because it lacked contrition: Guido could not have simultaneously willed a sin and repented for it. In this scene of otherworldly litigation, Dante relocates the instant of binding or "dressing" of the pact between God and man from formal act of absolution to the moment of consent (consent to sin, in this case). That shift in legal grounding (i.e., Dante's relocation of the moment of "dressing") is articulated within the canto as a disruption in narratological time. As soon as Guido gives his false counsel, the story jumps to the scene of his death, where he retrospectively discovers that, from the instant he transferred "title" over his soul, he has been stalked by the demonic magistrate: "dal quale in qua stato li sono a' crini" (from that time until now, I have been at his hair; *Inf.* 27.117).

Without too much exaggeration, the courtroom scene at Guido's death may be viewed as representing a crucial aim of the *Commedia* as a whole: the imaginative construction of a "higher" legal system capable of punishing hidden crimes and informal pacts. It is for this reason that the momentary confusion about who has jurisdiction over Guido's soul—and the possibility that even a saint in heaven might err on this account—is so emotionally charged. It foregrounds the stakes of Dante's project: to reinforce the external supports of human law by making the repercussions of failing to do as one *ought* as visible and tangible as possible. If the purpose of final justice is to reground the law and serve as a theological model for its legitimacy, it can bear no uncertainty, no contingency. To put it another way, to properly function as a reaction-formation to the dystopia of Boniface's Italy, the fantasy of ultimate justice can have no points in contact with that fallen world—and yet, in some darkly humorous way, the two worlds resemble each other.

I do not, of course, want to propose that God's justice is flawed. Even less do I view Dante's poem as deconstructing itself at this point, revealing the loopholes in its supposedly divine foundations. Medieval readers could take a joke, and the scene of an angel and a devil arguing over the ultimate fate of a soul was a familiar one, widely depicted in the theater and art of the period. The uncertainty raised by the jurisdictional conflict over Guido is fleeting, after all, and its potential Manichaeism much less pronounced than in the battle at the Gates of Dis in *Inferno* 8–9. Yet we also need to take into account the unease this scene has caused over the centuries. Even in its earliest reception, readers registered their anxiety about the episode by attempting to domesticate it, labeling the portrayal of St. Francis and the demon as somehow more fictional than the rest of the fiction. Fourteenth-century commentaries insisted, for instance, that the poet only "pretends" that the battle for Guido's soul took place.

I would suggest that Dante built this discomfort into the text fully expecting readers to respond to it. Through the comic exchange at Guido's death, he allows us to experience the terror of discovering that the fantasy of final justice is just one more contingent struggle, a scene of further conflict rather than revelation (*litigium* where one would expect *iudicium*). In essence, the poet stages the costs of not believing in his poem, and hence of losing faith in a master signifier, by giving us a glimpse of what such an infernal justice would look like. In this final court of appeals, the devil's advocate, like a clever canon lawyer, dominates through his superior scholastic training, and cloaks his brute violence in legal reasoning. As he assumes possession of Guido's eternal soul, the black cherub cannot resist a final quip in the chillingly sardonic style of Boniface: "Forse / tu non pensavi ch'io löico fossi!" (Perhaps you did not think I was a logician!; *Inf.* 27.122–23).

Guido's dramatic tale of moral shipwreck is often read in tandem with the actual shipwreck of Ulysses as a contrast between the ancient and the modern, tragedy and comedy, high and low styles.[27]

In fact, Ulysses's fateful tale is characterized by rhetorical grandiloquence, narrative linearity, and objective distance, while Guido's account is colloquial, imbued with sarcasm, temporally discontinuous, and entirely subjective. Faithfully keeping these styles separate, the character of Virgil allows Dante to speak to Guido, since he is a fellow Italian, but insists on interviewing Ulysses and Diomedes himself, assuming that as Greeks they would object to Dante's "detto" (speech; *Inf.* 26.75). Yet by juxtaposing the ancient hero with the modern trickster, Dante the poet may also be seen as commenting on the illusion of these distinctions when viewed from the perspective of salvation. In the end, Guido reveals what Ulysses would look like were he alive at the time: a foxlike scoundrel or, in Virgil's own words, an "contriver of crimes" (*Aeneid* 2.164) who cannot readjust to the norms of peacetime, having experienced the exhilaration of violating them in war.

Yet one clear distinction remains between ancient and modern civilizations as they are symbolically presented in this pair of cantos. In their interaction and negotiation, Virgil and Ulysses are still beholden to a shared aristocratic code and assumed good faith, while Dante and Guido navigate within the deregulated marketplace of naked pacts. In his merit-based arrangement with Ulysses and Diomedes, Virgil entices the Greek heroes to speak by referencing the value of the *fama* he has bestowed upon them: "S'io meritai di voi mentre ch'io vissi / s'io meritai di voi assai o poco/ quando nel mondo li alti versi scrissi" (If any merit I have won from you while I lived, if any merit, much or little, when in the world I wrote my high verses; *Inf.* 26.80–82). In contrast with this transparent and equitable transaction, Dante's deal with Guido is instead based on the false presumption that he will *not* write about him in the future, thereby leaving his reputation unmarred by *infamia*. In remaining silent, Dante's character outfoxes the fox. But he also reveals the perils of a Christian "style" that privileges consensus over type. Christ's Revelation may have rendered the old social and aesthetic distinctions obsolete, but the disintegration of these collective schemas, when not superseded by a universal belief in eternal rewards and punishments, risks leaving behind a power vacuum filled by mere greed and domination, as evident here in Hell but also in Romagna, a place Dante has described as never "sanza guerra" (without war; *Inf.* 27.38).

Even when faced with the institutional failures and obsolete models foregrounded in *Inferno* 27, Dante does not resign himself to the inevitability of a state of brute nature. Instead, he seeks new ground on which to forge the pacts between man and man, and between man and God. His exploration comes to the fore when we compare Guido's damnation with his son Buonconte's salvation in *Purgatorio* 5. As we have seen in chapter 1, Buonconte dies unshriven after a life given over to violent sin. Yet his informal acts of contrition—dying with "Maria" on his lips, his arms folded in the sign of a cross, having shed a "little tear" (*Purg.* 5.107)—are honored despite lacking institutional sanctification. After his exile, Dante similarly seeks to rethink what qualifies a contract between an author and his public. In the next section we will examine Dante's quest to find the new "garment" that would "dress" his work.

Naked Pacts and Poems Dressed:
"Tre donne intorno al cor mi son venute"

In a suggestive parallel to contemporary legal discourse, Dante also draws on the symbolic rituals of dressing female bodies to depict his poems as naked or dressed.[28] As is well known, the poet often personified his poetic compositions and spoke of them as young ladies, *figliole* or *pulzelle*. But the significance of what it means for Dante to dress these unmarried maidens has for the most part escaped critical attention. In several preexilic compositions, Dante considers the dressing of his work as the moment in which it was put to music and performed. In this traditional view, the text remained naked until it received collective ratification and recognition. After his exile, when he could no longer count on his poems being performed within known and trustworthy circles, he was forced to relocate the dressing of his text within the intrinsic form and content of the poem itself, effectively bypassing the mediation of communal performance. As we will soon see, in the canzone "Tre donne intorno al cor mi son venute," he assigns the vivifying moment of contract to the direct granting of consent by author and reader.

In two of his early works, "Se Lippo amico sè tu che mi leggi" (If it is you my friend Lippo who are reading me) and "Per una ghirlandetta" (For a floral wreath),[29] Dante alludes to the poems as naked, *nuda*, and incomplete; they require something outside themselves, an appropriate *vesta* (dress), before they can safely circulate in public. As Claudio Giunta has recently confirmed, the *vesta* necessary in order for "Se Lippo amico" and "Per una ghirlandetta" to be published almost certainly refers to an accompanying musical melody.[30] Dante tellingly imagines the future performance of these works as a *vestizione*—a nuptial ritual in which the husband would dress his young bride, publicly recognizing her as his wife and the household's mistress.[31]

The metaphorical parallel is especially developed in "Se Lippo amico." Spoken in the voice of the personified poem itself, the entire twenty-line *sonetto doppio* functions as an apostrophe to its intended recipient, Lippo. After an extended salutation, the sonnet-messenger beseeches Lippo to receive and clothe the "pulcella nuda" he is chaperoning, most likely the isolated stanza "Lo meo servente core" (My observant heart):

> Lo qual ti guido esta pulcella nuda
> che vien dirieto a me sì vergognosa
> ch'atorno gir non osa
> perch'ella non ha vesta in cui si chiuda;
>   e prego il cor gentil che 'n te riposa
> che la rivesta e tegnala per druda,
> sì che sia cognosciuda
> e possa andar là 'vunq'è disïosa.

> (I bring you this naked maiden who is following me all timidly and who dares not walk abroad, for she has not clothes to cover her: and I beg the gentle heart that dwells in you to clothe her and keep her as your friend; so that she may become known and be able to go wherever she pleases; 13–20)

In this detailed request, Lippo is asked to play the role of "drudo" (friend/lover) to the "pulcella" and to "clothe" her with a new status.

Only after a proper *vestizione* will she be free "to go wherever she pleases."

Of all Dante's compositions, why do "Lo meo servente core" and "Per una ghirlandetta" need to be dressed and married to a musical accompaniment before they can be published, and why would they be considered naked otherwise? The answer may lie in their overt status as genre poems. Neither "Lo servente meo core" nor "Per una ghirlandetta" attempts to identify its speaker with an autobiographical "I." Rather than projecting a lyric self, that is, both poems exemplify conventional Romance topoi: "Lo servente meo core" is a *canzone di lontananza* (distance song) while "Per una ghirlandetta" adopts a common pastoral motif. Irrespective of Dante's originality in his treatment of these well-established schemas, the poems' ultimate success depends on their being recognized, "cognosciuda," as a type. Since they are already, in a sense, theatrical "scripts" of highly conventionalized personae, only a public recital once they have been put to music will render them fully efficacious. Without the intervention of this larger symbolic order, their mimetic content remains effectively bare.

Despite the examples of "Se Lippo amico" and "Per una ghirlandetta," Dante's involvement with poetic genres intended for musical accompaniment must have been sporadic at best. His literary output consists primarily of lyric and doctrinal poems, whose complex metrical schemes indicate they were likely conceived without any subsequent musical component in mind. After his exile, the opportunities for Dante to collaborate with local musicians obviously greatly decreased; indeed, he was cut off from a range of municipal poetic rituals, and could no longer count on a stable and determined audience.

In his great poem of exile, "Tre donne intorno al cor mi son venute," Dante confronts this breakdown in the normal circuit of poem and public. In particular, he dramatizes how, when the public authorities abandon justice, both laws and poems must wander in a state of undress. The female speaker of "Tre donne"—a personification of *Drittura* (Justice)—not only lacks adequate attire but has been forcibly stripped and discarded. While retaining her inherent honor, she is deprived of her social effectiveness. This disabling of the source of the law forces Dante to rethink as well the relationship between reader and public, and to imagine a new scenario in which the poem, rather than awaiting external ratification, must dress herself.

In its intellectual scope, its balanced employment of abstract personification and striking realism, and above all its universalizing perspective on personal circumstances, "Tre donne" has no equal in Dante's corpus besides the *Commedia*. The *canzone* consists of five stanzas and two distinct *congedi* (shortened metrical units at the end of the composition in which the author directly addresses his personified poem). The first four stanzas depict three allegorical ladies on a visit to Dante's heart so that they may converse with Love, who resides therein. The first of these ladies identifies herself as Justice, "Drittura," and explains that, along with her daughter and granddaughter, she has been forcefully exiled from society. Beginning with the earliest gloss on the poem—by Dante's son, Pietro Alighieri—most critics have interpreted Drittura and her progeny as personifications respectively of natural law (*ius naturalis*), the law of nations (*ius gentium*), and positive law or legislation (*lex*).[32] In the fifth stanza, Dante suddenly projects himself onto the allegorical landscape, claiming that he now considers his exile an honor since it is shared with such lofty Virtues.

The primary consequence of Justice's exile from the world is that it has rendered her laws ineffectual. Without the backing of Love's weapons ("armi"; 61), the three ladies are powerless. Their downcast state exemplifies the type of obstructed justice Dante classified in *Monarchia* as impeded with regard to power, "contrarietatem . . . in posse" (*Mon.* 1.11.7), as opposed to impeded with regard to the will, "contrarietatem . . . in velle" (1.11.6).[33] The various laws have retreated to Dante's heart as to the house of a friend, "a casa d'amico" (17). But this withdrawal from the public to the private also belies a loss of capacity. Just as Dante may possess justice in his heart—as a characteristic virtue or *habitus*—but lack the political power to employ it, the laws themselves have been disarmed and reduced to mere ethical precepts.

The debilitated condition of the law is most concretely represented by Drittura's inappropriate dress. She wears a simple tunic that reveals her "nudo braccio" (naked arm; 22), and she is barefoot and ungirt. Most disturbingly, in a detail bordering on the porno-graphic, her torn gown reveals her genitalia, with the implication that she is either an actual or potential victim of sexual violence: "Come Amor prima per la rotta gonna / la vide in parte che 'l tacere è bello" (When Love first saw, through the torn dress, that part of her which it is not decent to name; 27–28).[34] Instead of a maiden awaiting her *vestizione*, Drittura is a married woman who has been undressed and divested of her status, a forerunner to Boccaccio's Griselda (or Dante's Costanza). Stripped of the clothing that would ensure that her authority be recognized, she is now without a house-hold, a mistress of her body alone: "sol di sé par donna" (26). In al-legorical terms, the normative pronouncements of Justice are no longer heeded by society; they have become mere declarative state-ments rather than efficacious speech acts.

Given that the barren state of the law is associated with a loss of marital status, Drittura's emphasis on virginity and virgin births is all the more striking. When she tells Love that she is the sister of his mother, Venus, Drittura allusively identifies herself as Astraea, the celestial virgin (Dante similarly identifies Justice with Astraea, "the Virgin," in Book One of *Monarchia*). She further explains that she delivered her daughter at the source of the Nile—most likely refer-ring to Eden—where the waves of the great river are still "virgin" (49). Drittura's daughter, in turn, bore her own daughter in similarly asexual circumstances. She gave birth by self-reflexively gazing at her own image, "mirando sé" (53), in the Nile's pure waters.

Through these Neoplatonizing births and virginal conceptions, Drittura depicts a legal universe devoid of masculine intervention, yet fully valid and autonomous. In Drittura's parable of generation, the law is a female body whose authoritative content requires no formalization. The creative power of the law belongs to its intrinsic nature rather than to any subsequent institutional sanction. Truly "mistresses of themselves," these laws possess a fertility that derives from their own substance, irrespective of any infusion of form by the political order. (This belief contrasted strongly with medieval theo-ries of conception, in which the active male seed provided the form necessary to vivify the female's passive material.)

By associating the asexual reproduction of the law with the fertility of the Nile and the fullness of Eden, Dante portrays a different vision of the female body than that of the early jurists, who found something lacking and incomplete in its naked form. Accursius had stated unequivocally that bringing a civil action on the grounds of a naked pact would have been like expecting "a virgin or sterile woman to give birth."[35] In contrast, Dante views such a miraculous conception as the very foundation of the law—a fusion of legal fertility and ethical virginity. Even if public authorities are not currently executing the law, its capacity to create natural obligations remains intact.

In the poem's conclusion, Dante associates his own political misfortunes with the stoic retreat of the laws to their source. Beginning the stanza with the adversative "Ed io" (But I; 73), the poet suddenly reconsiders the universalizing dialogue between Love and Justice from the viewpoint of his personal downfall. He now considers the exile imposed upon him an honor, "l'essilio che m'è dato onor mi tegno" (76), because Justice and Love are similarly banished along with him. Although he has been politically defeated and formally sentenced, Dante takes comfort in the fact that the laws themselves are shown to be literally on his side. In an unjust system, it is still praiseworthy to fall with the just: "cader co' buoni è pur di lode degno" (80).

This ethical rationalization of a legal outcome lasts only a few verses, however (the first two quatrains of the stanza). In the *sirma*, introduced by another adversative, the poet confronts the bleak realities of his political impasse. He finds the distance caused by his exile intolerable, as it has removed his love object from his sight: "E se non che degli occhi miei 'l bel segno / per lontananza m'è tolto dal viso / che m'have in foco miso" (And were it not that the fair goal of my eyes is removed by distance from my sight—and this has set me on fire; 81–83). That "fire" has so consumed the poet's "bones and flesh" (86) that he is near death. Dante concludes the stanza by asking to be pardoned—and, presumably, readmitted to Florence—for the unspecified "colpa" (fault; 88) for which he has already repented.

Critics are split on how to interpret the "bel segno" whose absence disturbs the poet's philosophical consolation.[36] Equally valid arguments have been put forth for identifying the "segno" either as the city of Florence or the poet's lady. The context seems to allow for both private desire and patriotic sentiment and, in my view, Dante fully intended such ambiguity. I would further argue that the two readings are related—that Dante's distance from Florence for political reasons (first reading) has devastated his relationship with the literary public for his love poetry, figured as the distant beloved (second reading). What Dante cannot abide in exile is the loss of a sphere of action for his poetic compositions. We can thus read the emphasis on *lontananza* in the stanza as an elegy for his former ability to participate in poetic genres such as the *canzone di lontananza*, which imply a ready-made public that can circulate, consume, execute, and hence "dress" one's works.

We can observe the effects of this loss on Dante in the directions he gives the canzone in the first *congedo*. In a personification that directly recalls the allegory of Drittura, the poet focuses obsessively on his poem's body and dress. He warns her:

Canzone, a' panni tuoi non ponga uom mano
per veder quel che bella donna chiude:
bastin le parti nude;
el dolce pome a tutta gente niega,
per cui ciascun man piega.

(Canzone, let no man touch your dress to see what a fair woman hides; let the uncovered parts suffice; deny to all the sweet fruit for which all stretch out their hands; 91–95)

Those readers who forcefully attempt to undress her should be allowed access only to that part of her body which is already uncovered, "le parti nude" (93), and be denied her sweet fruit, "dolce pome" (94). However, if she should encounter the type of virtuous reader who makes his request politely and respectfully, she should put on "color' novi" (fresh colors; 98), and "'l fior ch'è bel di fuori / fa disïar negli amorosi cori" (make the flower that has outward beauty be desired by hearts in love; 99–100).

Contrasting literal body to metaphorical or allegorical dress was, of course, a familiar way to speak about different levels of poetic meaning in Dante's time. Dante uses such language in the *Vita nova*, where he insists that a true poet should be able to "denude" a rhetorical figure to reveal its meaning in prose. In *Convivio*, he similarly compares the mere rhetorical *ornatus* of a lady's dress with the sententious content of her unadorned body, or *bellezza* (beauty) with *bontà* (goodness). In the *congedo* to "Tre donne," however, the traditional dichotomies of form/content, body/dress, and beauty/goodness are complicated. The full external beauty of the poem, the "'l fior ch'è bel di fuori," cannot be perceived unless its content is revealed. And what the privileged reader gains access to is not simply the poem's body, but that body wrapped in a renewed rhetorical garb, "color' novi."

The contradictory indications Dante gives his poem have often puzzled critics. But at least one rhetorical strategy of the *congedo* seems clear. Above all, the poem is represented as *dressing herself*. She alternatively hides her sweet fruit or puts on new colors for those she herself selects. In contrast to "Se Lippo amico," where the poetic composition needs to find a husband in order to circulate in public, Dante instead depicts the canzone "Tre donne" as a woman in control of her erotic power—and as one who employs the rituals of dress to her own advantage.

Through this representation of female autonomy, Dante construes his poetic artifact as intrinsically complete and qualified on its own—its "fertility" derives from authorial intention rather than public performance.[37] Of course, the relationship between poem and public remains a heterosexual arrangement: she still seeks out an appropriately virtuous male lover-reader, an "amico di vertù" (friend to virtue; 97). Yet the source of the poem's validity and efficacy is relocated from execution to hermeneutics. It does not need to be finished in the future through music; an original completeness already resides in the texture of the work. In the end, what brings the poem to life is a direct negotiation between the intentions of the author and the reader.

The stakes for these new postexilic poetics become clear when we consider the political allusion of the second *congedo*. In this coda, Dante directs the canzone to both "hawk" with the white birds and "hunt" with the black greyhounds (101–2)—an apparent reference to the White and Black parties of Florentine Guelphs. These few lines make several allusions to forgiveness and pardon: first, the "black greyhounds" from whom Dante is forced to flee could grant him the gift of peace, "di pace dono" (104), but they fail to do so because they do not realize who he really is: "Però nol fan, ché non san quel ch'io sono" (105). Second, in a final rhymed couplet, Dante concludes with an ethical *sententia* about forgiveness. He reminds the Blacks that "camera di perdon savio uom non serra / ché perdonare è bel vincer di guerra" (A wise man will not lock the chamber of forgiveness; for to pardon is a fine victory in war; 106–7).

Because no other poem of Dante's besides "Tre donne" includes a second *congedo*, critics have plausibly suggested that it may have been added to the already-finished poem at a later date. These last verses differ metrically from the rest of the composition, and they do not appear in part of the manuscript tradition. At the same time, though, the emphasis on reconciliation and pardon was a crucial theme in the main body of the text (especially so in the reference to the poet's "colpa" in the fifth stanza). It seems likely, therefore, that both the second *congedo* and the rest of "Tre donne," whether or not they were composed separately, can both be situated somewhere between 1304 and 1309—just after Dante and his fellow exiles suffered a series of military defeats against Florence. In these years, according to Leonardo Bruni, the poet was still seeking conciliation with his native city after having broken ranks with the White Guelphs, and he had yet to assume the violent polemics that followed Henry VII's failed coronation.[38]

The emphasis in this second *congedo* on pardon, reconciliation, and peace sheds light on the rhetorical context of "Tre donne," especially its role as a verbal act. With these lines, Dante aims to establish a peace treaty with the Blacks, who have remained in the city and in power. Dante thus finds himself in the position of the Colonna with respect to Pope Boniface—a defeated enemy who has lost certain protections under the law. The weakness of his position in negotiating this truce extends to another pact he vitally needs to establish: the one creating a new relationship with his literary public. In both cases he is compelled to offer what are, for all intents and purposes, naked pacts. Whether the pacts in question are established between private citizen and *civitas* or between poet and reader, Dante wants to effect the sanctioning of a legal contract or public performance: he needs what he says to count. Otherwise, his good intentions, unheeded and uncirculated, will be confined to the dormant realm of fantasy—protected but also trapped, like Justice within the "etterna rocca" (eternal fortress; 69).

In "Tre donne" Dante confronts the barren landscape of unprotected pacts that will come to characterize the *Commedia*. Excluded from the protections of municipal law as well as from the normal authoritative channels for bringing texts to life, he argues that the authority of both laws and poems resides in their intrinsic nature. In this vision of legal and literary rights, the poet possesses an individual dignity that allows him to negotiate the meaning of his work directly with readers, free from the mediation of public performance and rigidly standardized genres.

However, by the time Dante begins writing the *Commedia*, he is less sanguine about naked pacts and more doubtful that consensus alone could dress the pact between author and reader. The addresses to the reader in his masterpiece do indeed reproduce the unmediated negotiations between author and public that preoccupy the dual *congedi* of "Tre donne." But Dante simultaneously finds it necessary to clothe his poem in a collectively established genre, to name it a "comedy." While he recognizes the failure of present-day schemas to regulate contracts, be they legal or literary, he nonetheless attempts to adapt an authoritative model to the new conditions. The divide between Dante's title and the actual content of his poem, which has so troubled readers over the centuries, should be interpreted as his attempt to navigate between an unrestrained freedom to contract and a no longer viable system of standard types. In the section that follows, we will grapple with the question of what it meant when Dante identified his *Commedia* as a comedy.

Comedy as a Naked Pact

Dante calls his poem a "comedìa" twice in *Inferno*: "questa comedia" (this comedy; *Inf.* 16.128) and "la mia comedìa" (my comedy; *Inf.* 21.2). In *Monarchia*, he cross-references a passage found "in Paradiso Comedìe" (in the Paradiso of the Comedy; *Mon.* 1.12.6), and in the Epistle to Cangrande della Scala, he provides a brief definition of the title "Comoedia." The fourteenth-century commentators likewise refer to the work as a comedy when discussing its title, and the rubrics to the earliest manuscripts consistently entitle the poem *Comedia*. Although scholars have occasionally raised doubts about whether Dante intended "comedìa" to refer to the entire work or perhaps simply the first *cantica*, especially since in the *Paradiso* he will instead refer to it as "lo sacrato poema" (the consecrated poem; *Par.* 23.62) and "'l poema sacro" (the sacred poem; *Par.* 25.1), the current state of evidence favors the traditional title (minus the qualifying *Divina* which first appears in the sixteenth century).[39] But what did the poet mean by "comedìa" and how are we to understand the relationship of his text to this traditional genre?

In the epistle to his patron Cangrande, Dante begins an introduction to the *Paradiso* by examining the title of the text as a whole, giving four primary reasons as to why it is entitled "Comoedia." The first is etymological and sociological: the name *comedy* derives from *comos*, "village," and *oda*, "song." The second is based on its structure or plot: it begins horribly but ends happily, while tragedy begins happily but ends horribly. The third pertains to style: it is written in a lowly, humble style in contrast with the high, sublime style of tragedy. The fourth is linguistic: rather than in Latin, Dante wrote the work in the common vernacular, a language even simple women (*mulierculae*) would comprehend.

Although these definitions do describe in very general terms the form and content of Dante's poem, critics since Boccaccio have been understandably frustrated with their inadequacy in accounting for the boundless expressiveness and experimentalism of the *Commedia*. Given the limits of the Epistle,[40] modern scholars have turned their attention to Dante's uses of the term in the poem itself.[41] Their studies argue broadly that Dante seeks to extricate his work from conventional expectations of genre, paradoxically establishing a "genre that surpasses and eliminates genre: the *comedìa* that is higher than the highest *tragedìa*."[42] According to this line of inquiry, Dante employs the category of comedy only to highlight the extent to which his poem is unclassifiable and beyond genre; his particular brand of "comedy" rejects the separation of styles so as to more faithfully represent God's multifaceted creation.

Yet, as I hope to make clear, Dante was much less sanguine about the possibility, or even the advantage, of sidestepping the collective models for individual behavior, be they economic or literary. Because he viewed the system of genres as essentially productive rather than constraining, it makes little sense that he would want to call attention to his "freedom" from them in the naming of his poem. In contrasting his *comedìa* to Virgil's *tragedìa*, Dante's aim is not simply to declare the superiority of the former over the latter vis-à-vis its greater scope and flexibility, but to probe an ethically more complex situation: the role of the modern author caught at a crossroads between a system built around established types and one based on consensus alone. In order to more fully understand Dante's reaction to this crisis in categorization, I will focus on the poet's naming of his work as a reflection on the function of naming itself. Specifically, I will argue that while critics typically treat these "baptismal events" as unilateral pronouncements, they are in fact bilateral pacts—tentative agreements negotiated with readers. As a consequence, they will be read in relation to two crucial "pacts" that occur in the accompanying narrative: the pact with the monster Geryon to convey the travelers into the pit of Malebolge, and the pact with the Malebranche for safe conduct in the circle of the barrators.

Geryon

The monster Geryon appears at the end of canto 16. Having left the last group of sodomites, Virgil and Dante arrive at the edge of the fiery plain where punishment is meted out to the violent against God. Far beneath them is the eighth circle of simple fraud. The deadly drop between the regions is conveyed by the roar of the river Phlegethon, which plunges into the abyss below in a deafening waterfall. Dante removes a cord from around his waist at Virgil's request, and Virgil tosses it into the pit as a kind of bait to lure Geryon. The canto concludes in an atmosphere of suspense, as the poet swears to the truth of the unbelievable marvel he is about to describe:

Sempre a quel ver c'ha faccia di menzogna
de' l'uom chiuder le labbra fin ch'el puote,
però che sanza colpa fa vergogna:
ma qui tacer nol posso, e per le note
di questa comedìa, lettor, ti guiro,
s'elle non sien di lunga grazia vòte,
ch'i' vidi per quell'aere grosso e scuro
venir notando una figura in suso
maravigliosa ad ogne cor sicuro.

(Always to that truth that has the face of falsehood one should
close one's lips as long as one can, for without guilt it brings shame;
but here I cannot conceal it, and by the notes of the comedy, reader, I
swear to you, lest they fail to find long favor, that I saw, through that
thick dark air, a figure coming swimming upward, fearful to the most
confident heart; *Inf.* 16.124–32)

Canto 17 begins with a description of the hybrid monster, perhaps
Dante's most original contribution to the canon of underworld
guardians. This "sozza imagine di froda" (filthy image of fraud; *Inf.*
17.7) possesses the face of a "uom giusto" (just man; 10), the paws
of a lion, the body of a serpent, and the bifurcated tail of the scor-
pion. Virgil directs Dante to continue walking to the right so that
he may encounter a group of usurers punished at the outer edge of
the shelf, and thereby acquire "piena / esperïenza" (full experience;
Inf. 17.37–38) of this circle. In the meantime, Virgil will speak with
Geryon and convince him to bear them into the pit below.

After a brief visit with the usurers, the Pilgrim returns to Virgil,
who tells him to mount the monster and seat himself in front of
him, so that the guide may serve as a buffer between him and the
poisonous tail. The poet then describes in remarkably vivid detail
the terrifying blind flight on Geryon's back. As the monster descends
with his cargo in wide slow circles, the Pilgrim is aware of its move-
ment only by feeling the wind from below (eventually he will be able
to peer down and see the fires punishing the damned). Dante com-
pares his fear to that of Icarus and Phaeton, the protagonists of two
famous myths of doomed flights. But they land safely: Geryon de-

posits his charge at the base of the cliffs surrounding Malebolge and then quickly disappears, perhaps upset at having been tricked into giving something for nothing.

In this transition from middle to lower Hell, one narrative anomaly stands out. Dante separates from his guide in canto 17 at verse 43 and remains "tutto solo" (all alone; *Inf.* 17.44) until reuniting with him at verse 79. For the first time in the poem, Virgil's and Dante's experiences of the journey do not coincide. More importantly, although Virgil announces his intention to parley with Geryon—and we can deduce from his appearance astride the monster that the negotiation was successful—the actual interaction with the monster is never represented. Occurring at the same time as Dante's interview with the usurers, it happens offstage; a parallel event of which we become aware only after the fact.

Although the Pilgrim was similarly left alone when Virgil went to speak with the demons before the battle at the Gates of Dis (as we saw in chapter 3), in that case the separation lasted only a *terzina* and the diegetic events were never removed from the Pilgrim's visual field and subjective perspective. In canto 17 instead we have a doubling of the storyline but not of the mimesis. Virgil's negotiation with Geryon escapes briefly from the omniscient narration and consequently appears contiguous to the main action of the poem—the Pilgrim's acquiring of "full experience" of the otherworld. In contrast with his normal evocation of a transcendent public authority (epitomized in the formula "vuolsi così colà . . ."), Virgil's arrangement for safe conduct with Geryon results from a private agreement, from an autonomous freedom to contract "beside" the law.

Established at the edge of the known world, this deal with the enemy reveals in dramatic fashion the perils of naked pacts. Ulpian had metaphorically portrayed the consensual element at the root of every pact and contract as a physical meeting of those "who come together from different places."[43] Yet what kind of coming together is possible in this unfamiliar territory, outside of the limits of Christian empire? When Dante compares the bright patterns on Geryon's skin—the "nodi" (knots) and "rotelle" (little wheels; *Inf.* 17.15) that the monster uses to disorient his prey—to the textiles ("drappi"; 17.17) of the Turks and Tartars, he raises through this allusion to exotic luxury goods the ethical dilemma of the "merchant in the Sultan's lands" (*Inf.* 27.90): How can there be consent without a *sensus communis*—or *fides* with the infidel?

The Pilgrim's terror during the flight on Geryon's back is a reaction to the vulnerability of such "exposed" pacts, which are depicted as a blind descent into the void. Without the intervention of collective models and institutional guarantees, the only mediation, "mezzo" (*Inf.* 17.83), remaining between an individual and the sting of fraud's tail is one's own wit, as personified by Virgil. In this nightmarish reimagination of nascent international trade, the contracting parties are unrestrained, but also unprotected.[44]

At this point we must ask: Why does Dante wait until precisely this moment of the narrative to identify his poem as a "comedìa?" And what is the specific relation between this designation and the pact made with Geryon? Recent criticism has provided an answer to at least the first part of this question by demonstrating the ways in which Geryon is a symbol of the poem itself.[45] The hybrid monster represents an allegory of Dante's literary monstrosity, with its mixture of styles and generic hybridity.[46] As his character prepares to enter the circles of fraud, the poet swears to the reality of the fantastic Geryon, thus daringly associating his work with "quella sozza imagine di froda." As an emblem of fraud, Geryon has a face of truth but hides the body of a lie, while Dante claims that his poem contains a truth that has the face of falsehood: "quel ver c'ha faccia di menzogna" (*Inf.* 16.124).

Critics have justly celebrated this passage for its self-reflexiveness and its recognition of the potential "inauthenticity inherent in all narrative."[47] The line between a truthful lie and a lying truth is indeed a thin one. Yet by treating Geryon as a static image rather than as an actor within the episode, the critical conversation has neglected to take into account the significance of the *agreement* formed between this image of hybrid poetics and his passengers. In canto 16 Dante does not simply declare his poem a "comedìa"; he negotiates its status with readers, who need to accept the terms of his representational contract: "per le note / di questa comedìa, lettor, ti guiro" (by the notes of this comedy, reader, I swear to you; *Inf.* 16.127–28). Without their faith in his word and a corresponding suspension of disbelief, the text will lack public favor and thus be inefficacious, void of vivifying grace: "di lunga grazia vòte" (129). What brings the text to life is no longer the purely externalized sanction of musical accompaniment—the poem is itself already composed of musical "notes"—but recognition of common terms, agreement, consensus.

When Dante calls his work a "comedìa," then, it is not an authoritative decree, but a bilateral contract. Comedy, in this light, is not a stable and pre-authorized category, but neither is it an artistic free-for-all. Its conditions need to be defined directly between parties at the moment of contract. Although the poet could count on a variety of loose associations to accompany the term, his comedy, as scholars have long recognized and struggled with, is unlike any other. Even Dante's own categorizations, theorized both before and after writing the poem, do not do justice to its actual poetics. Lacking a determined a priori framework, the generic nature of the work is established above all performatively. As a result, when Dante finally announces its genre as comedy, he must solemnize it with an oath.

Yet something is amiss in Dante's oath. By invoking an outside authority as its guarantee, an oath normally serves to reinforce the relationship between word and deed in a statement. This external power functions both as a witness (what the speaker swears by) and a punishing authority (fulfilling the malediction component of the oath were it to be broken). But Dante does not swear by an external, mutually recognized authority, such as the gods or the Bible. He swears instead by the notes of the *Commedia* itself. That is, he guarantees the truth of his words by calling as witnesses those same words.

For the malediction component of the oath, Dante pledges the public favor he so fervidly wants his work to achieve. Were his words to be untrue, he vows, they should be stripped of any future acclaim— "s'elle non sien di lunga grazia vòte" (so may they not fail to find long favor; 129). Yet once again, this "grazia" (literally "grace") does not depend on a transcendent divine judge, but is instead contingent on the same readers to whom he is swearing. How can the poet offer up the future interest of his public at the very moment he is attempting to capture that interest? From an economic perspective, Dante submits to a conditional penalty using capital that—paradoxically—

belongs to the buyer, not the seller, and hence he comes perilously close to making a fraudulent deal.

In contrast to similar addresses to the reader in *Paradiso*, in which Dante swears to the truth of his vision by his desire to return to heaven, this infernal oath is based solely on accrued "interest"—in both its economic and aesthetic sense. Without a recognized transcendent authority and shared higher norms, the pact between reader and author remains claustrophobically closed in upon itself. In fact, when placed within the context of the fiction of the journey, the naming of the *Commedia* in *Inferno* 16 resembles a naked pact and, even more troublingly, a potentially usurious contract.

Dante portrays his poetics at this point as adapting to historical conditions. This adjustment to circumstance is symbolically represented when his character removes the cord around his waist in order to entice Geryon to the surface. Much attention has been paid to the precise allegorical meaning of this cord.[48] If, however, we think of the cord less as an object in itself and more in terms of the consequences of its removal, the meaning within the context of the narrative is more legible.

Like *Drittura* in "Tre donne," Dante is left ungirded for the rest of the journey through Hell, having been stripped of a key symbolic item of clothing. Although at the beginning of the canto the sodomites still identify him by his costume, Dante prepares to enter lower Hell by becoming more like the sinners he will encounter, at least in external appearance. From this point on, Dante's character, now undressed, will need to deal with a savage population of devils and damned, with whom he shares no common belief system or guaranteeing external authority. This, for Dante, is the new world of comedy, a world in which custom and costume no longer have a stable place. In this realm, genre can be "freely" negotiated between author and readers, but only because the mediating institutions have failed to intervene.

Malebranche

Dante and Virgil's dramatic interaction with the Malebranche is spread over two cantos, *Inferno* 21 and 22. These cantos describe the fifth, central ditch of Malebolge, in which the barrators are punished. (Barratry was a category of political corruption akin to graft.) As a consequence of their hidden dealings, which were perpetrated under the cover of political office, the barrators are submerged in boiling pitch or tar. Demon guards identified as the Malebranche (Evil Claws) circle the pitch, ensuring with their menacing hooked claws that the damned remain underneath.

The episode begins violently in canto 21, with a glimpse of one of the Malebranche throwing a barrator from Lucca, whom he has been carrying over his shoulder like a slaughtered carcass, into the pitch. When the barrator tries to come up for air, other demons immediately rip into him. Upon observing this mayhem, Virgil tells Dante's character to hide behind a rock while he goes to speak with them. Apparently immune to their threats, Virgil commands them to summon their leader. When he appears, Virgil reminds this demon leader, Malacoda (Evil Tail), of the divine authority, "voler divino e fato destro" (divine will and favorable fate; *Inf.* 21.82) guaranteeing Dante's voyage. At this information, Malacoda feigns defeat. He lets his hooks droop to the ground and tells the others in his double-speak: "Omai non sia feruto" (Now he musn't be gored; 21.87). Although Virgil assures Dante that it is now safe for him to emerge from sitting "quatto quatto" (all asquat; *Inf.* 21.89) behind the rock, the Pilgrim remains distrustful of the devils' intentions.

Next, Malacoda slyly informs the travelers that the bridge in front of them over the sixth *bolgia* has collapsed as a result of the earthquake at Christ's death: "Ier, più oltre cinqu' ore che quest'otta, / mille dugento con sessanta sei / anni compiè che qui la via fu rotta" (Yesterday, five hours later than now, one thousand two hundred and sixty-six years were completed since the way was broken here; *Inf.* 21.112–14). He directs them to the next bridge, and offers them a demon squadron to ensure their safe conduct there. Couched in precise truthful details, what this brilliant lie fails to reveal is that *all* of the bridges over the sixth *bolgia* collapsed during the earthquake, not just this one.

Inferno 22 continues the mischievous action established by the Malebranche in the previous canto—but with Virgil and Dante as more active participants after the capture of the damned barrator

Ciampolo, who lingers too long on the shore and is hooked by a devil. Virgil and Dante attempt to interview the sinner from Navarre while the demonic leader Barbariccia keeps the other Malebranche at bay. After describing his own story and naming his neighbors in the pitch, Ciampolo promises to supply the demons with many more Tuscans and Lombards if they will play along with his stratagem: If the demons retreat out of visual range, just behind the ridge, he will lure his fellow sinners onto the shore by whistling the all-clear sign. Although they suspect Ciampolo of treachery, the demons are overcome by their bloodlust and eventually agree to the plan. Yet just as they feared, as soon as their backs are turned, Ciampolo extricates himself from Barbariccia's grasp and leaps back into the pitch. Enraged at being duped, two of the demons fruitlessly chase after Ciampolo before taking out their frustration on each other. These two end up themselves mired in the boiling tar, and Virgil and Dante take advantage of the melee to make their escape.

Dante names his poem a comedy for the second and last time before the episode's action begins: "Così di ponte in ponte, altro parlando / che la mia comedìa cantar non cura" (Thus we went from bridge to bridge, speaking of other things my comedy does not record; *Inf.* 21.1–2). As with the lead-in to the Geryon scene, Dante again asks readers to commit themselves to his representational terms. While in canto 16 he swore to the unbelievable truth of something he was depicting, here he asks us to proceed as if there existed a reality outside of the one found on the page—an "unpublished" dialogue between the two travelers. This readerly contract follows closely Virgil's mention of "l'alta mia tragedìa" (my high tragedy; *Inf.* 20.113) at the end of the previous canto, setting up a deliberate contrast between tragedy and comedy, high and low styles.[49]

Readers have long noted the connection between Dante's categorization of his work as a "comedìa" at this point and the conspicuously comic nature of these cantos, exemplified by the mock heroic simile opening *Inferno* 22, in which the demon leader's fart is compared to various other military signals.[50] In fact, the episode of the barrators draws heavily on the physical comedy of popular contemporary theater and festivals. The Malebranche, in particular, with their mixture of gallows humor and sadism, resemble the demonic figures represented in medieval mystery plays—a far cry from the other monsters Dante appropriates from classical myth.[51] These "vernacular" guardians, with their appropriately animalesque and harsh-sounding names, give the episode a farcical tone, and they administer an abject universe of dog-eat-dog subhumanity (*homo homini lupus*) which is insistently untranscendent and unheroic. As the damned attempt to sneak out of the swamp, the Malebranche swipe at them with their hooks, like cooks poking at meat in a cauldron (*Inf.* 21.55–57). The resulting cat-and-mouse games account for much of the slapstick humor of the episode, which culminates with the two struggling demons landing together in the pitch.

Recent criticism has focused on the differing manners in which Virgil's character and Dante's character engage with the Malebranche—their respective effectiveness at navigating the devils' duplicitous "baratta" (deal; *Inf.* 21.63).[52] For his part, Virgil hopes to enlist the demonic police force as chaperones through the circle, and so he maintains a lofty and formal style when he addresses them. He requests to speak with their leader, invokes divine will and the Pilgrim's fated voyage in his plea, and believes Malacoda when he promises to provide them safe conduct to the next bridge. In the end, however, he is chastened for his trust. He learns, from one of the hypocrites no less, that no such bridge exists and that—astonishingly—the Devil is a liar: "Io udi' già dire a Bologna / del diavol vizi assai, tra ' quali udi' / ch'elli è bugiardo e padre di menzogna" (In Bologna I once heard many vices of the devil told, among which I heard that he is a liar and the father of lies; *Inf.* 23.142–44). Confronted with the true nature of evil, higher learning and reason prove less effective than proverbial truths.

Dante's character is far more suspicious from the start. Although Virgil tells him he can emerge safely, "sicuramente" (*Inf.* 21.90), from his hiding place, he notices the demons lunging at him and fears that they will not honor their "pact": "e i diavoli si fecer tutti avanti, / sì ch'io temetti ch'ei tenesser patto" (and the devils all started forward so that I was afraid they would not keep the pact; *Inf.* 21.92–93). His precarious situation reminds him of a scene he had observed firsthand as a Guelph soldier at the battle of Caprona (1289), when he saw the defeated Ghibellines timorously exiting their captured stronghold under a treaty of surrender or "patteggiati" (*Inf.* 21.95). Even after he returns to Virgil's side, Dante's character remains focused on the fierce visages of the demons, whose pornographic intentions to hook Dante on the rump, "in sul groppone" (*Inf.* 21.101), are only barely suppressed by their squadron leader. Understandably wary of such bestial company, the Pilgrim begs Virgil to decline Malacoda's offer of safe-conduct, and to let them instead try to reach the next circle by themselves; he is unable to trust, as Virgil does, that the demons' menacing gestures—their fierce expressions and grinding teeth—are reserved for the sinners alone. In each of these cases, instead of simply accepting Malacoda's words, the pilgrim "reads" the demons' body language as well. He ends up, of course, being the better judge of character.

Following the lead of Robert Hollander,[53] many scholars view Virgil's humiliation at the hands of the devils as a commentary on the anachronistic poetics he symbolizes. According to this interpretation of the episode, Dante is taking a swipe at his guide for his overconfidence, his naiveté, and, most of all, his incapacity to free himself from the high style—notwithstanding its gross inappropriateness given the surrounding circumstances. Unable to extricate himself from aristocratic convention, Virgil becomes a victim of farce, in which every attempt to maintain a superior ethical code is made to look ridiculous. Dante's character, on the other hand, is quick to adapt, embodying the proverb "in church with the saints, and in the tavern with the gluttons" (*Inf.* 22.14–15). He displays a realistic appraisal of the situation and an understanding of evil that his predecessor fails to grasp. In this way, comic realism is shown to trump tragic idealism.

Yet is the main source of Virgil's error really overconfidence or hubris, as Hollander suggests?[54] More importantly, is Dante the poet really leveraging Virgil's errors of judgment to undermine the ethos of epic poetry? Several elements of the episode indicate that he is not. These elements are at odds with its supposed anti-Virgilian subtext.

First and most noticeably, there is Virgil's selfless courage. With the devils still in hot pursuit at the beginning of canto 23, Virgil grabs the Pilgrim and slides down the embankment into the next ditch, clasping him to his chest "come suo figlio, non come compagno" (like his son, not like his companion; *Inf.* 23.51). Virgil's spontaneous and immediate care for his charge is compared to a mother's protective instinct (38–42); in this instance, Virgil's absolute fusion with an epic ideal is shown in a clearly positive light. His heroism manifests not as some narcissistic artifice, but as an utterly ingrained second nature. Similarly, the old poet's comprehensible and momentary "crankiness" at discovering he has been tricked by Malacoda reveals his humanity, not his ridiculousness. If it were the latter, such a spectacle would be hard to reconcile with the Pilgrim's reverence in following "dietro a le poste de le care piante" (behind the prints of his dear feet; *Inf.* 23.148) at the end of the episode—a filial gesture worthy of pious Aeneas.

By neglecting or ironizing these passages,[55] critics have reduced the complex psychological depictions of Pilgrim and guide in these cantos to a simple contrast between stuffy elitism and pragmatic street smarts. More critically, by reading the diverse interactions of these characters with the Malabranche as just another opportunity for Dante the poet to tout the superiority of his Christian comedy vis-à-vis pagan tragedy,[56] they have missed the force of the vernacular poet's critique of *contemporary* culture. After all, the root of Virgil's miscalculation is his failure to recognize that the world around him has dramatically changed. Embodying an ethos in which military values were upheld even among enemies, Virgil still believes in the laws of war. According to the conventions of epic, the "pact" established between wanderers and guardians, although bare, would command respect, since it remained protected by an aristocratic code of conduct. If anything, rather than exposing his arrogance, Virgil's mistake brings him closer to readers by revealing his vulnerability. It is meant to elicit our sympathy, not our ridicule, for this representative of a bygone and less debased era.

Dante's character certainly understands the new rules of engagement much better than his guide, and is savvier when it comes to dealing with these low-life figures. He is also well aware that higher principles can no longer be taken for granted in the enforcement of pacts (which is what makes his evocation of the captured Ghibelline troops at Caprona, and the frailty of their truce, so chilling). No doubt Dante portrays himself here as the poet better equipped to represent this erosion of distinctions and long-standing convention, the one ready to morally and stylistically "squat down." But at what cost? In representing the greater scope of his masterpiece, the poet clearly views his artistic modernity as being tinged with loss. After all, the comedic style he lays claim to in these cantos is much darker than is generally recognized—encompassing the detached, sneering irony of the devils and the doomed cynicism of the damned. It conveys a horror that cannot be represented within the bounds of tragedy, as evident, for instance, in the pleasure that the dramatic torture of Ciampolo conveys. Everyone involved in this chaotic scene—sinners, guards, even the Pilgrim himself—is eventually reduced to the same subhuman level. Dante's poetics, in this sense, are not simply beyond genre; they are also beneath it.

The historical Dante was himself sentenced to exile for the crime of barratry. Scholars have long found an autobiographical resonance in the encounter with the barrators, not entirely without cause.[57] In broad terms, the bullying administrators of this ditch of Malebolge, the black demons, can indeed be seen as dramatically reproducing the persecution of Florentine citizens by the Black Guelphs once they took power in a coup d'état in 1301. And in both cases Dante makes a narrow escape. But attempts to find a one-to-one relationship between Dante's life and art in these cantos—identifying, for example, the Malabranche with specific members of the Black party—are inevitably less successful. It is only when we turn to the episode's global message about justice that its autobiographical backdrop emerges as necessary and compelling.

In "Tre donne," Dante reflects at length about "laws without teeth," and about what happens when the judicial system lacks an enforcing political authority. In the circle of the grafters, he presents laws with plenty of teeth—but no conscience. This pouch of Malebolge might seem particularly lawless at first, but the rule-bound nature of its "ludo" (game; *Inf.* 22.118) is actually quite apparent. Ciampolo and the other damned understand perfectly well the laws governing their allotted place in Hell, and for the most part these laws are vigilantly, even zealously, enforced by the devils. That sinners attempt to circumvent these laws whenever they find themselves beyond detection does not, therefore, result from a lack of law and order. Rather, the relationship between the demonic police and the condemned barrators illustrates the shortcomings of a legal order based solely on legislation and enforcement. The devils' claws are not sufficient to generate obedience among the damned, just as Virgil's threat of divine punishment does not trigger compliance among the Malabranche. In this corrupt polity, the laws are neither followed nor enforced out of an underlying sense of their righteousness or reason. Instead, on the one side, fear produces a charade of obedience, while on the other, administrative office provides a legitimate veneer for sadism and a relish of violence.

The broken pacts in these cantos represent the limits of the law, or what happens when positive laws, such as the municipal statutes, are divorced from higher norms. After all, from a purely technical standpoint, Malacoda's promise to Virgil and Dante—that they will be safe *until*, "infin" (*Inf.* 21.125), the next bridge—is perfectly legal. Yet legality and justice are obviously wrenched apart here, as Dante no doubt felt had been the case with his technically legal conviction. On the surface, the public authority and its institutions continue to function properly, but they have become detached from the original principles they were created to uphold. Dante defines barratry as what happens when public officials turn "no" into "yes" for money: "Del *no*, per li denar, vi si fa *ita*" (*Inf.* 21.42). When even its most elemental capacity to constrain—to say "no"—is undermined, the law becomes just another way of sanctioning power.

Dante elects to call attention to the title of his work within a nightmare of deregulation, implicitly associating his comic poetics with naked pacts. In this way he clearly indicates that his artistic vision is more equipped to deal with the fallen state of civilization than Virgil's epic tragedy would be. At the same time, he balks at the free fall that resorting to a contractual model based on consensus alone would entail. The conventional genres may no longer respond to contemporary exigencies, but the shape of promises, vows, and literary texts cannot be left simply to individual choice. Cognizant that there is no going back to Virgil's world, Dante nonetheless attempts to stave off a descent into a state of nature by expanding and adapting the traditional schemata as much as possible. In a heroic, if doomed, act of cultural conservation, he insists on the value of a name.

Conclusion
"Se mai continga . . ."

I began this book by asking why Dante rejected an amnesty that would have allowed him to reenter Florence. I want to conclude it by examining the conditions under which Dante would *not* have rejected an amnesty: the ideal reconciliation the poet himself came to envision in *Paradiso* 25. These differing views on civic reintegration will serve as a final clarification on the distinction I have been drawing between a "state" and a "system" of exception in Dante's work.

In the sphere of the fixed stars, at the threshold between material and spiritual realities, Dante's character must undergo one last test before entering the Empyrean. He is interrogated about the three theological virtues of faith, hope, and charity by their respective representatives: Peter, James, and John the Evangelist (*Par.* 24–26). At the conclusion of *Paradiso* 24, Peter celebrates Dante's successful passing of his examination on Faith, which the Pilgrim defines in Pauline terms as "the substance of things hoped for and proof of those unseen" (*Par.* 24.64–65), by encircling him three times in a crown of light. At the beginning of canto 25, directly after the coronation but before James questions the pilgrim on Hope, the poet interrupts the catechism with one of his most personal and affecting autobiographical asides:

Se mai continga che 'l poema sacro
al quale ha posto mano e cielo e terra
sì che m'ha fatto per più anni macro,
vinca la crudeltà che fuor mi serra
del bello ovile ov'io dormi' agnello,
nimico ai lupi che li danno guerra,
con altra voce omai, con altro vello
ritornerò poeta, e in sul fonte
del mio battesmo prenderò 'l cappello:
però che ne la fede, che fa conte
l'anime a Dio, quivi intra' io, e poi
Pietro per lei sì mi girò la fronte.

(Should it ever come to pass that the sacred poem, to which both heaven and earth have set their hand so that for many years it has made me lean, should overcome the cruelty that locks me out of the fair sheepfold where I slept as a lamb, an enemy of the wolves that make war on it, I shall return as a poet, with another voice by then, with another fleece, and at the font of my baptism I shall accept the wreath: for there I entered the faith that makes souls known to God, and later Peter so circled my brow because of it; *Par.* 1–12).

Here, as his character triumphantly prepares to surpass the confines of time and space, Dante the poet allows himself one last glance at the tragic circumstances of his life on earth.[1] Between nostalgia for an innocent past and longing for an unlikely and ever-diminishing future, the poet imagines returning home—now gray-haired ("with another fleece") and with an aged voice—to be honored as both citizen and poet at the baptismal font of San Giovanni. Despite his viciously attacking Florence and Florentines throughout the *Commedia*, it seems that Dante still holds out hope for a final reconciliation.

Critics have rightly celebrated this bittersweet fantasy of homecoming for the insight it offers into the poet's mindset near the end of his life. Yet this autobiographical reference also serves a structural and heuristic role within the poem, by connecting the return of the Pilgrim to his celestial home with the return of the poet to his native city. Just as the pilgrim is welcomed back from his Egyptian exile by the citizens of this New Jerusalem (*Par.* 25.55–56), so Dante imagines being re-embraced by the Florentine community.

Of course, the benefits of citizenship in this "Rome of which Christ is a Roman" (*Purg.* 32.102) are more reliably awarded than those of contemporaneous Florence. Dante presents his spiritual homecoming as more or less theologically assured once he passes his last examination. In contrast with this meritocracy, the optative subjunctives *continga* and *vinca* suggest that Dante's reentry into Florence depends on circumstances outside of his control—namely, the softening of the Florentines' hardened hearts.

Given this disparity between theological certainty and political contingency, it is tempting to dismiss the dream of personal homecoming as a false shadow of universal Christian homecoming—a shadow Dante prepares to leave behind. In this sense it acts as one more instance of the Augustinian contrast between the fallen earthly city and New Jerusalem. Yet Dante's dramatic juxtaposition of these homecomings resists such a clear-cut distinction. After all, the poet's earthly coronation is modeled on Peter's heavenly coronation—not the other way around. The regime of reconciliation the Pilgrim encounters in these cantos establishes the theological basis for its secular echo. Dante exploits the spiritual trope of reintegration to construct its civic *figura*.

In establishing this metaphysics of amnesty, Dante continuously returns to the exceptionality of his journey, reemphasizing the special dispensation he has received to travel to the world beyond. For instance, when Beatrice addresses the host of the Church Triumphant, he has her request their support for his journey by reminding them that "per grazia di Dio questi preliba / di quel che cade de la vostra mensa / prima che morte tempo li prescriba" (by God's Grace this man has a foretaste of what falls from your table before death sets a limit to his time; *Par.* 24.4–6). In this episode, the poet underscores that such a privilege is grounded in an objective higher cause. Indeed, James opens his interrogation of the Pilgrim by commenting on the exceptionality of the heavenly voyage, which he acknowledges has been undertaken for the greater good:

Poi per grazia vuol che tu t'affronti
lo nostro Imperadore, anzi la morte,
ne l'aula più secreta co' suoi conti,
sì che, veduto il ver di questa corte,
la spene, che là giù bene innamora,
in te e in altrui di ciò conforte.

(Since our Emperor in his grace wills that before your death you confront his counts in the innermost hall, so that, having seen the truth of this court, you may strengthen the hope of it in yourself and others, that hope which makes those down there love well; *Par.* 25.40–45).

This is the definitive answer to the questions Dante's character posed in *Inferno* 2: "Ma io perché venirvi? O chi 'l concede?" (But I, why come there? Or who grants it?; 31). The divine emperor grants the exceptional journey for an explicit purpose: just as Paul was raised to heaven to "strengthen" ("recarne conforto"; *Inf.* 2.29) the faith, Dante is provided a vision that will "strengthen" ("conforte") hope. '

Dante further suggests, for the first and only time in the poem, that he has earned his special grace through personal merit. As Beatrice explains, on account of the Pilgrim's unrivaled hope, he has been granted entry into Jerusalem out of Egypt "anzi che 'l militar li sia prescritto" (before his militancy is concluded; *Par.* 25.57). The suspension of the Pilgrim's exile is thus both justified and deserved. It is an exception to what has been decreed, "prescritto," but it is an exception that does not violate higher norms.

Dante thus ties the rescission of his sentence of exile from the New Jerusalem to the revocation of his sentence of exile from Florence—deliberately invoking the "system of exception" in divine justice as a model for its earthly counterpart. Specifically, he suggests that since he has been singularly invited to walk the inner halls of the celestial emperor's court, the fruit of this fated journey, the "poema sacro" testifying to his vision, should procure him re admittance to his birthplace. After long years sacrificed for the collective good,[2] the poet has earned his repatriation (as Jason earned his triumphant return after heroically attaining the Golden Fleece). In other words, Dante harnesses the dispensation his character enjoys in a fictive poetic universe to argue for a political-juridical exemption in the real world. To this end he implicitly asks his readers to use their discretion—a discretion that has been cultivated and vicariously exercised throughout the poem—in measuring the general rule against his individualized case. They should show mercy for his circumstances ("vinca la crudeltà che fuor mi serra") not only out of pity, but also out of an underlying sense of fairness.

This is not the first time Dante has conceived of his poetry as a medium for diplomacy. We have already seen how in the *congedo* of "Tre donne" Dante takes leave of his poem by asking her to "hunt" with the Black Guelphs remaining in Florence, who have forced him to flee but who can still bestow the gift of peace: "di pace dono" (104). He concludes the *canzone* with an explicit request for pardon: "camera di perdon savio uom non serra / ché perdonare è bel vincer di guerra" (A wise man will not lock the chamber of forgiveness; for to pardon is a fine victory in war; 106–7). Reusing the rhyme words *guerra* and *serra* and similarly requesting—albeit less directly and now much less plausibly—to be allowed to return home, Dante recalls this *congedo* in the proem of *Paradiso* 25.[3] In both the lyric poem and the epic narrative, the text itself is imagined as politically efficacious, rhetorically moving readers toward clemency.

Yet by the time Dante wrote these final cantos of the *Paradiso*, he had dramatically altered his terms for reconciliation: he now firmly rejects a pardon that would require any admission of guilt. In "Tre donne" the author still alludes to an undefined "colpa" (blame; 88) for which he has repented. In the *Commedia*, on the other hand, Dante carefully separates the penitential motif of the poem from the politics of his reconciliation. This penitential narrative culminates in his character's public confession to Beatrice in Eden. The subsequent absolution and rebaptism of the Pilgrim in the river of Lethe would seem the natural locus for the poet to seek his civic absolution and recall his original baptism. Instead, Dante waits until the examination on the outer edges of the universe to deliberately connect his spiritual homecoming with the desired earthly one.

If Dante had accepted a governmental pardon, his participation in its penitential regime would have implicitly negated the "system of exception" he developed so painstakingly in the *Commedia*. As we have seen in the epistle "To a Florentine Friend," Dante rejected the proposed amnesty because it would have forced him to act as a suppliant and perform an oblation: to be paraded along with other infamous citizens into the Baptistery of San Giovanni—carrying a penitential candle, clothed in sackcloth, and crowned with a mitre. Refusing to sanction the gestures of this top-down, unilateral conception of absolution, the Pilgrim dramatically concludes the letter by asserting his indifference to offers of mere "humanitarian" sustenance: "Quippe nec panis deficiet!" (Certainly bread will not fail me).[4]

In lieu of undergoing such a legally debilitating disgrace, in *Paradiso* the poet imagines his return to Florence with full citizenship and honors, crowned at the Baptistery not with a dunce cap but with a laurel wreath.[5] Rather than paying a fine to those enemies whom he still resented, he would ransom his return by offering his fellow citizens his consecrated poem—a horizontal agreement grounded in principles of fairness. Dante's personal return is thus contingent on the restoration of a system of equity that simultaneously underwrites and exceeds specific legislation. Within this flexible jurisprudential regime, that return functions as a justified exception— acquired by a privilege "above the law," supported by a poetic fame "below the law," enabled by a discretional act of mercy "beyond the law," and recognized within that legitimate space "beside the law" of the peace settlement.

If the reconciliation offered by the Florentine amnesty depended on municipal statutes that were directly enforceable but not necessarily just (in Dante's view), the reconciliation the poet imagines in *Paradiso* relies on transregional norms that were just but not necessarily enforceable (especially in light of the vacant seat of empire). It is the role of the poem itself to span this gap between validity and enforcement, between the possibility of *continga* and *vinca* and the certainty of *ritonerò* and *prenderò*. For this reason, Dante situates his fantasy of homecoming within the proem to a canto dedicated to theological hope.

Throughout the poem, the poet expresses an unrelentingly pessimistic vision of contemporary society, a pessimism still amply on display in Peter's vehement denouncement of the Church's hierarchy in *Paradiso* 27. Given this sustained critique, Beatrice's bold claim that the Pilgrim's hope exceeds that of any other living Christian— "La Chiesa Militante alcun figliuolo / non ha con più speranza" (The Church Militant has no son with more hope; *Par.* 25.52–53)—is unexpected, even contradictory. In another apparent irony, just as the poet's ultimate mission is unveiled—to comfort the people with hope as Paul had comforted them with faith—the means to fulfill that mission are temporarily withheld. James reveals that Dante has been allowed to *see* the truth of the heavenly court so that, "veduto il ver," he may foster hope by attesting to its reality. Yet when the pilgrim strives to discern whether John the Evangelist already possesses his resurrected body, he is scolded by the apostle:

> Perché t'abbagli
> per veder cosa che qui non ha loco?
> In terra è terra il mio corpo, e saragli
> tanto con li altri che 'l numero nostro
> con l'etterno proposito s'agguagli.

(Why do you dazzle yourself to see what has no place here? On earth my body is earth, and it will remain there with the others until our number equals the eternal purpose; *Par.* 25.122–26).

Finally, after staring too intently at Beatrice, Dante's character finds himself at the close of the canto in total blindness.

At the very moment Dante is rebaptized the poet of hope, he is denied visual evidence of the "double raiment" (*Par.* 25.92). This situation perfectly encapsulates, however, the paradoxical and elusive purpose of the author's overarching poetic mission—to imaginatively sustain the faithful during the messianic in-between time of the interregnum. In the absence of a discernible imperial authority, allegiance to a nonterritorialized law is all the more dependent on the power of a collective imaginary. This, ultimately, is the challenge for Dante as he conjoins heavenly and earthly justice—to convince readers to remain committed to the law while awaiting the resurrection of the sovereign's body.

Notes

Introduction

1. Text and translations from the *Commedia* based on *The Divine Comedy of Dante Alighieri*, trans. Robert M. Durling, 3 vols. (New York and Oxford: Oxford University Press, 1996–2011). Citations and translations from the *Digest* based on *The Digest of Justinian*, ed. Theodor Mommsen and Paul Krueger, trans. Alan Watson (Philadelphia: University of Pennsylvania Press, 1985). All other translations, unless otherwise noted, are my own.

2. There is no comprehensive study of Dante and the law. For Dante and justice, however, see among the most important contributions Anthony K. Cassell, *Dante's Fearful Art of Justice* (Toronto and Buffalo: University of Toronto Press, 1984); Allan H. Gilbert, *Dante's Conception of Justice* (Durham, NC: Duke University Press, 1925); and Giuseppe Mazzotta, "Metaphor and Justice," in *Dante's Vision and the Circle of Knowledge* (Princeton, NJ: Princeton University Press, 1993), 75–95. For Dante's intervention in the legal battles between Church and Empire, see Charles Till Davis, *Dante and the Idea of Rome* (Oxford: Clarendon Press, 1957); Michele Maccarrone, "Teologia e diritto canonico nella *Monarchia* III, 3," *Rivista di storia della chiesa* 5 (1951): 7–42; and Bruno Nardi's introduction in Dante Alighieri, *Opere minori* (Milan and Naples: Ricciardi, 1979), 3:241–69. The tide, however, may be turning regarding studies of Dante and the law. See, for example, the following recent contributions: Claudia Di Fonzo, "Dante tra diritto, letteratura e politica," *Forum Italicum* 41:1 (spring 2007), 5–22; Sabrina Ferrara, "Tra pena giuridica e diritto morale: L'esilio di Dante nelle *Epistole*," *L'Alighieri* 40 (2012), 45–65; Steven Grossvogel,

"Justinian's *Jus* and *Justificatio* in *Paradiso* 6.10–27," *Modern Language Notes* 127.1 (supplement, 2012 Jan), 130–37; and Loren Michael Valterza, "Infernal Retainers: Dante and the Juridical Tradition," PhD dissertation, Rutgers University (2011).

3. On the pluralism of the medieval legal order, see Paolo Grossi, *L'ordine giuridico medievale* (Rome and Bari: Laterza, 1991).

4. On the state of exception see Giorgio Agamben, *Homo Sacer: Sovereign Power and Bare Life*, trans. Daniel Heller-Roazen (Stanford, CA: Stanford University Press, 1998), 11–29; Giorgio Agamben, *State of Exception*, trans. Kevin Attell (Chicago: University of Chicago Press, 2005); and Carl Schmitt, *Political Theology: Four Chapters on the Concept of Sovereignty*, ed. and trans. George Schwab (Chicago: University of Chicago Press, 1985).

5. For medieval law as a *system* of exception, see the essays collected in Massimo Vallerani, ed., "Sistemi di eccezioni," a volume of *Quaderni storici* 131 (2009), especially Massimo Meccarelli, "Paradigma dell'eccezione nella parabola della modernità penale: Una prospettiva storico-giuridica," 493–521; Sara Menzinger, "Pareri eccezionali: Procedure decisionali ordinarie e straordinarie nella politica comunale del XIII secolo," 399–410; Giuliano Milani, "Legge ed eccezione nei comuni di Popolo del XIII secolo (Bologna, Perugia, Pisa)," 377–98; and Massimo Vallerani, "Premessa," 299–312. See also Massimo Vallerani, "Paradigmi dell'eccezione nel tardo medioevo," *Storia del pensiero politico* 2 (2012), 3–30. In partial contradiction to his portrayal of the medieval ban in *Homo Sacer*, in *State of Exception* Agamben declares that "the idea that a suspension of law may be necessary for the common good is foreign to the medieval world," 26.

6. Dante's own conviction was, after all, perfectly legal from a procedural standpoint.

7. Ernst Hartwig Kantorowicz, *The King's Two Bodies: A Study in Medieval Political Theology* (Princeton, NJ: Princeton University Press, 1997).

8. See, most recently, Stephen Greenblatt, *Shakespeare's Freedom* (Chicago: University of Chicago Press, 2010); Lorna Hutson, *The Invention of Suspicion. Law and Mimesis in Shakespeare and Renaissance Drama* (Oxford: Oxford University Press, 2007); Lorna Hutson, "Imagining Justice: Kantorowicz and Shakespeare," *Representations* 106 (Spring 2009), 118–42; Victoria Kahn, "Political Theology and Fiction in *The King's Two Bodies*," *Representations* 106 (Spring 2009), 77–101; Julia Reinhard Lupton, *Citizen-Saints: Shakespeare and Political Theology* (Chicago: University of Chicago Press, 2005); and Eric L. Santner, *The Royal Remains: The People's Two Bodies and the Endgames of Sovereignty* (Chicago: University of Chicago Press, 2011).

9. See especially Kantorowicz, *The King's Two Bodies*, 493.

10. See the review of critical views in Bernhard Jussen, "*The King's Two Bodies* Today," *Representations* 106 (2009), 102–17.

11. For the latter, see especially Kahn, "Political Theology and Fiction," and Jennifer Rust, "Political Theologies of the Corpus Mysticum: Schmitt, Kantorowicz, and de Lubac," in Graham Hammill and Julia Reinhard Lupton, eds., *Political Theology and Early Modernity* (Chicago: University of Chicago Press, 2012), 102–23.

12. Ernst Hartwig Kantorowicz, "The Sovereignty of the Artist: A Note on Legal Maxims and Renaissance Theories of Art," in *Selected Studies* (Locust Valley, NY: J. J. Augustin, 1965), 352–65.

13. See especially Schmitt, *Political Theology*, 36–37: "The idea of the modern constitutional state triumphed together with deism, a theology and metaphysics

that banished the miracle from the world. This theology and metaphysics rejected not only the transgression of the laws of nature through an exception brought about by direct intervention, as is found in the idea of a miracle, but also the sovereign's direct intervention in a valid legal order. The rationalism of the Enlightenment rejected the exception in every form."

14. For a modern example of the politicization of the miracle, see Bonnie Honig, *Emergency Politics: Paradox, Law, Democracy* (Princeton, NJ: Princeton University Press, 2009), 87–111.

Chapter 1

1. On the events leading to Dante's exile and the legal documents pertaining to it, see Bernardino Barbadoro, "La condanna di Dante e le fazioni politiche del suo tempo," *Studi danteschi* 2 (1920), 5–74; Bernardino Barbadoro, "La condanna di Dante e la difesa di Firenze guelfa," *Studi danteschi* 8 (1924), 111–27; Giuliano Milani, *L'esclusione dal commune: Conflitti e bandi politici a Bologna e in altre città italiane tra XII e XIV secolo* (Rome: Istituto Storico Italiano per il Medio Evo, 2003), 416–23; Giuliano Milani, "Appunti per una riconsiderazione del bando di Dante," in *Bollettino di Italianistica* 8/2 (2011), 42–70; and Randolph Starn, *Contrary Commonwealth: The Theme of Exile in Medieval and Renaissance Italy* (Berkeley: University of California Press, 1982), 60–85.

2. On the "notam oblationis," see Oddone Zenatti, *Dante e Firenze: Prose antiche con note illustrative ed appendici* (Florence: Sansoni, 1902; reprint, 1984), 509. Text of the letter in Dante Alighieri, *Opere minori,* ed. Domenico De Robertis et al. (Milan and Naples: Ricciardi, 1979), 2:594–97 (596). Translation based on Dante Alighieri, *Epistolae; The Letters of Dante,* trans. Paget Toynbee (Oxford: Clarendon Press, 1966).

3. "Absit a viro predicante iustitiam ut perpessus iniuras, iniuriam inferentibus, velut benemerentibus, pecuniam suam solvat" (Far be it from a man preaching justice, who has suffered injuries, to pay his money to the offending parties, as if they deserved a reward; 2:596).

4. Medieval glosses were based on Callistratus's definition of "existimatio" in *Digest* 50.13.5.1: "Existimatio est dignitatis inlaesae status, legibus ac moribus comprobatus, qui ex delicto nostro auctoritate legum aut minuitur aut consumitur." (Status is a position of unimpaired standing, which is approved by laws and customs and under the authority of the laws may be diminished or extinguished by our misdeeds). On the glossators' definition of *infamia* as a privation of *fama* and its relation to *existimatio,* see Livingston, "Infamy and the Decretists," 3–6, and Migliorino, *Fama e infamia,* 73–78. On *fama* as a synonym for "existimatio," see also Zvi Yavetz, "Existimatio, Fama and the Ides of March," *Harvard Studies in Classical Philology* 78 (1974), 35–65.

5. For the causes and effects of legal infamy in the Middle Ages, see the following works: G. Dalla Torre, Jr., "Infamia (dir. canonico)," in *Enciclopedia del diritto,* vol. 21, 387–91; Thomas Kuehn, "*Fama* as a Legal Status in Renaissance Florence," in *Fama: The Politics of Talk and Reputation in Medieval Europe,* ed. Thelma Fenster and Daniel Lord Smail (Ithaca, NY: Cornell University Press, 2003), 27–46; Peter Landau, *Die Entstehung des Kanonischen Infamienbegriffs von Gratian bis zur Glossa ordinaria,* Cologne and Graz: Böhlav Verlag, 1966; John Livingston, "Infamia in the Decretists from Rufinus to Johannes Teutonicus," PhD dissertation, University of Wisconsin, 1962; Aldo Mazzacane, "Infamia (storia)," in *Enciclopedia del diritto,* vol. 21, 383–87; Francesco Migliorino, *Fama e infamia: Problemi della so-*

cietà medievale nel pensiero giuridico nei secoli XII e XIII (Catania: Editrice Giannotta, 1985); Edward Peters, "Wounded Names: The Medieval Doctrine of Infamy," *Law and Mediaeval Life and Thought*, ed. Edward B. King and Susan J. Ridyard (Sewanee, TN: Press of the University of the South, 1990), 43–89; Chris Wickham, "Fama and the Law in Twelfth-Century Tuscany," in *The Politics of Talk and Reputation in Medieval Europe*, 15–26. The synthesis of legal infamy presented in this chapter is especially indebted to Migliorino's treatment of the various doctrinal questions.

6. See the discussions of Roman legal infamy in A. H. J. Greenidge, *Infamia: Its Place in Roman Public and Private Law* (Oxford: Clarendon Press, 1894); Peter Garnsey, *Social Status and Legal Privilege in the Roman Empire* (Oxford: Oxford University Press, 1970), 185–204; Max Kaser, "Infamia und Ignominia in den römischen Rechtsquellen," in *Zeitschrift der Savigny-Stiftung für Rechtsgeschichte. Romanistische Abteilung* 27 (1956), 220–78; J. M. Kelly, *Studies in the Civil Judicature of the Roman Republic* (Oxford: Oxford University Press, 1970), 185–204; and Alberto Maffi, "La costruzione giuridica dell'infamia nell'ordinamento romano," in Paolo Prodi, ed., *La fiducia secondo i linguaggi del potere* (Bologna: Il Mulino, 2008), 41–51 (42–43).

7. See the list of punishments in *Digest* 50.13.5.

8. See the discussion of the three types of legal infamy in Livingston, "*Infamia* in the Decretists," 8–12 and Migliorino, *Fama e infamia*, 85–138.

9. The idea that a stain or, more specifically, a scar remained even after a sentence had been completed was commonplace in legal writings about infamy, especially among canon lawyers. Dante's familiarity with this figure is evident in his Letter to the Cardinals, in which he claims that even if the cardinals were to repent for their avarice, they would still be marked with the scar of infamy ("nota cicatrix infamis"). For the scar of infamy in canon law doctrine, see the passages cited in Stephen Kuttner, *Kanonistische Schuldlehre von Gratian bis auf die Dekretalen Gregors IX* (Vatican City: Biblioteca Apostolica Vaticana, 1935), 18, notes 4 and 5.

10. "Quod homines alicuius civitatis. . . . communiter opinantur et existimant, sive sentiunt . . ." Thomas de Piperata, *De fama*, in *Tractatus universi iuris*, vol. 11 (Venice, 1584), fol. 8a, n. 1. Thomas clearly distinguishes at the beginning of his treatise between *fama* as reputation, which he will not discuss ("de illa fama . . . curandum non est"), and his main topic, *fama* as circumstantial evidence.

11. On the emergence of *fama* as a form of proof in the ecclesiastical justice system, see Julien Théry, "Fama: L'opinion publique comme preuve judiciare. Aperçu sur la révolution médiévale de l'inquisitoire (XIIe-XIVe siècles)," in *La preuve en justice, de l'antiquité à nos jours*, ed. Bruno Lemesle (Rennes: Presses Universitaires de Rennes. 2002), 119–47.

12. For Innocent's contribution to the concept of infamy, see Massimo Vallerani, *La giustizia pubblica medievale* (Bologna: Il Mulino, 2005), 34–36, and, by the same author, "Modelli di verità: Le prove nei processi inquisitori," in *L'enquête au Moyen Âge*, ed. Claude Gauvard (Rome: Ecole française de Rome, 2008), 123–42.

13. For the phenomenon of canonical purgation, see Antonia Fiore, *Il giuramento di innocenza nel processo canonico medievale: Storia e disciplina nella "purgatio canonica"* (Frankfurt: Klostermann, 2013).

14. "Respondemus, nullum esse pro crimine, super quo aliqua non laborat infamia . . . cum inquisitio fieri debeat solummodo super illis, de quibus clamores aliqui praecesserunt" (We respond that it is not considered a crime when there is no pressing infamy . . . since an inquest should proceed only against those

about whom an outcry has already arisen). X 5. 1. 21, in "Decretales Gregorii IX" (Leipzig, 1879; reprint, Graz: Akademische Druck- u.Verlagsanstalt, 1955), 2: 742. On the concept that the Church does not judge hidden crimes, which are left to God's judgment and the internal forum of conscience, the classic study remains Stephan Kuttner's "Ecclesia de occultis non iudicat: Problemata ex doctrina poenali decretistarum et decretalistarum a Gratiano usque ad Gregorium PP. IX," in *Acta congressus iuridici internationalis, Romae 1934* (Rome: Pontificum Institutum Utriusque, 1936), vol. 3, 225–46. But see now also Jacques Chiffoleau, "'Ecclesia de occultis non judicat?' L'Église, le secret et l'occulte du XIIe au XVe siècle," *Micrologus: Nature, Sciences and Medieval Societies*, 13 (2005), 359–481; Henry Ansgar Kelly, "Inquisitorial Due Process and the Status of Secret Crimes," in *Proceedings of the Eighth International Congress of Medieval Canon Law* (UCSD 1988), ed. Stanley Chodorow (Vatican City: Biblioteca Apostolica Vaticana, 1992), 407–28; and Lotte Kéry, "Non enim homines de occultis, sed de manifestis iudicant: La culpabilité dans le droit pénal de l'Église à l'époque classique," *Revue du droit canonique* 53/2 (2003), 311–36.

15. For the development and transformation of canonical infamy in urban contexts, see Richard M. Fraher, "Conviction According to Conscience: The Medieval Jurists' Debate Concerning Judicial Discretion and the Law of Proof," *Law and History Review* 7 (1989), 23–88; Vallerani, *La giustizia medievale*, 39–57; and Vallerani, "Modelli di verità," 131–34.

16. *Interest re: publice ne maleficia remeneant impunita*. For the origins of this maxim, see Richard M. Fraher, "The Theoretical Justification for the New Criminal Law of the High Middle Ages:'Rei publicae interest, ne crimina remaneant impunita,'" *University of Illinois Law Review* (1984), 577–95. For the increased public prosecution of crimes, see also Susanne Lepsius, "Public Responsibility for Failure to Prosecute Crime? An Inquiry into an Umbrian Case by Bartolo da Sassoferrato," in *A Renaissance of Conflicts: Visions and Revisions of Law and Society in Italy and Spain*, ed. John A. Marino and Thomas Kuehn (Toronto: Center for Reformation and Renaissance Studies, 2004), 131–70, and Mario Sbriccoli, "'Vidi communiter observari': L'emersione di un ordine penale pubblico nelle città italiane del secolo XIII," *Quaderni fiorentini: Per la storia del pensiero giuridico moderno* 27 (1998), 231–68.

17. See Mario Sbriccoli, "Giustizia negoziata, giustizia egemonica: Riflessione su una nuova fase degli studi di storia della giustizia criminale," in *Criminalità e giustizia in Germania e in Italia. Pratiche giudiziarie e linguaggi giuridici tra tardo medioevo ed età moderna*, ed. Marco Bellabarba, Gerd Schwerhoff, and Andrea Zorzi (Bologna: Il Mulino/Istituto storico italo-germanico in Trento, 2001), 345–64.

18. "Quoniam per inquisitionem non requirantur multe solemnitates, et sic facilius poterit culpa inveniri." Text from the *Tractatus de maleficiis* in Hermann U. Kantorowicz, ed., *Albertus Gandinus und das Strafrecht der Scholastik*, vol. 2 (Berlin and Leipzig: Walter de Gruyter, 1926) (hereafter "Tractatus de maleficiis"), 47. I cite throughout from a translation of this edition prepared by Patrick Lally and edited by Osvaldo Cavallar and Julius Kirshner. I am grateful to these scholars for generously providing me with this unpublished text.

19. X 5 .3. 31, *Licet Heli*: "Non tanquam sit idem ipse accusator et iudex, sed, quasi fama deferente vel denunciante clamore"; repeated verbatim in X.5.1.24, *Qualiter et quando*.

20. See the transcription of Dante's sentence on January 27, 1302, in Renato Piattoli, ed., *Codice Diplomatico dantesco* (Florence: L. Gonnelli, 1950), 103–7, esp.

105. A philologically superior edition can now be found in Maurizio Campanelli, "Le sentenze contro i bianchi fiorentini del 1302. Edizione critica," *Bullettino dell'Istituto Storico Italiano per il Medio Evo* 108 (2006), 224–28 (226).

21. *Codice Diplomatico dantesco*, 105; Campanelli, "Le sentenze contro i bianchi," 226.

22. The relationship between infamy and credibility is suggestively explored in Giacomo Todeschini, *Visibilmenti crudeli: Malviventi, persone sospette e gente qualunque dal Medioevo all'età moderna* (Bologna: Il Mulino, 2007).

23. 1.2.1. Text from Dante Alighieri, *Il Convivio*, ed. Domenico de Robertis and Cesare Vasoli, in *Opere minori*, vol. 1, pt. 2 (Milan and Naples: Ricciardi, 1988). English translation based on Dante Alighieri, *Dante's Il Convivio (The Banquet)*, trans. Richard Lansing (New York: Garland Publishing, 1990).

24. For an influential study of the relationship between these stains and Dante's rhetoric of authority, see Albert Russell Ascoli, *Dante and the Making of a Modern Author* (New York: Cambridge University Press, 2008), 67–129.

25. "L'una è quando senza ragionare di sé grande infamia o pericolo non si può cessare; e allora si concede" (1.2.13).

26. "E questa necessitate mosse Boezio di se medesimo a parlare, acciò che sotto pretesto di consolazione escusasse la perpetuale infamia del suo essilio, mostrando quello essere ingiusto" (1.2.13).

27. "Ahi piaciuto fosse al Dispensatore de l'universo che la cagione de la mia scusa mai non fosse stata! ché né altri contr'a me avria fallato, né io sofferto avria pena ingiustamente, pena, dico, d'essilio e di povertate. Poi che fu piacere de li cittadini de la bellissima e famossissima figlia di Roma, Fiorenza, di gittarmi fuori del suo dolce seno—nel quale nato e nutrito fui in fino al colmo de la vita mia, e nel quale, con buona pace di quella, desidero con tutto lo cuore di riposare l'animo stancato e terminare lo tempo che m'è dato—, per le parti quasi tutte a le quali questa lingua si stende, peregrino, quasi mendicando, sono andato, mostrando contra mia voglia la piaga de la fortuna, che suole ingiustamente al piagato molte volte essere imputata. Veramente io sono stato legno sanza vela e sanza governo, portato a diversi porti e foci e liti dal vento secco che vapora la dolorosa povertade; e sono apparito a li occhi a molti che forse che per alcuna fama in altra forma m'aveano immaginato, nel conspetto de' quali non solamente mia persona invilio, ma di minor pregio se fece ogni opera, sì già fatta come quella che fosse a fare." (1.3.3–5).

28. "La fama buona principalmente è generata da la buona operazione ne le mente de l'amico, e da quella e prima partorita; chè la mente del nemico, avvegna che riceva lo seme, non concepe. Quella mente che prima la partorisce, sì per far più ornato lo suo presente, sì per la caritade de l'amico che lo riceve, non si tiene a li termini del vero, ma passa quelli."

29. "Fama, malum qua non aliud velocius ullum / mobilitate viget virisque adquirit eundo" (Rumor, of all evils the most swift. Speed lends her strength, and she wins vigor as she goes). Text and translation of the *Aeneid* based on Virgil, *Eclogues. Georgics. Aeneid I–VI* and *Aeneid VII–XII*. Rev. edn. by G.P. Goold, trans. H. Rushton Fairclough. Volumes 63–64 of the The Loeb Classical Library (Cambridge, MA: Harvard University Press, 1999–2000). Gandinus's citation is found in *Tractatus de maleficiis*, 64–65. Dante paraphrases Virgil's denigration of *fama* in *Convivio* 1.3.10: "La Fama vive per essere mobile, e acquista grandezza per andare."

30. "Sì come la parte sensitiva dell'anima ha suoi occhi, colli quali aprende la

differenza delle cose in quanto elle sono di fuori colorate, così la parte razionale ha suo occhio, collo quale aprende la differenza delle cose in quanto sono ad alcuno fine ordinate: e questo è la discrezione" (1.11.3).

31. Gherardo Ortalli, *La pittura infamante nei secoli XIII-XVI* (Rome: Jouvence, 1979), 8.

32. According to the jurist Ugolino dei Presbiteri, in such cases it was as if the law itself marked a culprit with infamy (*quasi ipsa lex notet talem*). Quoted in Migliorino, 94.

33. For a recent study on rhetorical *circumstantiae*, see Michael C. Sloan, "Aristotle's *Nicomachean Ethics* as the original locus for the *septem circumstantiae*," *Classical Philology* 105 (2010), 236–51. On rhetoric and philosophical probability, see John Glucker, "*Probabile, Veri Simile*, and Related Terms," in *Cicero the Philosopher: Twelve Papers*, ed. J. G. F. Powell (Oxford: Oxford University Press, 1995), 115–43, and James Franklin, *The Science of Conjecture: Evidence and Probability before Pascal* (Baltimore: Johns Hopkins University, 2001), 102–30.

34. On the jurist's and judge's use of verisimilitude as an argument for sentencing, see Julius Kirshner, "Custom, Customary Law and *Ius Commune* in Francesco Guicciardini," in *Bologna nell'età di Carlo V e Guicciardini*, ed. Emilio Pasquini and Paolo Prodi (Bologna: Il Mulino, 2002), 174–76; Isabella Rosoni, *Quae singula non prosunt collecta iuvant* (Milan: Giuffrè, 1969), 97–119; Mario Sbriccoli, *L'interpretazione dello statuto: Contributo allo studio della funzione dei giuristi nell'età comunale* (Milan: Giuffrè, 1969), 376–81; and Massimo Vallerani, "Il giudice e le sue fonti," 8–11, and "Modelli di verità." For the influence of rhetorical theory on medieval theories of evidence and probability, see Alessandro Giuliani, "The Influence of Rhetoric on the Law of Evidence," *Juridical Review* (1962), 216–51; James Franklin, *The Science of Conjecture*, 12–39; and Barbara J. Shapiro, *"Beyond a Reasonable Doubt" and "Probable Cause": Historical Perspectives on the Anglo-American Law of Evidence* (Berkeley: University of California Press, 1991).

35. "Nam, cum videatur probatum, eum captum fuisse alias hominem male fame, dici potest, quod adhuc tempore criminis, de quo queritur, esse presumitur eiusdem condicionis et fame. quia ea, que in preterita vera fuerunt, sic esse vera et in eo statu hodie presumuntur, et ideo presumendum videtur, eum aliquam huius delicti conscientiam habuisse potius quam alium hominem condicionis alterius. Unde, cum magis de isto verisimilius videatur, et in oscuris et in dubiis iudex habet imitari et inspicere ea, que verisimiliora et vero aptiora esse videntur, videtur quod possit et in questionibus adhiberi" (Since it seems to have been proven that the man seized was in other respects a man of ill repute, it may be said that at the time of the crime that is being investigated, he is presumed to have been of the same status and reputation, because what was true about his status in the past, is presumed to be true also today. For this reason, it seems we ought to presume that he is more likely to have had some knowledge of the crime than another man of a different reputation. Thus, since there seems a distinctly greater plausibility in his regard, and since in obscure and doubtful events a judge must examine and reconstruct what appears more likely and more fitting, it seems right that he may also be tortured). Gandinus, *Tractatus de maleficiis*, 66.

36. See also Laura Hutson's brilliant analysis of how the forensic narrative of the orators influenced later literary models of mimesis in *The Invention of Suspicion: Law and Mimesis in Shakespeare and Renaissance Drama* (Oxford: Oxford University Press, 2007).

37. See especially Erich Auerbach, "Farinata and Cavalcante," in *Mimesis: The Representation of Reality in Western Literature* (Princeton, NJ, and Oxford: Princeton University Press, 2003), 174–202.

38. See Gratian, *Decretum*, C. 2, q. 1, c. 20. For Gratian, in contrast with Innocent III, God's descent to verify the facts of Sodom was a warning against presumptive judgment, not a model for proactive investigation.

39. See Jacques Chiffoleau, "Dire l'indicibile: Osservazioni sulla categoria del 'nefandum' dal XII al XV secolo," in *La parola all'accusato*, ed. Jean-Claude Maire Vigueur and Agostino Paravicini Bagliani (Palermo: Sellerio, 1991), 43–73, and Livingston, "Infamy in the decretists," 103, 104, 111, 116–17.

40. "Si per clamorem et famam ad aures superioris pervenerit." See Innocent's gloss of Genesis 18:16 in X 3.2.8 *Qualiter et quando*, and X 5.3.3.1, *Licet Heli*.

41. "Quod ad aures nostras et curie nostre notitiam, fama publica referente, pervenit" (because it has reached our ears and the notice of the court, with public fame indicting). *Codice diplomatico dantesco*, 105; Campanelli, "Le sentenze contro i bianchi," 226.

42. Given the lack of such evidence, some scholars argue that that the sin punished in these cantos is not in effect sodomy. See Peter Armour, "Dante's Brunetto: The Paternal Paterine?" *Italian Studies* 38 (1983), 1–38; Richard Kay, *Dante's Swift and Strong: Essay on "Inferno XV* (Lawrence: Regents Press of Kansas, 1978); and André Pézard, *Dante sous la pluie de feu* (Paris: Vrin, 1950).

43. See especially John Freccero, "The Eternal Image of the Father," in *The Poetics of Allusion: Virgil and Ovid in Dante's Commedia* (Stanford, CA: Stanford University Press, 1991), 62–76; Ronald L. Martinez, "Dante and Brunetto Latini," in the notes to the Durling translation of *Inferno*, 557–59; and Manlio Pastore Stocchi, "Delusione e giustizia nel canto XV dell'Inferno," *Letture classensi* 3 (1970), 219–54. In her commentary, Chiavacci Leonardi instead locates Dante's ambiguity toward Brunetto (as poet, not only as character) in the contradictions inherent in Brunetto himself—an admirable citizen but a private sinner. In the same vein, see Ernesto Giacomo Parodi, "Il caso di Brunetto Latini," in *Poesia e storia nella "Divina Commedia*," ed. by Gianfranco Folena and P. V. Mengaldo (Vicenza: Neri Pozza Editore, 1965), 163–200.

44. For Dante's equivocal view of homosexual relations and potential homosexuality, see Gary Cestaro, "Pederastic Insemination, or Dante in the Grammar Classroom," in *The Poetics of Masculinity in Early Modern Italy and Spain*, ed. by Gerry Milligan and Jane Tylus (Toronto: Centre for Reformation and Renaissance Studies, 2010), 41–73; Massimiliano Chiamenti, "Dante Sodomita?" *L'Alighieri* 34 (2009), 133–48; and Joseph Pequigney, "Sodomy in Dante's *Inferno* and *Purgatorio*," *Representations* 36 (1991), 22–42.

45. The exposure of societal misrecognition emerges as a pivotal theme of this canto, one neglected by critics who focus exclusively on Dante's interpersonal drama. Distinguished by their "fama" (fame) (*Inferno* 16.31) and "grado" (rank) (*Inferno* 16.36), the sodomites are uniquely divided into discrete "families." Yet unlike Dante's character, who is identified by his Florentine style of dress, these illustrious citizens now roam naked within an extraurban no-man's-land in which the former markers of status no longer apply.

46. On immortality versus eternity, see Hannah Arendt, *The Human Condition* (Chicago and London: University of Chicago Press, 1958), 12–21.

47. See the selection of the *Rettorica* in *Medieval Grammar and Rhetoric: Lan-*

guage Arts and Literary Theory, AD 300–1475, ed. Rita Copeland and Ineke Sluiter (Oxford: Oxford University Press, 2009), 753–86.

48. See the discussion on infamy by punishment in Migliorino, *Fama e infamia,* 129–38.

49. On the differing views on infamy "ex genere poenae," see Migliorino, *Fama e infamia,* 129–38. Contradictory passages in the *Corpus iuris* about whether punishment could defame on its own added to the confusion. In several passages in the *Digest,* penalties affecting reputation (*ad existimationem*) are distinguished from capital and monetary penalties (esp. *Dig.* 48.19.29). Yet *Dig.* 3.22.22 clearly states that in punishments such as whipping, the cause for which a penalty has been incurred defames, not the punishment.

50. *Summa theologiae* IIa IIae, 61, 4, resp.; see the helpful summary of Aristotle's and Aquinas's views in Giuseppe Mazzotta, "Metaphor and Justice," in *Dante's Vision and the Circle of Knowledge* (Princeton, NJ: Princeton University Press, 1993), 75–95 (esp. 79–80). For a thorough examination of the sources of the *contrapasso,* see Peter Armour, "Dante's *Contrapasso*: Context and Texts," *Italian Studies* 55 (2000), 1–20.

51. On Dante's representation of Mohammed and anti-Islamic discourse, see Otfried Lieberknecht, "A Medieval Christian View of Islam: Dante's Encounter with Mohammed in Inferno XXVIII," available at www.lieberknecht.de/~diss/ papers/p_moham.pdf; Karla Mallette, "Muhammad in Hell," *Dante Studies* 125 (2007), 207–24; and Ronald L. Martinez, "Dante between Hope and Despair: The Tradition of Lamentations in the *Divine Comedy,*" *Logos: A Journal of Catholic Thought and Culture* 5:3 (2002), 45–76.

52. See Paola Allegretti, "Canto XXVIII," in *Lectura Dantis Turicensis: L'Inferno,* ed. Georges Guntert and Michelangelo Picone (Florence: Franco Cesati Editore, 2000), 393–406; Pietro G. Beltrami, "Metrica e sintassi nel canto XXVIII dell' *Inferno,*" *Giornale storico della letteratura italiana* 162 (1985), 1–26; and Ronald L. Martinez, "The Poetry of Schism," in Dante Aligheri, *Inferno,* ed. Durling and Martinez, 573–76.

53. For the most exhaustive recent account of these allusions, see Allegretti, "Canto XXVIII."

54. See Robert Hollander, "Dante and the Martial Epic," *Mediaevalia: A Journal of Medieval Studies* 12 (1989), 67–91.

55. On the role of Bertran's poetry in this canto, see especially Teodolinda Barolini, *Dante's Poets: Textuality and Truth in the Comedy* (Princeton, NJ: Princeton University Press, 1984), 164–73; Martinez, "The Poetry of Schism"; and Michelangelo Picone, "I trovatori di Dante: Bertran de Born," *Studi e problemi di critica testuale* 19 (1979), 71–94.

56. Barolini, *Dante's Poets,* 166.

57. In my portrayal of the tension between equality and equity in *Inferno* 28, I am indebted to Mazzotta's "Metaphor and Justice" and his discussion of the problematic qualities of arithmetic justice.

58. "Manifestum est enim quod maius est nocumentum cum aliquis percutit principem, per quod non solum personam ipsius sed totam rempublicam laedit, quam cum percutit aliquam privatam personam. Et ideo non competit iustitiae in talibus simpliciter contrapassum." *Sententia Libri Ethicorum*: Lib. 5 lec. 8 n. 5. Translation in text adapted from Thomas Aquinas, *Commentary on the Nicomachean Ethics,* translated by C. I. Litzinger, O.P. (Chicago: Henry Regnery Company, 1964).

59. See Mario Sbriccoli, "'Vidi communiter observari.' L'emersione di un ordine penale pubblico nelle città italiane del secolo XIII," *Quaderni fiorentini per la storia del pensiero giuridico moderno* 27 (1998), 231–68; and Massimo Vallerani, "Il giudice e le sue fonti. Note su inquisitio e fama nel *Tractatus de maleficiis* di Alberto da Gandino," *Rechtsgeschichte: Zeitschrift des Max-Planck-Instituts für europäische Rechtsgeschichte* 14 (2009), 40–61.

60. See in particular Julien Théry, "'Atrocitas/enormitas.' Per una storia della categoria di 'crimine enorme' nel basso Medioevo (XII–XV secolo)," *Quaderni storici* 131.2 (2009), 329–76; but see also these general studies: Jacques Chiffoleau, "Le crime de majesté, la politique et l'extraordinaire: Note sur les collections érudites de procès de lèse-majesté du XVIIᵉ siècle français et sur leurs exemples médiévaux," in *Le proces politique: XIVᵉ–XVIIᵉ siècle*, ed. Yves-Marie Bercé (Rome: École française de Rome, 2007), 577–662; and Edward Peters, "'Crimen exceptum': The History of an Idea," in *Proceedings of the Tenth International Congress of Medieval Canon Law: Syracuse, New York, 13–18 August 1996* (Vatican City: Biblioteca Apostolica Vaticana, 2001), 137–94.

61. On the city as injured *publica persona*, see Sbriccoli, "Vidi communiter observari," 236.

62. Scholars disagree, however, on how to characterize Dante's response to the question of vengeance raised by Geri. Some critics view it as evidence that Dante condoned the medieval tradition of private vengeance and the necessity of defending one's blood ties. Others see in Dante's pity for Geri a departure from both the vengeful impasse of the Law and the retaliatory violence characterizing Virgil's epic. Instead of piety toward his clan, Dante's character now feels pity for another human being, even one behaving like his enemy. The most sophisticated treatment of these views is found in Lino Pertile, "Canto XXIX: Such Outlandish Wounds," *Lectura Dantis: Inferno*, ed. Allen Mandelbaum, Anthony Oldcorn, and Charles Ross (Berkeley and Los Angeles: University of California Press, 1998), 378–91.

63. This exclusivity would have been especially shocking for Dante's contemporaries, since various categories of people were entitled to bear arms in medieval city-states. See Osvaldo Cavallar, "Regulating Arms in Late Medieval Italy," in *Privileges and Rights of Citizenship: Law and the Juridical Construction of Civil Society*, ed. Julius Kirshner and Laurent Mayali, (Berkeley: Robbins Collection Publications, University of California, 2002), 57–126.

64. See the allusion to the betrayal at Ceperano, *Inf.* 28, 16–18.

65. John Freccero, "Manfred's Wounds and the Poetics of the *Purgatorio*," in *Dante: The Poetics of Conversion*, ed. Rachel Jacoff (Cambridge, MA: Harvard University Press, 1986), 195–208. Now see also Adriana Cassata Contin, "Le ferite di Manfredi: Un ipotesi,"*Giornale storico della letteratura italiana* 183 (2006), 96–130.

66. See the essay "Odysseus' Scar," in *Mimesis*, 3–23.

67. See Erich Auerbach, "Figura," in *Scenes from the Drama of European Literature: Six Essays* (Minneapolis: University of Minnesota Press, 1984), 11–76. But see also the chapter on Dante in *Mimesis*, "Farinata and Cavalcante," 174–202.

68. Freccero, "Manfred's Wounds," 198.

69. For the treatment of war dead in ancient epic, see Jean-Pierre Vernant, "A 'Beautiful Death' and the Disfigured Corpse in Homeric Epic," in Jean-Pierre Vernant, *Mortals and Immortals: Collected Essays*, ed. Froma I. Zeitlin, (Princeton, NJ: Princeton University Press, 1991), 50–74.

70. On Dante's critique of crusades against Christian political enemies, see Ronald L. Martinez, "Dante between Hope and Despair," 59.

Chapter 2

1. Ernst Hartwig Kantorowicz, "The Sovereignty of the Artist: A Note on Legal Maxims and Renaissance Theories of Art," in *Selected Studies* (Locust Valley, NY: J. J. Augustin, 1965), 352–65.

2. Kantorowicz, "The Sovereignty of the Artist," 364.

3. Ernst Hartwig Kantorowicz, *The King's Two Bodies: A Study in Medieval Political Theology* (Princeton, NJ: Princeton University Press, 1997), 494. Victoria Kahn argues that Kantorowicz's focus in Dante on the "new model of the sovereign subject" and a "protoliberal ideal of human autonomy" was a response to Carl Schmitt's political theology. See Victoria Kahn, "Political Theology and Fiction in *The King's Two Bodies*," *Representations* 106 (2009), 77–101 (92).

4. Kantorowicz, *The King's Two Bodies*, 451–95.

5. For Kantorowicz's misreading of medieval texts from the perspective of the modern constitutionalist state, see Bernhard Jussen, "The *King's Two Bodies* Today," *Representations* 106 (2009), 102–17.

6. See, for example, Mario Caravale, *Ordinamenti giuridici dell'Europa medievale* (Bologna: Mulino, 1994), 538–41; Ennio Cortese, *La norma giuridica: Spunti teorici nel diritto comune classico*, 2 vols. (Milan: Giuffrè, 1962), 2:203–30; Kenneth Pennington, *The Prince and the Law, 1200–1600: Sovereignty and Rights in the Western Legal Tradition* (Berkeley: University of California Press, 1993).

7. Albert Russell Ascoli, *Dante and the Making of a Modern Author* (Cambridge: Cambridge University Press, 2008), 330. For other readings of the coronation scene and Dante's liberty, see Gianfranco Contini, "Alcuni appunti su Purgatorio XXVII," in *Un' idea di Dante: Saggi danteschi* (Turin: Giulio Einaudi, 1970), 171–90; Joan M. Ferrante, *The Political Vision of the Divine Comedy* (Princeton, NJ: Princeton University Press, 1984), 243–52; Ernesto G. Parodi, "La *Divina Commedia*, poema della libertà dell'individuo e il canto XXVII del *Purgatorio*," in Alojzij Res, ed., *Dante: Raccolta di studi (Per il Secentenario della morte di Dante 1321)* (Gorizia: Paternolli, 1921), 9–41; John A. Scott, *Dante's Political Purgatory* (Philadelphia: University of Pennsylvania Press, 1996), 179–84; and Charles S. Singleton, *Dante Studies 2: Journey to Beatrice* (Cambridge, MA: Harvard University Press, 1958), 57–71.

8. On the concept of negative freedom, see especially Isaiah Berlin, "Two Concepts of Liberty," in Isaiah Berlin, *Liberty*, ed. Henry Hardy (Oxford: Oxford University Press, 2002), 166–217.

9. For the buffered versus the porous self, see Charles Taylor, *A Secular Age* (Cambridge, MA: Harvard University Press, 2007).

10. See Dante's Epistle to the Florentines (VI): ". . . laws whose observance—if it is joyful and free—not only can be seen to involve no element of coercion, but rather on closer inspection, reveals itself to be nothing less than perfect liberty itself. For what is liberty if not the free translation of the will into action, which the laws facilitate to those who obey them? Therefore, since only those who obey the laws on their own free will are truly free, who do you think you are, who pretend to love liberty, but who break off all laws in conspiring against the Prince who is the source of law." Dante targets in particular in this letter the argument for Florentine autonomy based on "prescription"—the legal institution whereby

rights are acquired over a territory after extended neglect by its rightful owner (in this case caused by the vacancy of the emperor's seat). Given this forceful rejection of Florentine self-governance as a form of "captivity" masquerading as liberty, it is highly unlikely that Dante would claim a similar "pseudo-liberty" for himself in the crowning scene of *Purgatorio* 27. English translation of the letter from Dante Alighieri, *Four Political Letters*, trans. Claire E. Honess (London: Modern Humanities Research Association, 2007), 66–67. Latin text in Dante Alighieri, *Opere minori*, ed. Domenico De Robertis et al. (Milan and Naples: Ricciardi, 1979), 2:550–60 (558).

11. Jonathan Lear, *Radical Hope: Ethics in the Face of Cultural Devastation* (Cambridge, MA: Harvard University Press, 2006).

12. Gianfranco Contini describes Dante's singular journey and crowning in *Purgatorio* as "exceptional, I would say emergency measures" necessitated by the vacancy of the Empire in "Alcuni appunti su Purgatorio XXVII," 173.

13. For an excellent introductory summary, see J. B. Korolec, "Free Will and Free Choice," in *The Cambridge History of Later Medieval Philosophy: From the Rediscovery of Aristotle to the Disintegration of Scholasticism, 1100–1600*, eds. Norman Kretzmann, Anthony Kenny, and Jan Pinborg (Cambridge: Cambridge University Press, 1982), 629–41.

14. On Dante's intellectualist approach to free choice, see Robert M. Durling, "The Primacy of the Intellect, the Sun, and the Circling Theologians," in Dante Alighieri, *Paradiso*, ed. and trans. Robert M. Durling (Oxford and New York: Oxford University Press, 2011), 708–14; Paolo Falzone, "Psicologia dell'atto umano in Dante: Problemi di lessico e di dottrina," in *Filosofia in volgare nel medioevo: Atti del Convegno della Società italiana per lo studio del pensiero medievale (S.I.S.P.M.), Lecce, 27–29 settembre 2002*, ed. Nadia Bray and Loris Sturlese (Louvain-la-Neuve: Fédération internationale des instituts d'études médiévales, 2003), 331–66; Bruno Nardi, "Il libero arbitrio e la storiella dell'asino di Buridano" in Bruno Nardi, *Nel mondo di Dante* (Rome: Edizioni di Storia e Letteratura, 1944), 287–303; and Giorgio Stabile's definitive treatment under the entry "Volontà" in *Enciclopedia Dantesca*, Vol. 5, 1134–40. See also the overviews of "free will" in Dante in Patrick Boyde, *Perception and Passion in The Dante's Comedy* (Cambridge: Cambridge University Press, 1993), 197–208; Warren Ginsberg, "Free Will" in *The Dante Encyclopedia*, 425–27; and Sofia Rovighi Vanni, "Arbitrio" in *Enciclopedia Dantesca* 1:345–48.

15. "Si ergo iudicium moveat omnino appetitum et nullo modo preveniatur ab eo, liberum est; se vero ab appetitu quocunque modo preveniente iudicium moveatur, liberum esse non potest, quia non a se, sed ab alio captivum trahitur" (Now if judgment controls desire completely and is in no way at all preempted by it, it is free; but if judgment is in any way at all preempted and thus controlled by desire, it cannot be free, because it does not act under its own power, but is dragged along captive by another). Text and translations (slightly adapted) from *Monarchia* based on Dante Alighieri, *Monarchia*, ed. and trans. by Prue Shaw (Cambridge and New York: Cambridge University Press, 1995).

16. See Korolec, "Free Will and Free Choice," 634.

17. My understanding of *arbitrium* owes a great debt to the work of Massimo Meccarelli, even on those points where my interpretation differs from his own. See especially *Arbitrium: Un aspetto sistematico degli ordinamenti giuridici in età di diritto comune* (Milan: Giuffrè, 1998) and "Paradigma dell'eccezione nella parabola della modernità penale: Una prospettiva storico-giuridica," *Quaderni storici 131* (2009), 493–522.

18. "Omne arbitrium debet regi tanquam equus a freno et navis a clavo." Quoted in Meccarelli, *Arbitrium*, 67.

19. See language cited in Meccarelli, *Arbitrium*, 10.

20. For the role of *arbitrium* in the establishment of the *signori*, see Jane Black, "The Visconti in the Fourteenth Century and the Origins of their *Plenitudo Potestatis*," in *Poteri signorili e feudali nelle Campagne dell'Italia settentrionale fra Tre e Quattrocento: Fondamenti di legittimità e forme di esercizio*, eds. Federica Cengarle, Giorgio Chittolini, and Gian Maria Varanini (Florence: Firenze University Press, 2005), 11–30; idem, *Absolutism in Renaissance Milan: Plenitude of Power under the Visconti and the Sforza 1329–1535* (Oxford: Oxford University Press, 2009); Giovanni Cassandro, "Signoria," in *Novissimo Digesto Italiano*, 17 vols. (Turin: UTET, 1957); G. De Vergottini, "Vicariato imperiale e signoria" and "Signorie e principati" in *Scritti di storia del diritto italiano* (Milan: G. Rossi, 1977), 615–36 and 637–70; Gino Masi, *Verso gli albori del principato in Italia: Note di storia del diritto pubblico* (Bologna: N. Zanichelli, 1936); Meccarelli, *Arbitrium*, 188–93; and G. B. Picotti, "Qualche osservazione sui caratteri delle signorie italiane," *Rivista storica italiana* (1926), 7–30.

21. This *translatio* from *repubblica* to *signoria* is one of the most studied and contested topics of Italian historiography. For recent work focusing especially on the legal aspects, see Andrea Gamberini, *Lo stato visconteo: Linguaggi politici e dinamiche costituzionali* (Milan: Franco Angeli, 2005); Claudia Storti Storchi, *Scritti sugli statuti Lombardi* (Milan: Giuffrè, 2007); and Andrea Zorzi, "Bien commun et conflits politiques dans l'Italie communale," in *De Bono Communi : The Discourse and Practice of the Common Good in the European City (13th–16th c.)*, ed. Elodie Lecuppre-Desjardin, Anne-Laure Van Bruaene (Turnhout: Brepols, 2010), 267–90.

22. On the relation between the Scaligeri and local laws, see Silvana Anna Bianchi and Gian Maria Varanini, "Statuti comunali e signoria: Verona e gli Scaligeri," in *Gli statuti di Verona del 1327*, ed. Silvana Anna Bianchi and Rosalba Granuzzo (Rome: Jouvence, 1992), 11–62; Andrea Castagnetti and Gian Maria Varanini, eds., *Il Veneto nel medioevo: Le signorie trecentesche, Verona* (Milan: Mondadori, 1995); and Andrea Di Salvo, "Il signore della Scala: Percezione e rielaborazioni della figura di Cangrande nelle testimonianze del secolo XIV," *Rivista storica italiana* 108 (1996), 36–87.

23. Massimo Vallerani emphasizes the restrictions placed on *arbitrium* in *La giustizia pubblica medievale* (Bologna: Il Mulino, 2005), 218–31 and 251–59.

24. On the two types of *arbitrium*, see the discussions in Cortese, *Norma giuridica* 2:228–29; Charles Lefebre, *Les pouvoirs du Juge en droit canonique* (Paris: Thèse Droit, 1938), 84–86; and Meccarelli, *Arbitrium*, 97–128.

25. On the limits on free discretion in Bartolus and Baldus, see Black, "The Visconti in the Fourteenth Century," 21; Ennio Cortese, "Nicolaus de Ursone de Salerno: Un'opera ignota sulle lettere arbitrarie angione nella tradizione dei trattati sulla tortura" in *Scritti*, eds. Italo Birocchi and Ugo Petronio, 2 vols. (Spoleto: Centro italiano di studi sull'alto Medioevo, 1999), 1:379–90 (368–70); and Nicolini, *Il principio di legalità*, 396–97.

26. Ascoli, *Dante and the Making of a Modern Author*, 332, note 39, is a notable exception.

27. On the historical semantics of *arbitrium*, see in particular Meccarelli, *Arbitrium*, 43–53.

28. See Pennington, *The Prince and the Law*, 31–35, for a copious bibliography and important qualifications of this maxim.

29. Text from the epistle based on Dante Alighieri, *Epistole* in *Le Opere di Dante*, ed. Ermenegildo Pistelli (Firenze: Società Dantesca Italiana, 1960). English translation based on *Epistolae: The Letters of Dante*, trans. Paget Toynbee (Oxford: Clarendon Press 1966).

30. Text and translation based on Dante Alighieri, *De vulgari eloquentia*, ed. and trans. Steven Botterill (New York and Cambridge, Cambridge University Press, 1996).

31. Critics have tended to read the construction of Babel as a wholesale critique of Italian municipal life. I have argued that Dante specifically targets magnate culture. See Ascoli, *Dante and the Making of a Modern Author*, 171; Corti, "Dante e la torre" in *Il viaggio testuale* (Turin: Einaudi, 1978), 245–56 (255); and Justin Steinberg, *Accounting for Dante: Urban Readers and Writers in Late Medieval Italy* (Notre Dame, IN: University of Notre Dame Press, 2007), 95–123.

32. For the contrast between the aristocratic Tower of Babel and the civic construction of Dido's Carthage, see Steinberg, *Accounting for Dante*, 116–18.

33. For the role of Nimrod in the discussion of primeval property rights, see Brian Tierney, *The Idea of Natural Rights: Studies on Natural Rights, Natural Law, and Church Law, 1150–1625* (Grand Rapids, MI, and Cambridge, UK: Eerdmans, 2001), 140–41, and especially the glosses on the *Decretum* cited in Rudolf Weigand, *Die Naturrechtslehre der Legisten und Dekretisten von Irnerius bis Accursius und von Gratian bis Johannes Teuononicus* (Munich: Hueber, 1967), 337–39.

34. See also *Convivio* 1.5.8, where Dante describes the vernacular as constructed "a piacimento" (at will).

35. "Hinc moti sunt inventores gramatice facultatis: que quidem gramatica nichil aliud est quam quedam inalterabilis locutionis ydemptitas diversibus temporibus atque locis. Hec cum de comuni consensu multarum gentium fuerit regulata, nullo singolari arbitrio videtur obnoxia, et per consequens nec variabilis esse potest. Adinvenerunt ergo illam ne, propter variationem sermonis arbitrio singularium fluitantis, vel nullo modo vel saltim imperfecte antiquorum actingeremus autoritates et gesta, sive illorum quos a nobis locorum diversitas facit esse diversos."

36. On the Neoplatonic patterns of *De vulgari*, see Giorgio Stabile, "Sì-oc-öil: In signum eiusdem principii. Dante contro le barriere di confini e linguaggi" in *Dante e la filosofia della natura: Percezioni, linguaggi, cosmologie* (Florence: SLSMEL, Edizioni del Galluzzo, 2007), 253–70.

37. "In quantum ut homines cives agimus, habemus legem, secundum quam dicitur civis bonus et malus; in quantum ut homines latini agimus, quedam habemus simplicissima signa et morum et habituum et locutionis, quibus latine actiones ponderantur et mensurantur" (Insofar as we act as human beings who are citizens, we have the law, by whose standards we describe a citizen as good or bad; insofar as we act as human beings who are Italians, there are certain very simple features, of manners and appearance and speech, by which the actions of the people of Italy are weighed and measured).

38. "Vide ergo, lector, quanta licentia data sit cantiones poetantibus, et considera cuius rei causa tam largum arbitrium usus sibi asciverit; et si recto calle ratio te duxerit, videbis autoritatis dignitate sola quod dicimus esse concessum."

39. Text of the *Vita nova* cited from Dante Alighieri, *Vita nova*, ed. Stefano Carrai (Milan: BUR, 2009).

40. For the centrality of the concept of "just cause" in medieval legal thought, see Cortese, *La norma giuridica*, 1:183–296.

41. A paraphrase of *Digest* 1.4.2: "In rebus novis constituendis evidens esse utilitas debet, ut recedatur ab eo iure, quod diu aequum visum est."

42. (1.1.1.) See the section "Lucidare discretionem" in the essay by Francesco di Capua, "Insegnamenti retorici medievali e dottrine estetiche moderne nel *De vulgari eloquentia* di Dante," in *Scritti minori* (Rome: Desclée, 1959), 302–14.

43. For the connections between the license Dante allows himself in "Amor, tu vedi ben che questa donna" and another investiture ceremony, see Robert M. Durling and Ronald L. Martinez, *Time and the Crystal: Studies in Dante's Rime Petrose* (Berkeley and Los Angeles: University of California Press, 1990), 261–67.

44. The broad distinction I draw between promulgated law and binding conventions obviously does not take into consideration the complex legal debates in the period over the nature of customary law, which often took the form of written municipal statutes. See Gianfranco Garancini, "'Consuetudo et statutum ambulant pari passu': La consuetudine nei diritti italiani del basso medioevo," in *Rivista di storia del diritto italiano* 58 (1985), 19–55; Paolo Grossi, *L'ordine giuridico medievale* (Bari: Laterza, 1995), 182–90; Julius Kirshner, "Custom, Customary Law and *Ius Commune* in Francesco Guicciardini," in *Bologna nell'età di Carlo V e Guicciardini*, ed. Emilio Pasquini and Paolo Prodi (Bologna: Il Mulino, 2002), 151–79; Laurent Mayali, "La coutume dans la doctrine romaniste au Moyen Age" in *La coutume-Custom*, a special issue of *Recueils de la Société Jean Bodin* 52 (1990), 11–31; and Laurent Leo Jozef Maria Waelkens, *La théorie de la coutume chez Jacques de Révigny: Edition et analyse de sa repetition sur la loi 'De quibus' (D. 1. 3. 32)* (Leiden: Brill, 1984).

45. Alessandro Passerin d'Entrèves interprets this "gratiosum lumen rationis" as representing natural law, the same "impressio divini luminis" (impression of divine light) that, according to Aquinas, allows human beings to discern good from evil. He takes issue with previous identifications of it with the *ratio scripta* of Roman law. For Passerin d'Entrèves, Dante's use of *ratio* and *ragione* is more akin to the concept of *ius*, a norm derived from natural equity, than to the *lex* of imperial positive laws. However, by the later Middle Ages, the most widespread instances of positive law and legislation were not imperial *leges* but the municipal statutes. Roman civil law instead consisted primarily of a corpus of deterritorialized and dehistoricized *iura*. See, with further bibliography, the essay "Gratiosum lumen rationis" in Alessandro Passerin d'Entrèves, *Dante as a Political Thinker* (Oxford: Oxford University Press, 1952), 76–97.

46. On the role of tacit consent in customary norms, see Grossi, *L'ordine giuridico*, 186; and Kirshner, "Custom, Customary Law, and *Ius Commune*," 153–54.

47. See Teodolinda Barolini, "Minos's Tail: The Labor of Devising Hell (*Aeneid* 6.431–33 and *Inferno* 5.1–23)," in *Dante and the Origins of Italian Literary Culture* (New York: Fordham University Press, 2006), 132–50.

48. For the reception of these verses with further bibliography, see Barolini, "Minos's Tail," 144–46.

49. On confession in the *Commedia*, see Peter Brooks, *Troubling Confessions: Speaking Guilt in Law and Literature* (Chicago: University of Chicago Press, 2000), 97–100; and Matthew Senior, *In the Grip of Minos: Confessional Discourse in Dante, Corneille, and Racine* (Columbus: Ohio State University Press, 1994), 27–74.

50. According to *Digest* 22.5.2, judges were to examine "the status, faith

(*fides*), morals, and gravity of witnesses." On the judge's role in assessing the credibility of witnesses, see Meccarelli, *Arbitrium*, 245 (see note on Bartolus); Antonio Padoa Schioppa, "La coscienza del giudice," in *Italia ed Europa nella storia del diritto: Collezione di testi e di studi* (Bologna: Il Mulino, 2003), 251–92; and Walter Ullmann, "Medieval Principles of Evidence," *Law Quarterly Review* (1946), 77–87.

51. Jean-Claude Maire Vigueur, "Giudici e testimoni a confronto," in *La parola all'accusato*, eds. Jean-Louis Biget, Jean-Claude Maire Vigueur, and Agostino Paravicini Bagliani. (Palermo: Sellerio, 1991), 105–23 (110–11).

52. The bibliography on torture in the Middle Ages is vast. For the tensions between doctrine and practice, see, at least, Ennio Cortese, "Casi di giustizia sommaria: Le lettere arbitrarie angione," in *Forme stragiudiziali o straordinarie di risoluzione delle controversie nel diritto comune e nel diritto canonico (atti del covnegno di studi, Teramo, 21–22 Aprile 2004)*, ed. Piero Antonio Bonnet and Luca Loschiavo (Naples: Edizioni Scientifiche Italiane, 2009), 79–90; Maire Vigueur, "Giudici e testimoni a confronto"; and Mario Sbriccoli, "'Tormentum idest torquere mentem': Processo inquisitorio e interrogatorio per tortura nell'Italia comunale," in *La parola all'accusato*, 17–32.

53. On the threshold of proof required for conviction and torture, see Richard M. Fraher, "Conviction According to Conscience: The Medieval Jurists' Debate Concerning Judicial Discretion and the Law of Proof," *Law and History Review* 7 (1989), 23–88; and Vallerani, *La giustizia pubblica medievale*, 45–47.

54. On the *lettere arbitrarie*, see Federico Ciccaglione, "Le lettere arbitrarie nella legislazione angiona," *Rivista italiana per le scienze giuridiche* 28 (1899), 254–89; Cortese, "Casi di giustizia sommaria"'; and Ennio Cortese, "Nicolaus de Ursone de Salerno: Un'opera ignota sulle lettere arbitrarie angione nella tradizione dei trattati sulla tortura," in *Scritti* 1, 379–90.

55. "Iunxta tuum arbitrium Deum tamen et iustitiam habendo pro oculis." Quoted in Cortese, "Casi di giustizia sommaria," 85.

56. See Cortese, "Casi di giustizia sommaria," 85–86; and Cortese, "Nicolaus de Ursone." Even Thomas and Gandinus, after permitting torture in cases with minimal evidence, are careful to add that judges could not ignore all legal solemnities, proceeding with no respect for the law whatsoever: "Licet in procedendo et in maleficium cognoscendo possint omittere ordinem et solemnitatem iuris ex consuetudinaria et communi interpretatione arbitrii, non tamen prorsus non possunt vel debent omittere" (Although in investigating and trying crimes they may omit the order and solemnity of the trial, according to the customary and common interpretation of *arbitrium*, they nonetheless cannot and should not omit these elements altogether). From Thomas de Piperata, *De fama*. Gandinus again is very close to Thomas: "Nam licet in processu potestas possit ex suo arbitrio multa de iuris solemnitate omittere, non tamen potest prorsus omittere" (For although the *podestà* in a trial, because of his *arbitrium*, may omit many of the solemnities of law, he nonetheless cannot omit them altogether). *Tractatus de maleficiis* 2:176.

57. On the materiality of Piero's speech, see Leo Spitzer, "Speech and Language in Inferno XIII," *Italica* 19 (1942), 77–104.

58. On the style and language of *Inferno* 13, see especially Ettore Paratore, "Analisi 'retorica' del canto di Pier della Vigna," *Studi danteschi* 42 (1965), 281–336; and Spitzer, "Speech and Language."

59. See Anthony K. Cassell, *Dante's Fearful Art of Justice* (Toronto: University of Toronto Press, 1984).

60. For Dante's rewriting of Virgil's text, see Giuseppe Mazzotta, *Dante, Poet*

of the Desert: History and Allegory in the Divine Comedy (Princeton, NJ: Princeton University Press, 1979), 188–91; and Paratore, "Analisi 'retorica,'" 187–98.

61. For the judge's discretion in punishing culprits, see Cortese, *La norma giuridica*, 2, 170–77; Laurent Mayali, "The Concept of Discretionary Punishment in Medieval Jurisprudence," in *Studia in honorem Eminentissimi Cardinalis Alphonsi M. Stickler*, ed. Rosalio José Castillo Lara (Rome: Libreria Ateneo Salesiano, 1992), 299–315; Meccarelli, *Arbitrium*, 226–35; Meccarelli, "Paradigma dell'eccezione," 497–98; and Nicolini, *Il principio di legalità*, 89–113.

62. "Quia in talibus ordinem iuris non servare est iuris ordinem observare." Gandinus, *Tractatus de maleficiis* 2:104. King Robert is even more explicit in the letter "Si cum sceleratis": "Quia in talibus est ordo ordinem non servare, qui nullum iuris ordinem observarunt" (because with those who have in no way observed the rule of law it is the rule not to observe the rules). Quoted in Ciccaglione, "Le lettere arbitrarie," 276.

63. An example of the suspect who lies to avoid torture can be found among the damned, in the barrater Ciampolo. Captured by the demon police in *Inferno* 22, Ciampolo interrupts their sadistic attacks—and Dante and Virgil's questioning—by promising false information on how to seize his infernal compatriots.

64. In contrast with the critical consensus, John Ahern argues that the central moral dilemma of this canto resides in the Pilgrim's mirroring of the damned: "Canto XXXII: Amphion and the Poetics of Retaliation," in *Lectura Dantis: Inferno. A Canto by Canto Commentary*, ed. Allen Mandelbaum, Anthony Oldcorn, and Charles Ross (Berkeley: University of California Press, 1998), 413–23.

65. See Virgil's description of the examples of compassion and envy:

Questo cinghio sferza
la colpa di invidia, e però sono
tratte d'amore le corde de la ferza.
Lo fren vuol esser del contrario suono

(This circle whips the guilt of envy, and therefore the cords of the whip are braided of love. The bridle nees to be of the opposite sound; *Purgatorio* 13.37–40).

66. While critics are divided as to whether the exceptional freedom the Pilgrim achieves in Eden is unique or potentially imitable, readers are clearly meant to experience these disciplinary spectacles vicariously.

67. See Pierre Bourdieu, "Bodily Knowledge," in *Pascalian Meditations*, trans. Richard Nice (Stanford, CA: Stanford University Press, 2000), 128–63.

68. On the nature of Dante's mimesis on the terrace of pride, see especially Barolini, *The Undivine Comedy*, 122–36; and Nancy J. Vickers, "Seeing is Believing: Gregory, Trajan, and Dante's Art," *Dante Studies* 101 (1983), 67–85.

69. For background on theological views of conscience, especially on how they relate to natural law, see Timothy C. Potts, "Conscience," in *The Cambridge History of Later Medieval Philosophy: From the Rediscovery of Aristotle to the Disintegration of Scholasticism, 1100–1600*, ed. Norman Kretzmann, Anthony Kenny, and Jan Pinborg (Cambridge and New York: Cambridge University Press, 1982), 687–704; and Sofia Vanni Rovighi, "Legge e coscienza in San Tommaso," *Vita e pensiero*, n.s. 10 (1971), 787–93. On the jurists' classification on public conscience, see Meccarelli, *Arbitrium*, 104–6.

70. See John Freccero, "Manfred's Wounds and the Poetics of the *Purgatorio*," in *Dante: The Poetics of Conversion* (Cambridge, MA: Harvard University Press 1996), 195–208; Peter S. Hawkins, "Dido, Beatrice, and the Signs of Ancient Love," in *The Poetry of Allusion: Virgil and Ovid in Dante's Commedia*, ed. Rachel Jacoff and Jeffrey T. Schnapp (Stanford, CA, Stanford University Press, 1991),113–30; and Mazzotta, *Dante, Poet of the Dessert*, 185–88.

71. For the effacement of Virgil, see Freccero, "Manfred's Wounds," 207–208.

Chapter 3

1. See the discussions of the two definitions in Ennio Cortese, *La norma giuridica: Spunti teorici nel diritto comune classico*, 2 vols. (Milan: Giuffrè, 1962), 1:103–4 and 2:44–46; Vincenzo Del Giudice, "Privilegio, dispensa, ed epicheia nel diritto canonico," in *Scritti in Memoria del Prof. Francesco Innamorati* (Perugia: Tip. G. Guerra, 1932), 227–81 (260); André Gouron, "La notion de privilège dans la doctrine juridique du douzième siècle," in Barbara Dölemeyer and Heinz Mohnhaupt, eds., *Das Privileg im Europäischen Vergleich*, 2 vols. (Frankfurt am Main: Klostermann, 1999), 1:1–16; Vincenzo Piano Mortari, "Ius sigulare e privilegium nel pensiero dei glossatori," *Rivista italiana per le scienze giuridiche* 9 (1957–58), 271–350 (299–307); Massimo Vallerani, "Premessa," *Quaderni storici* 131.2 (2009), 299–312 (301–2).

2. The formula can be found in various sources. See the *Libellus de verbis legalibus*, Hermann Fitting, ed., *Juristische Schriften des früheren Mittelalters* (Halle: Buchhandlung des Waisenhauses, 1876), 196. For discussion and other sources, see Cortese, *La norma giuridica*, 2:44–46; Gouron, "La notion de privilège," 3–4; Piano Mortari, "Ius singulare e privilegium," 304–7.

3. In order to contain the potential antinomy of imperial and papal privileges, they classified various types according to a sophisticated ladder of validity (at the top of which were privileges already contained within the *Corpus iuris civilis*, while the lowest rung was occupied by those for which no higher cause or utility justified their divergence from preexisting law). See the discussion of the tree of rescripts included in the *Summa Trecensis* in Cortese, *La norma giuridica*, 1:258; and Gouron, "La notion de privilège," 8.

4. "Iura non in singulas personas sed generaliter constituuntur." See Del Giudice, "Privilegio, dispensa, ed epicheia," 256; and Piano Mortari, "Ius singulare e privilegium," 316–17.

5. "Leges non sunt conditae ut haec habeat locum in persona huius, illa in persona alterius . . . sed generaliter in omnibus personis." Quoted in Piano Mortari, "Ius singulare e privilegium," 316–17.

6. "Privilegium dicitur, quod per hoc leges sua generalitate privantur." See the examples given of this definition by the Bolognese jurists in Piano Mortari, "Ius singulare e privilegium," 306.

7. Cicero's critique of *privilegia*, most likely the source of Isidore's definition, conceives of privileges as special laws enacted to prejudicially harm particular persons or groups. The view of privileges as a special benefit or favor bestowed upon one by the law, an advantage rather than a handicap, was developed later.

8. With the same subjective perspective on the law, Virgil obeys Beatrice because he recognizes that the sovereign will back her requests, the "talento" (81) underlying the "comandamento" (79).

9. On Beatrice's advent in limbo and prevenient grace, see Amilcare A. Ian-

nucci, "Beatrice in Limbo: A Metaphoric Harrowing of Hell," *Dante Studies* 97 (1979), 23–45; and Singleton, *Journey to Beatrice*, 48–54.

10. On the "sanctity" of the ambassador in Roman law, see Marcian, *Dig.* 1.8.8.1; Pomponius, *Dig.* 50.7.18; and the interpretation of these passages, in David J. Bloch, "Res sanctae in Gaius and the Founding of the City," *Roman Legal Tradition* 4 (2006), 48–64 (53–54). For the medieval reception of this concept, see Sara Menzinger, "Verso la costruzione di un diritto pubblico cittadino," in the introduction to Emanuele Conte and Sara Menzinger, eds., *La Summa trium librorum di Rolando da Lucca (1195–1234). Fisco, politica, scientia iuris* (Rome: Viella, 2012), cxliii–cxlix.

11. See Giorgio Lombardi, "Spazio e frontiera. Tra eguaglianza e privilegio: Problemi costituzionali tra storia e diritto," in *La frontiera da Stato a Nazione: Il caso Piemonte*, eds. C. Ossola, C. Raffestin, and M. Ricciardi (Rome: Bulzoni, 1987), 385–406; Paolo Marchetti, *De iure finium: Diritto e confini tra tardo medievo ed età moderna* (Milan: Giuffrè, 2001), 58–60; and, for an excellent overview of the distinctions between medieval and modern immunity, Garrett Mattingly, *Renaissance Diplomacy* (Baltimore: Penguin, 1955), 15–54; and Donald E. Queller, *The Office of Ambassador in the Middle Ages* (Princeton, NJ: Princeton University Press, 1967), 175–84.

12. Marchetti, *De iure finium*, 54–56.

13. See Natalino Sapegno's commentary to *Inferno* 3.95 in *La Divina Commedia* (Milan and Naples: Ricciardi, 1957), but the sentiment is widespread among *dantisti*.

14. On the theological debates about the limits of God's omnipotence (especially on the distinction between absolute and ordained powers discussed below in the text), see Luca Bianchi, "'Cotidiana miracula,' comune corso della natura e dispense al diritto matrimoniale: Il miracolo fra Agostino e Tommaso d'Aquino," *Quaderni storici* 131.2 (2009), 313–28; William J. Courtenay, *Capacity and Volition: A History of the Distinction of Absolute and Ordained Power* (Bergamo: P. Lubrina, 1990); Francis Oakley, "The Absolute and Ordained Power of God in Sixteenth- and Seventeenth-Century Theology," *Journal of the History of Ideas* 59.3 (1998), 437–61 (440–49); Francis Oakley, *Omnipotence, Covenant, and Order: An Excursion in the History of Ideas from Abelard to Leibniz* (Ithaca, NY: Cornell University Press, 1984); and Eugenio Randi, *Il sovrano e l'orologiaio: Due immagini di Dio nel dibattito sulla "potentia absoluta" fra XIII e XIV secolo* (Florence: La Nuova Italia, 1987).

15. Augustine, *De natura et gratia*, 7–8, CSEL 60, 237. Discussed in Courtenay, *Capacity and volition*, 55.

16. "And therefore it is not only in God, but in every free agent that can either act in accord with the dictates of a just law or go beyond or against that law, that one distinguishes between absolute and ordained power; therefore, the jurists say that someone can act *de facto*, that is, according to his absolute power, or *de jure*, that is, according to his ordained legal power." Text and translation in *Duns Scotus on the Will and Morality*, ed. and trans. Allan B. Wolter (Washington: Catholic University of America Press, 1986), 254–55. See discussion in Courtnenay, *Capacity and Volition*, 100–103; and Randi, 56–65.

17. In treating a similar question in *Paradiso* 5, Dante also denied that the pope could abrogate religious vows. See Manlio Pastore Stocchi, "Il canto V del *Paradiso*," *Nuove letture dantesche*, vol. 5 (Florence: Le Monnier, 1972), 341–74.

18. "Non de potestate ordinata, sed de absoluta." Hostiensis to X 3. 35. 6, *Cum ad monasterium: Lectura in quinque Decretalium Gregorianarum libros* (Venice:

1581, repr. 1965), III, fol. 134r. See discussion in Courtenay, *Capacity and Volition*, 92–95; and Oakley, "Absolute and Ordained," 446.

19. On the historical background of the debate, see Yves M. J. Congar, "Aspects ecclésiologiques de la querelle entre mendiants et séculiers dans la seconde moitié du XIIIe siècle et le début du XIVe siècle," in *Archives d'Histoire Doctrinale et Littéraire du Moyen Âge* 36 (1961), 35–151; D. L. Douie, *The Conflict between the Seculars and the Mendicants at the University of Paris in the Thirteenth Century* (London: Blackfriars, 1954); and Palémon Glorieux, "Prélats français contre religieux mendicants: Autour de la bulle 'Ad fructus uberes' (1281–1290)," in *Revue d'Histoire de l'Église de France* 11 (1925), 309–31.

20. According to the Fourth Lateran Council (1215), it was necessary to confess at least once a year to one's parish priest. Mendicant theologians argued that only sins not already confessed to friars needed to be confessed to local priests.

21. For the role played by privileges in this debate, see Alain Boureau, "Privilege in medieval societies from the twelfth to the fourteenth centuries, or: How the exception proves the rule," in *The Medieval World*, ed. by Peter Linehan and Janet L. Nelson (London and New York: Routledge, 2001), 621–34, esp. 627–28.

22. On the distinction in Henry of Ghent, see Courteney, *Capacity and Volition*, 98–100; John Marrone, "The Absolute and Ordained Powers of the Pope: A Quodlibetal Question of Henry of Ghent," *Mediaeval Studies* 36 (1974), 7–27; and Pasquale Porro, "Henry of Ghent on Ordained and Absolute Power, in *Henry of Ghent and the Transformation of Scholastic Thought: Studies in Memory of Jos Decorte*, ed. Guy Guldenstops and Carlos Steel (Leuven: Leuven University Press, 2003), 387–408.

23. Courtenay, 25–41.

24. On the divine intervention in cantos 8–9 as a metaphor for Christ's Advent or Harrowing, see Eric Auerbach, *Literary Language and its Public in Latin Antiquity and in the Middle Ages*, trans. Ralph Manheim (Princeton, NJ: Princeton University Press, 1993), 228–33; Denise Heilbronn, "Dante's Gate of Dis and the Heavenly Jerusalem," *Studies in Philology* 72 (1975), 167–92; Peter S. Hawkins, "Descendit ad inferos," in *Dante's Testaments: Essays in Scriptural Imagination* (Stanford, CA: Stanford University Press, 1999), 99–124 (110–14); Amilcare Iannucci, "Dottrina e allegoria in *Inferno VIII*, 67-IX, 105," in *Dante e le forme dell'allegoresi*, ed. Michelangelo Picone (Ravenna: Longo, 1987), 99–124; and Mark Musa, *Advent at the Gates* (Bloomington: Indiana University Press, 1974).

25. See Hollander's useful summary of allegorical interpretations in Dante Alighieri, *Inferno*, trans. Jean and Robert Hollander (New York: Random House, 2002), 170.

26. On the episode as an interpretive trap, see Freccero's influential reading of the figure of Medusa: "Medusa: The Letter and the Spirit," now in *Dante: The Poetics of Conversion*, ed. Rachel Jacoff (Cambridge, MA: Harvard University Press, 1986), 119–35.

27. On the Pilgrim's and Cavalcanti's similar interpretive errors in cantos 9 and 10, see Zygmunt Barański, "Inferno IX," in *Lectura Dantis Bononiensis*, ed. Emilio Pasquini and Carlo Galli (Bologna: Bononia University Press, 2012), 2:101–26.

28. On the standoff at the gates as an ironic anti-siege, see Zygmunt Barański, "'E Cominciare stormo': Notes on Dante's Sieges," in *"Legato con amore in un volume": Essays in Honour of John A. Scott*, ed. John J. Kinder and Diana Glenn (Florence: Olschki, 2012).

29. On the theological consequence of the *rex inutilis*, see Giorgio Agamben, *Il regno e la gloria: Per una genealogia teologica dell'economia e del governo* (Turin: Bollati Borighieri, 2009), esp. 99 and 113–14.

30. Dante's "Letter to the Florentines" deals with precisely this situation: a rebellious city's challenge to the sanctity of Henry VII's ambassadors. For background on Henry's failed descent into Italy, see William M. Bowsky, *Henry VII in Italy: The Conflict of Empire and City-State, 1310–1313* (Lincoln: University of Nebraska Press, 1960); and John A. Scott, *Dante's Political Purgatory* (Philadelphia: University of Pennsylvania Press, 1996), 40–50. For an introduction, helpful commentary and a translation of the "Letter to the Florentines" (Epistle VI), see Claire E. Honess, trans., *Dante Alighieri: Four Political Letters* (London: Modern Humanities Research Association, 2007), 57–68.

31. For the history of medieval diplomatic safe-conducts and the difficulties of ensuring their enforcement, see Gian Piero Bognetti, *Note per la storia del passaporto e del salvacondotto (a proposito di documenti genovesi del Sec. XII)* (Pavia: Tip. già cooperativa, 1933); and Donald E. Queller, *The Office of Ambassador*. In particular, see Bognetti, 265–66: "Too often Italian subjects would close the gates of the city before the sovereign and forbid passage to the emperor."

32. For the role of the legislator's will in ratifying privileges, a prime example of the subjective authority of the law, see Cortese, *La norma giuridica*, 2:39–99.

33. The quote from the jurist Baldus about the emperor's limitless jurisdiction is cited in Piero Bellini, "*Dominus totius mundi*: L'imperatore dei romani e i popoli estranei al popolo romano (sec. XII–XIV)," in *Popoli e spazio romano tra diritto e profezia* (Napoli: Edizioni scientifiche italiane, 1986), 247–71 (251).

34. On the special risk of reprisals for foreigners and diplomats, see William M. Bowsky, "Medieval Citizenship: The Individual and the State in the Commune of Siena, 1287–1355," *Studies in Medieval and Renaissance History* 4 (1967), 193–43 (236–37); and Queller, *The Office of Ambassador*, 176. This is precisely what the Furies threaten when they summon Medusa: vengeance for crimes previously committed in their territory by others of his mortal kind (in this case, the attempted abduction of Persephone by Theseus and Pirithoüs).

35. For an overview of these various identifications, see Alison Cornish, "Messo celeste," in *The Dante Encyclopedia*, 609–10; and Silvio Pasquazi, "Messo celeste," in *Enciclopedia dantesca* 3:201–7.

36. See Tobias Foster Gittes, "'O vendetta di Dio': The Motif of Rape and Retaliation in Dante's *Inferno*," *Modern Language Notes* 120 (2005), 1–29.

37. The relation between law and violence in the establishment of the Roman Empire had long preoccupied Dante. In *Monarchia* he tells us that as a young man he formerly believed that the Roman people had attained their supremacy "not by right but only by force of arms" (*nullo iure sed armorum tantummodo violentia*; 2.2). By the time of writing the *Convivio*, however, he seeks to counter that argument, that the Roman Empire was obtained by "forza" (force) rather than "ragione" (reason), by demonstrating that it was willed by divine providence. Expanding on this line of argument in Book Two of *Monarchia*, in response to whether universal Roman rule was acquired de jure or de facto, he asserts that the Roman victories were the result of a contest that revealed the judgment of God.

38. For the resemblances between Dante's portraits of Cato and of Moses as lawgiver, see Robert Hollander, *Allegory in Dante's Commedia* (Princeton, NJ: Princeton University Press, 1969), 124–26.

39. For Cato as a *figura* of Christian conversion, see Erich Auerbach, "Figura"

in *Scenes from the Drama of European Literature: Six Essays* (Minneapolis: University of Minnesota Press, 1984), 11–76 (64–67).

40. For overviews of the question of Cato's salvation, with pertinent bibliography, see Ronald L. Martinez, "Cato of Utica," in *The Dante Encyclopedia*, 146–49; and Scott, *Dante's Political Purgatory*, 69–84.

41. On the contrast between the violence of Caesar and Cato's "cult of justice," see Scott, *Dante's Political Purgatory*, 79–80. For the uses of Lucan in Dante's text, see in addition "Lucano e Dante," in *Antico e nuovo* (Rome: Salvatore Sciascia Editore, 1965), 165–210.

42. *Pharsalia* 9.279. English translation from Lucan, *Civil War*, trans. Susan H. Braund (Oxford and New York: Oxford University Press, 2008)

43. Giuseppe Mazzotta argues that in his portrayal of Cato, Dante emphasizes the continuity between the old man and the spiritual renewal of the new man in *Dante, Poet of the Desert: History and Allegory in the Divine Comedy* (Princeton, NJ: Princeton University Press, 1979), 36–65.

44. For interpretations of this rebuke as a palinode of Dante's philosophical poetry in the *Convivio*, see John Freccero, "Casella's Song: *Purgatorio* II, 12," in *Dante: The Poetics of Conversion*, ed. Rachel Jacoff (Cambridge, MA: Harvard University Press, 1986), 186–94; and Robert Hollander, "*Purgatorio* II: Cato's Rebuke and Dante's scoglio," *Italica* 52 (1975), 348–63.

45. "Dicitur autem privilegium quasi lex privata, id est, unius ante alios honor et dignitas aut immunitas eorum quae aliis communi iure incumbant." Quoted from the *Libellus de verbis* by Cortese (*La norma giuridica*, 2:46) as part of his illustration of how the two definitions and conceptualizations of *privilegium*—as private law and as immunity—often converged.

46. See Roberto Esposito, *Communitas: Origine e destino della comunità* (Turin: Einaudi, 2006), vii–xxii; and, by the same author, *Immunitas: Protezione e negazione della vita* (Turin: Einaudi, 2002), 5–9.

47. See discussion in Piano Mortari, "Ius singulare e privilegium," 295–96.

48. On the privileges and exemptions for the clergy in local regulations, see Bowsky, "Medieval citizenship," 235; and Menzinger,"Verso la costruzione," clxxi–clxxvi. For the specific privileges of the Jovial Friars, see the entry "Gaudenti" in Alessandro Lisini, ed., *Il costituto del Comune di Siena volgarizzato nel MCCCIX–MCCCX*, 2 vols. (Siena: Sordmuti di L. Lazzeri, 1903).

49. For the social and political context of the Jovial Friar order, see especially Antonio De Stefano, *Riformatori ed eretici del Medioevo* (Palermo: Società siciliana per la storia patria, 1990), 229–56.

50. "Quia nolunt communicare aliis bona sua, sed volunt tantummodo sibi habere." Quoted in De Stefano, *Riformatori ed eretici*, 221.

51. For the connection between the the Jovial Friar Catalano's use of "privilegio" in *Inferno* 23 and Guinizzelli's use of the term when comparing the Jovial Friar and poet Guittone d'Arezzo unfavorably to Dante in *Purgatorio* 26, see Ezio Raimondi, "I canti bolognesi dell'inferno dantesco," in *Dante e Bologna nei tempi di Dante* (Bologna: Commissione per i testi di lingua, 1967), 229–49; and Justin Steinberg, *Accounting for Dante: Urban Readers and Writers in Late Medieval Italy* (Notre Dame, IN: University of Notre Dame Press, 2007), 45–48.

52. For an incisive and still fundamental treatment of hypocrisy in this canto, see Raimondi, "I canti bolognesi." See now also Catherine Keen, "Fathers of Lies: (Mis)readings of Clerical and Civic Duty in *Inferno* XXII," in Paolo Acquaviva and Jennifer Petrie, ed., *Dante and the Church: Literary and Historical Essays* (Dublin:

Four Courts Press, 2007), 173–207. Citation and translation of Uguccione from the Durling/Martinez commentary of *Inferno*, 356.

53. The emphasis is in line with medieval theologians such as Peter Lombard, who held that the essential trait of hypocrisy was pride, not deceit. The hypocrite desires to obtain for himself a greater share of glory. See Silvana Vecchio, "Segreti e bugie: I peccata occulta," *Micrologus* 14 (2006), 41–58.

54. "Peso" (weight; 70); "la grave stola" (the weighty stole; 90); "sono di piombo sì grosse / che li pesi fan così cigolar le lor bilance" (They are so thick with lead that the weights make the balances creak; 101–2); "come pesa" (how he weighs; 120); and "li 'ncarcati" (the burdened ones; 147). In punishing the hypocrites with heavy weights, Dante may have had in mind a passage from the Matthew 23:4 which attacks the Pharisees for not bearing the weight they impose upon their flock: "For they bind heavy and insupportable burdens [*onera gravia et importabilia*] and lay them on men's shoulders: but with a finger of their own they will not move them."

55. The counterpart to the hypocritical friars, who are now charged, "'ncarcati" (*Inf.* 23.147), against their will, are the hypocritical public officials Dante describes in *Purgatorio* 6. Those venal officials jostle to bear the public charge, "lo comun incarco" (*Purg.* 6.133), for private gain.

56. See the discussion in Robert Durling's note "Christ in Hell," in Dante Alighieri, 1:580–81.

57. See Ernst Hartwig Kantorowicz, "*Pro Patria Mori* in Medieval Political Thought," in *Selected Studies* (Locust Valley, NY: J. J. Augustin, 1965), 308–324.

58. Aristocratic knights had long enjoyed immunities and advantages before the law, in part as remuneration for their service in the city's cavalry (for which they had to provide their own armor and maintain a warhorse). Many of these privileges and social distinctions are alluded to in *Paradiso* 15–16, especially in Cacciaguida's depiction of old Florence. Those distinctions included the right to bear arms, patrilineal inheritance of martial architecture ("Montemurlo" [*Par.* 16.64]), modes of dress reserved for nobles by the sumptuary laws ("manto" [mantle; *Par.* 16.7]), titles ("voi"), use of a family surname, and special access to public office ("degne di più alti scanni" [worthy of the highest seats; *Par.* 16.27]). On the privileges and duties of the medieval aristocratic knights, see Jean-Claude Maire Vigueur, "I privilegi della *militia*," in *Cavalieri e cittadini: Guerra, conflitti e società nell'Italia comunale* (Bologna: Mulino, 2004), 207–67; and Menzinger, "Verso la costruzione," cxxviii–cxxxviii.

59. On Dante's refashioning of the Virgilian epoch in these central cantos, see Jeffrey T. Schnapp, *The Transfiguration of History at the Center of Dante's Paradise* (Princeton, NJ: Princeton University Press, 1986).

60. On Dante and nobility, in addition to the essays cited below, see Girolami Arnaldi, "La nobiltà di Dante e Cacciaguida, ovvero la provvidenzialità della mobilità sociale," *La cultura* 2 (2003), 203–15 (208); Enrico Fiume, "Fioritura e decadenza dell'economia fiorentina," *Archivio storico italiano* 30 (1957), 399–401; M. Sanfilippo, "Dante nobile?" *Problemi* 63 (1982), 89–96 and 190–91.

61. Umberto Carpi, "La nobiltà di Dante (A proposito di *Paradiso* XVI)," *Rivista di letteratura italiana* 8 (1990), 229–60 (234–37).

62. John M. Najemy, "Dante and Florence," in *The Cambridge Companion to Dante*, ed. by Rachel Jacoff (Cambridge: Cambridge University Press, 1993), 80–99 (93).

63. Carpi apparently conflates magnates with nobles, and *popolani* with

merchants. Instead, the powerful banking families of Tuscany were typically allied with the ruling noble elite and were accordingly the primary targets of the anti-magnate laws. Jurists were similarly considered lords (*domini*) and were entitled to many of the same privileges of the ruling classes.

64. See especially Silvana Anna Bianchi and Gian Maria Varanini, "Statuti comunali e signoria: Verona e gli Scaligeri," and Gian Maria Varanini, "Propoganda dei regimi signorili: Le esperienze venete del Trecento," in *Le forme della propaganda politica nel Due e nel Trecento* (Rome: École française de Rome, 1994), 311–43.

See also Arnaldi's revisionary stance on Dante's supposed conservatism and condemnation of social mobility in "La nobiltà di Dante," 209–15.

65. "Civitas Sibi Faciat Civem: Bartolus of Sassoferrato's Doctrine on the Making of a Citizen," *Speculum* 48.4 (1973), 694–713; "'Ars Imitatur Naturam': A Consilium of Baldus on Naturalization in Florence," *Viator* 5 (1974), 289–332; "Baldo Degli Ubaldi's Contribution to the Rule of Law in Florence," in *VI centenario della morte di Baldo degli Ubaldi 1400–2000*, ed. Maria Grazia, Nico Ottaviani, Carla Frova, and Stefania Zucchini (Perugia: Università degli studi, 2005), 313–64.

66. On acquiring legal capacity and citizenship as a means of social ascendency, see Peter N. Reisenberg, "Citizenship and Law in Late Medieval Italy," *Viator* 5 (1974), 333–46.

67. Kirshner, "Civitas Sibi Faciat Civem," 309–10.

68. New citizens might be exempt from certain taxes for a period of five or ten years and even, on occasion, from building a house or providing services. See Bowsky, "Medieval Citizenship," 213.

69. On the legal and social problem of "sylvan citizens," see Bowsky, "Medieval Citizenship," 210–12.

70. Bowsky, "Medieval Citizenship," 210–11.

71. Riesenberg discusses Gandinus's and Baldus's views about loss of citizenship for nonperformance of civic duties in "Citizenship and Law," 341–42.

72. On Dante as warrior and knight, see Robert M. Durling and Ronald L. Martinez, *Time and the Crystal: Studies in Dante's Rime Petrose* (Berkeley and Los Angeles: University of California Press, 1990), 261–67.

73. See Jeffrey T. Schnapp, "Sant' Apollinare in Classe and Dante's Poetics of Martyrdom," in *The Transfiguration of History*, 170–238. On the political theology of citizenship, see also Julia Reinhard Lupton, *Citizen-Saints: Shakespeare and Political Theology* (Chicago: University of Chicago Press, 2005).

74. Simone Weil, *The Need for Roots: Prelude to a Declaration of Duties towards Mankind* (New York: G. P. Putnam's Sons, 1955); "Draft for a Statement of Human Obligations & Human Personality," in *Two Moral Essays by Simone Weil: Draft for a Statement of Human Obligations & Human Personality*, ed. Ronald Hathaway, trans. Richard Rhees (Wallingford, PA: Pendle Hill Pamphlet, 1981). For medieval views of citizenship based primarily on *munera* rather than *privilegia*, see Julius Kirshner, "Genere e cittadinanza nelle città-stato del Medioevo e del Rinascimento," in Giulia Calvi, ed. *Innesti: Donne e genere nella storia sociale* (Rome: Viella, 2004), 21–37 (23); and Menzinger, "Verso la costruzione," ccx.

Chapter 4

1. Although "nudum" in Roman law is often translated as "mere," I adopt the more literal "bare" or "naked" to preserve the metaphorical usage of medieval glossators, who spoke of "dressing" naked pacts and providing them with "garments."

2. The bibliography is vast. See the fundamental accounts in Guido Astuti, "Contratto (diritto intermedio)," in *Enciclopedia del diritto*, vol. 9, 759–74; Italo Birocchi, *Causa e categoria del contratto. Un problema dogmatico nella cultura privatistica dell'età moderna. I. Il cinquecento*. (Turin: G. Giappichielli editore, 1997), esp. 1–94; Francesco Calasso, *Il negozio giuridico: Lezioni di storia del diritto italiano* (Milan: Giuffrè, 1959); James Gordley, *The Philosophical Origins of Modern Contract Law* (Oxford: Oxford University Press, 1991); Paolo Grossi, *L'ordine giuridico medievale* (Rome and Bari: Laterza, 1995); esp. 242–53; Paolo Grossi, "Proprietà e contratto," in Maurizio Fioravanti, ed. *Lo Stato moderno in Europa: Istituzioni e diritto* (Rome and Bari: Laterza, 2002), 128–38; Paolo Grossi, "Sulla 'natura' del contratto (qualche nota sul 'mestiere' di storico del diritto, a proposito di un recente 'corso' di lezioni)," *Quaderni fiorentini* 15 (1986), 593–619; Raffaele Volante, *Il sistema contrattuale del diritto commune classico: Struttura dei patti e individuazione del tipo. Glossatori e Ultramontani* (Milan: Giuffrè editore, 2001); and Reinhard Zimmermann, *The Law of Obligations: Roman Foundations of the Civilian Tradition* (Oxford: Oxford University Press, 1996), 508–46 and 551–52.

3. Once one party had performed his or her side of the arrangement, however, even unnamed contracts might be enforceable. On innominate real contracts, see Zimmermann, *The Law of Obligations*, 532–37.

4. See Astuti's critical comments about the "Trionfo del principio consensuale" in "Contratto," 760.

5. Informal "consensual contracts" were restricted to those immediately recognizable transactions most important to daily life, such as sale, lease, mandate, and partnership. On consensual contracts, see Max Kaser, *Roman Private Law*, trans. Rolf Dannenbring (Pretoria: University of South Africa, 1980), 57 and 198–99; and Zimmerman, *The Law of Obligations*.

6. *Dig.* 2.14.7.4, *Iuris gentium*, § *Sed cum nulla subest*. In practice, naked pacts were not entirely without legal consequences, even in Roman law. For example, although a claimant could not bring a lawsuit on the basis of a *pactum nudum*, the debtor in a suit could assert an informal release from (or modification to) an obligation as a viable defense. See Zimmerman, *The Law of Obligations*, 508–9.

7. For medieval theories of vestments, see especially the excellent account in Birocchi, *Causa e categoria*, 31–94.

8. On the *quid* capable of dressing a pact, see Birocchi, *Causa e categoria*, 51.

9. The most complex and thorough account of these divergences is found in Volante, *Il Sistema Contrattuale*, which gives particular emphasis to the ultramontane school of jurists and their recognition of natural obligations as legally binding. For a synthetic account in English, see Gordley, *The Philosophical Origins*, 41–45.

10. See Grossi, *L'ordine giuridico medievale*, 245–46; Robert S. Lopez and Irving W. Raymond, ed. and trans., *Medieval Trade in the Mediterranean World: Illustrative Documents* (New York: Columbia University Press, 2001); Vito Piergiovanni, "Diritto commerciale nel diritto medievale e moderno," in *Digesto delle discipline privatistiche: Sezione commerciale* (Turin: UTET, 1989), 333–45; and Umberto Santarelli, *La categoria dei contratti irregolari: Lezioni di storia del diritto* (Turin: G. Giappichelli, 1984).

11. See the Ordinary Gloss to *Decretum Gratiani*, C.12, q. 2, c. 66, s. u. *promiserint*. On the role of the Church in the development of enforceable naked pacts, see Astuti, "Contratto," 774–75; Piero Bellini, *L'obbligazione da promessa con oggetto temporale nel sistema canonistico* (Milan: Giuffrè, 1964); Calasso, *Il negozio giuridico*,

261–83; James Gordley, "Good faith in contract law in the medieval *ius commune*," in *Good Faith in European Contract Law*, ed. Reinhard Zimmerman and Simon Whittaker (Cambridge: Cambridge University Press, 2000), 93–117 (99–100); and Zimmerman, *The Law of Obligations*, 542–44.

12. For the development of the concept of *causae* as related to medieval theories of contract, see especially Birocchi, *Causa e categoria generale*, 31–94; and Gordley, *The Philosophical Origins*, 49–45. For an in-depth look at the basis on which jurists qualified specific contracts in the period, see Andrea Massironi, *Nell'officina dell'interprete: La qualificazione del contratto nel diritto comune (secoli XIV–XVI)* (Milan: Giuffrè, 2012).

13. See Erich Auerbach, *Dante: Poet of the Secular World* (Chicago and London: University of Chicago Press, 1961); and *Literary Language and Its Public in Late Latin Antiquity and in the Middle Ages*, trans. Ralph Manheim (Princeton, NJ: Princeton University Press, 1993), esp. chapter 1, "Sermo Humilis."

14. See especially "'Tres enim sunt manerie dicendi . . .': Some Observations on Medieval Literature, 'Genre,' and Dante," in *Libri poetarum in quattuor species dividuntur": Essays on Dante and "Genre"*, ed. Zygmunt G. Barański (Reading, UK: University of Reading, 1995), 9–60; and the entries "Comedy" and "Commedia. Title and Form" in *The Dante Encyclopedia*, 180–81 and 184–88.

15. Barański, "Tres enim sunt," 18.

16. Barański, "Commedia. Title and Form," 186.

17. Barański, "Tres enim sunt," 10.

18. H. R. Jauss, "Theory of Genres and Medieval Literature," in *Toward an Aesthetic of Reception*, trans. Timothy Bahti (Minneapolis: University of Minnesota Press, 1982), 76–109.

19. On this "locus in life," see Jauss, "Theory of Genres," 102–3.

20. The terms of the debate were established in the works of Astuti and Calasso cited above. For a concise account, see Grossi, *L'ordine giuridico*, 243–45.

21. Dante uses a similarly nautical image of coasting into harbor to describe Guido favorably in *Convivio*, as an example of one who changed his way of life near the end as his soul prepared to return to God. Yet here in *Inferno* Guido reveals the dramatic circumstances that led to his moral backsliding and late shipwreck.

22. In his oft-cited definition, Ulpian derived the terms *pactum* (pact) and *pactio* (agreement) from the word for peace, *pax*. See *Dig.* 2.14.1.1, *Huius edicti*, § *Pactum autem a pactione*: "Pactum autem a pactione dicitur (inde etiam pacis nomen appellatum est)" (Moreover, pact is derived from agreement [the word peace comes from the same origin]).

23. For the *lex regia* and how it applied to the pope, see Ernst H. Kantorowicz, *The King's Two Bodies: A Study in Medieval Political Theology* (Princeton, NJ: Princeton University Press, 1997), 129–30.

24. On the distinction in Aquinas between the coercive and directive aspects of the law (cf. *Summa theologiae* IIa IIae, 96.5), see the discussion in Cortese, *Norma giuridica*, 1:151. On Accursius's qualifications of absolutist formulas found in Roman law, see Brian Tierney, "'The Prince Is Not Bound by the Laws': Accursius and the Origins of the Modern State," in *Comparative Studies in Society and History* 5 (1963), 378–400.

25. See Francis Oakley, *Omnipotence, Covenant, and Order: An Excursion in the History of Ideas from Abelard to Leibniz* (Ithaca, NY: Cornell University Press, 1984), 84–85.

26. On the reliability of the divine sovereign's covenant in theological discus-

sions, see William J. Courtenay, *Covenant and Causality in Medieval T. Studies in Philosophy, Theology, and Economic Practice* (London: Variorum, 1984) and Oakley, *Omnipotence, Covenant, and Order*.

27. See the especially suggestive readings by Robert Pogue Harrison, "Comedy and Modernity: Dante's Hell," *Modern Language Notes* 102.5 (1987), 1043–61; and Giuseppe Mazzotta, "The Light of Venus and the Poetry of Dante: *Vita Nuova* and *Inferno* XXVII," in *Modern Critical Views: Dante*, ed. Harold Bloom (New York: Chelsea, 1986), 189–204.

28. Although not immune from fashion and the marketplace, modes of dress were rigidly linked to status and social group in Dante's time, and these connections were further policed by local sumptuary laws. See Maria Giuseppina Muzzarelli, *Gli inganni delle apparenze* (Milan: Scriptorium, 1996); and Catherine Kovesi Killerby, *Sumptuary Law in Italy 1200–1500* (Oxford: Oxford University Press, 2002).

29. Text of poems in this section from Claudio Giunta's edition of the *Rime* in Dante Alighieri, *Opere*, vol. 1, ed. Marco Santagata (Milan: Mondadori, 2011). Translation based on Dante Alighieri, *Dante's Lyric Poetry*, ed. Kenelm Foster and Patrick Boyde, 2 vols. (Oxford: Oxford University Press, 1967).

30. Claudia Giunta, "Sulla 'vestizione' delle ballate nel medioevo," in *Codici: Saggi sulla poesia del Medioevo* (Bologna: Il Mulino, 2005), 239–52. See also his commentary of "Se Lippo amico" and "Per una ghirlandetta" in Dante Alighieri, *Opere*, ed. Santagata, 123–32 and 172–81.

31. In *De vulgari eloquentia* Dante speaks of a *canzone* being "wedded" ("nupta"; 2.8.5) to music. On the role of *vestizione* in Florentine and Tuscan society, especially for its legal status, see Julius Kirshner, "*L: emergent bisogni matrimoniali* in Renaissance Florence," in *Society and Individual in Renaissance Florence* (Berkeley: University of California Press, 2002), 79–109; and Christiane Klapisch-Zuber, "Zacharias, or the Ousted Father: Nuptial Rites in Tuscany between Giotto and the Council of Trent" and "The Griselda Complex: Dowry and Marriage Gifts in the Quattrocento," now in *Women, Family, and Ritual in Renaissance Italy*, trans. L. G. Cochrane (Chicago: University of Chicago Press, 1985), 178–212 and 213–46.

32. See the brief, lucid explanation given in Kenelm Foster, "Dante's Canzone 'Tre donne,'" *Italian Studies* 9 (1954), 56–68 (62).

33. See Ronald L. Martinez, "'Nasce il Nilo': Justice, Wisdom, and Dante's Canzone 'Tre donne intorno al cor mi son venute,'" in *Dante Now: Current Trends in Dante Studies*, ed. Theodore J. Cachey, Jr. (Notre Dame, IN: University of Notre Dame Press, 1995), 115–53, esp. 118. My reading of "Tre donne" owes much to this essay.

34. For the relationship of Drittura's vulnerability to that of personifications of Jerusalem in Lamentations, Lady Philosophy in Boethius's *Consolation of Philosophy*, and Lorenzetti's Justice in his fresco of Bad Government, see Martinez, "Nasce il Nilo," 124.

35. Gloss to *Dig.* 2.14.6: "Cum pactum nudum parere actionem tale sit ac si prorsus sterilis mulier generaret vel virgo pariat." Quoted in Astuti, "Contratto," 771.

36. See the recent review of arguments in Stefano Carrai, "Il doppio congedo di 'Tre donne intorno al cor mi son venute," *Le Rime di Dante: Gargnano del Garda (25–27 settembre 2008)*, ed. Claudia Berra and Paolo Borsa (Milan: Cisalpina, 2010), 197–211.

37. In a similar manner, in *De vulgari* 2.8.6 Dante describes the process of binding words together in a harmonious relationship as in itself a self-contained, completed action ("actio completa") whether or not these words are eventually set to music. This binding action lends the poem the name "canzone," not its "mar-

riage" to music and performance. Like certain Roman contracts, it is internally dressed and named.

38. For the historical context and date of composition of "Tre donne" see, most recently, the notes in Giunta's edition, with bibliography in *Opere*, ed. Santagata, 518–19.

39. Bibliography on Dante's title is obviously vast. See, among other works, Zygmunt G. Barański, "*Comedìa*: Notes on Dante, the Epistle to Cangrande, and Medieval Comedy," *Lectura Dantis* 8 (1991), 26–55; Barański, "Commedia: Title and Form," 184–88; Alberto Casadei, "Il titolo della *Commedia* e l'Epistola a Cangrande," *Allegoria* 60 (2009), 167–81; "*Commedia*. 1. Titolo" in the *Enciclopedia Dantesca*, 79–81; Lino Pertile, "*Canto-cantica-comedìa* e l'Epistola a Cangrande" *Lectura Dantis* 9 (1991), 105–23.

40. For a forceful denial of the Epistle's paternity based on the utter conventionality of its definitions of comedy, see Barański, "Comedìa: Notes on Dante, the Epistle to Cangrande, and Medieval Comedy."

41. See, for example, in addition to the works mentioned below for the Geryon scene in particular, Teodolina Barolini, *Dante's Poets: Textuality and Truth in the Comedy* (Princeton, NJ: Princeton University Press, 1984), 269–86; Franco Ferrucci, "Comedìa," *Yearbook of Italian Studies* 1 (1971), 29–52; and Amilcare A. Ianucci, "Dante's Theory of Genres and the *Divina Commedia*," *Dante Studies* 91 (1973), 1–25.

42. Barolini, *Dante's Poets*, 273.

43. *Dig.* 2.14.1.3, *Huius edicti*, § *Conventionis verbum generale*.

44. In this context, the allusion to Phaeton's fall in this canto is even more significant than previously thought. According to the Ovidian myth, the origin of Phaeton's mad flight was an equally rash pact—the promise, solemnized with an oath, on the part of the sun god to provide his son with any proof of paternity he wished.

45. See Zygmunt G. Barański, "The 'Marvelous' and the 'Comic': Toward a Reading of *Inferno* XVI," *Lectura Dantis*, 7 (1990), 72–95; Barolini, *Dante's Poets*, 213–14; Teodolina Barolini, *The Undivine Comedy: Detheologizing Dante* (Princeton, NJ: Princeton University Press, 1992), 58–73; Theodore J. Cachey, Jr., "Dante's Journey between Fiction and Truth: Geryon Revisited," in *Dante, da Firenze all'aldilà: Atti del terzo Seminario dantesco internazionale, Firenze, 9–11 giugno 2000*, ed. Michelangelo Picone, (Florence: Franco Cesati Editore, 2001), 75–92; and Ferrucci, "Comedìa."

46. For Geryon as a symbol of the hybridity of Dante's poem, monstrously violating Horatian decorum, see Barański, "The 'Marvelous' and the 'Comic,'" and Claudia Villa, "Per una tipologia del commento mediolatino: *L'Ars poetica* di Orazio," in *Il commento ai testi: Atti del seminario di Asona 2–9 ottobre 1989*, ed. Ottavio Besomi and Carlo Caruso (Basel, Boston, and Berlin: Birkhäuser, 1992), 19–42 (39).

47. Barolini, *The Undivine Comedy*, 59.

48. For a summary of view on the meaning of the cord, see commentary to Dante Alighieri, *The Divine Comedy of Dante Alighieri: Inferno*, trans. Robert M. Durling (Oxford and New York: Oxford University Press, 1996), 257–58.

49. The employment of the Florentine term "introque" (meanwhile; 20.13)–a word Dante eschews in the *De vulgari eloquentia* as unworthy of the illustrious vernacular (1.13.2)—as the last rhyme-word of canto 20 pre-announces the comic interlude of the next two cantos.

50. The bibliography is extensive, but in addition to contributions cited elsewhere in the notes and modern commentaries, see especially Antonio Pagliaro, "La rapsodia dei diavoli," in *Ulisse: Ricerche semantiche sulla Divina Commedia* (Messina and Florence: G. D'Anna, 1967), 311–24; Luigi Pirandello, "Il canto XXI dell'Inferno," in *Letture dantesche*, ed. G. Getto (Florence: Sansoni, 1964), 393–414; and Leo Spitzer, "The Farcical Elements in *Inferno*, Cantos XXI–XXIII," *Modern Language Notes* 59.2 (1944), 83–88.

51. See Guido Favati, "Il 'Jeu di Dante' (Interpretazione del canto XXI dell'*Inferno*)," *Cultura neolatina* 25 (1965), 34–52; and D. D. R. Owen, "Hell on the Stage," in *The Vision of Hell: Infernal Journey in Medieval French Literature* (Edinburgh: Scottish Academic Press, 1970), 224–52.

52. See Barolini, *Dante's Poets*, 222–23; Robert Hollander, "Virgil and Dante as Mind Readers (*Inferno* XXI and XXIII)," *Medioevo romanzo* 9 (1984), 85–100; Christopher Kleinhenz, "Deceivers Deceived: Devilish Doubletalk in Inferno 21–23," *Quaderni d'italianistica* 10 (1989), 133–56; and C. J. Ryan, "*Virgil and Dante: A Study in Contrasts,*" in *Italica* 59 (1982), 16–31.

53. Hollander's conviction that Dante continuously undercuts Virgil throughout the poem and in these cantos in particular is neatly summarized in his commentary to *Inferno* 21 in Dante Alighieri, *The Inferno*, trans. Robert Hollander and Jean Hollander (New York: Random House, 2002). See, for example: "Virgil's aplomb, his 'high style' contrasting with demonic 'vernacular,' serves at once to set him apart from the 'low-life' devils and their leader Malacoda, but also to make him seem slightly ridiculous" (395); and "Virgil's response to Dante's question, based on correct observation and resultant correct interpretation of the devils' true motives, marks yet another moment in this canto in which the reader is nearly forced to observe how harshly the guide is being treated by the author" (397).

54. In addition to this commentary, see especially "Virgil and Dante as Mind-Readers."

55. An egregious example of the latter can be found in Sam Guyler's interpretation of Virgil's last-minute rescue as an expression of his hypocrisy: "Virgil has been guilty of hypocrisy in his attempt to preserve the façade of authority" (35). See Sam Guyler, "Virgil the Hypocrite—Almost: A Re-interpretation of Inferno XXIII," *Dante Studies* 90 (1972), 25–42.

56. "As poet, Dante, with a snicker, has subtly pointed out the superiority of his own Christian poem to that of its pagan model." Guyler, "Virgil the Hypocrite," 39–40. This sentiment has become commonplace.

57. For a balanced account of the use of autobiography in these cantos, see Robert M. Durling, "Autobiography in Cantos 21–23," in his translation of *Inferno*, 567–68. For a recent reexamination of the autobiographical references behind the names of the Malebranche, see, with further bibliography, Simone Marchesi, "Distilling Ovid: Dante's Exile and Some Metamorphic Nomenclature in Hell," in *Writers Reading Writers: Intertextual Studies in Medieval and Early Modern Literature in Honor of Robert Hollander*, ed. Janet Levarie Smarr (Newark: University of Delaware Press, 2007), 21–39.

Conclusion

1. The poet's final reminiscence of that sheepfold wherein he slept as a lamb among wolves parallels the Pilgrim's last glance at earth, which appears to him from the heights of the stars as a mere "threshing floor" (*Par* 22.151).

2. In this sense the *poema sacro* may be *sacer* not only because of its sacred

subject matter but also because it is "consecrated, "sacrato" (*Par.* 23.62), as an inviolable collective good, like the city walls or the baptistery itself.

3. The *congedo* to another of Dante's late lyrics, "Amor, da che convien pur ch'io mi doglia" (Love, since after all I am forced to grieve)—the so-called "canzone montanina" (mountain song)—is linguistically even closer to *Paradiso* 25's proem. In its conclusion, Dante tells the poem that if "she" enters Florence she should assure its residents that, since he is now under the spell of a harsh woman, he can no longer wage war, "guerra" (81), against them. Likewise, even if they were to relax their harshness, "piega vostra crudeltate" (83), he would not be free to return. Compare also "fuor di sé mi serra" (locks me out from her; 78) and "fuor mi serra" (*Par.* 25.4).

4. Dante Alighieri, *Opere minori*, 2:596.

5. The first Florentine commentary to the poem similarly views Dante's imagined homecoming as deliberately reversing his legal infamy. See the gloss to "altra voce" (*Par.* 25.7): "Così com'io mi stii infamato *de crimine lesae majestatis*, così vi ritornerò con fama pura, netta da' vizii, ed accompagnato da virtù, e d'avere fatto giovamento alla repubblica di tutto il mondo con questa Commedia" (Just as I was defamed there by the crime of lese-majesty, I will return accompanied by virtue and with an intact fame, one unblemished by vices, having aided the republic and the entire world with this *Commedia*). *L'Ottimo commento della Divina Commedia: Testo inedito d'un contemporaneo di Dante citato dagli Accademici della Crusca*, ed. A. Torri, 3 vols. (Pisa: N. Capurro, 1827–29), 3:544.

Bibliography

Primary Sources

Alighieri, Dante. *Il Convivio*. Edited by Domenico de Robertis and Cesare Vasoli, in *Opere minori*, vol. 1, pt. 2. Milan and Naples: Ricciardi, 1988.

———. *De vulgari eloquentia*. Edited and translated by Steven Botterill. New York and Cambridge: Cambridge University Press, 1996.

———. *Dante's Il Convivio (The Banquet)*. Translated by Richard Lansing. New York: Garland Publishing, 1990.

———. *Dante's Lyric Poetry*. Edited by Kenelm Foster and Patrick Boyde, 2 vols. Oxford: Oxford University Press, 1967.

———. *The Divine Comedy of Dante Alighieri*. Translated by Robert M. Durling, 3 vols. New York and Oxford: Oxford University Press, 1996–2011.

———. *Epistolae: The Letters of Dante*. Translated by Paget Toynbee. Oxford: Clarendon Press, 1966.

———. *Four Political Letters*. Translated by Claire E. Honess. London: Modern Humanities Research Association, 2007.

———. *Inferno*. Translated by Jean and Robert Hollander. New York: Random House, 2002.

———. *Monarchia*. Edited and translated by Prue Shaw. Cambridge and New York: Cambridge University Press, 1995.

———. *Opere*. Edited by Marco Santagata. Milan: Mondadori, 2011.

———. *Le Opere di Dante*. Edited by Ermenegildo Pistelli. Florence: Società Dantesca Italiana, 1960.

———. *Opere minori*. Edited by Domenico De Robertis et al. Milan and Naples: Ricciardi, 1979.

———. *Vita nova*. Edited by Stefano Carrai. Milan: BUR, 2009.

Aquinas, Thomas. *Commentary on the Nicomachean Ethics*. Translated by C. I. Litzinger, O. P. Chicago: Henry Regnery Company, 1964.

Augustine of Hippo, *De natura et gratia*. Edited by Karl F. Urba and Joseph Zycha. Corpus Scriptorum Ecclesiasticorum Latinorum, 60. Vienna: Tempsky, 1913.

Gandinus, Albertus, *Tractatus de maleficiis*. In Hermann U. Kantorowicz, ed., *Albertus Gandinus und das Strafrecht der Scholastik*, vol. 2. Berlin and Leipzig: Walter de Gruyter, 1926.

Gratian, *Decretum*. In *Corpus iuris canonici*, vol. 1, edited by E. Friedberg. Leipzig: 1879 (reprinted Graz: Akademische Druck-u.Verlagsanstalt, 1955).

Decretales Gregorii IX. In E. Friedberg, ed. *Corpus iuris canonici*, vol 2. Leipzig: 1879 (reprinted Graz: Akademische Druck-u.Verlagsanstalt, 1955).

Hostiensis, *Lectura in quinque Decretalium Gregorianarum libros*. Venice: 1581 (reprinted 1965).

Justinian. *The Digest of Justinian*. Edited by Theodor Mommsen and Paul Krueger, translated by Alan Watson. Philadelphia: University of Pennsylvania Press, 1985.

Latini, Brunetto. *Rettorica*. In *Medieval Grammar and Rhetoric: Language Arts and Literary Theory, AD 300–147*. Edited by Rita Copeland and Ineke Sluiter. Oxford: Oxford University Press, 2009.

Lucan, *Civil War*. Translated by Susan H. Braund. Oxford and New York: Oxford University Press, 2008.

Piperata, Thomas de. *De fama*. In *Tractatus universi iuris*, vol. 11. fol. 8a, n. 1. Venice: 1584.

Scotus, John Duns. *Duns Scotus on the Will and Morality*. Edited and translated by Allan B. Wolter. Washington: Catholic University of America Press, 1986.

Virgil, *Aeneid*. Edited by H. Rushton Fairclough and William Heinemann,.2 vols. Cambridge, MA, and London: Harvard University Press, 1930.

Secondary Sources

Agamben, Giorgio. *Homo Sacer: Sovereign Power and Bare Life*. Translated by Daniel Heller-Roazen. Stanford, CA: Stanford University Press, 1998.

———. *Il regno e la gloria: Per una genealogia teologica dell'economia e del governo*. Turin: Bollati Boringhieri, 2009.

———. *State of Exception*. Translated by Kevin Attell. Chicago: University of Chicago Press, 2005.

Ahern, John. "Canto XXXII: Amphion and the Poetics of Retaliation." In *Lectura Dantis: Inferno. A Canto by Canto Commentary*, edited by Allen Mandelbaum, Anthony Oldcorn, and Charles Ross, 413–23. Berkeley: University of California Press, 1998.

Allegretti, Paola. "Canto XXVIII." In *Lectura dantis turicensis: L'Inferno*, edited by Georges Guntert and Michelangelo Picone, 393–406. Florence: Franco Cesati Editore, 2000.

Arendt, Hannah. *The Human Condition*. Chicago and London: University of Chicago Press, 1958.

Armour, Peter. "Dante's Brunetto: The Paternal Paterine?" *Italian Studies* 38 (1983), 1–38.

———. "Dante's *Contrapasso*: Context and Texts." *Italian Studies* 55 (2000), 1–20.

Arnaldi, Girolami. "La nobiltà di Dante e Cacciaguida, ovvero la provvidenzialità della mobilità sociale." *La cultura* 2 (2003), 203–15.

Ascoli, Albert Russell. *Dante and the Making of a Modern Author.* New York: Cambridge University Press, 2008.

Astuti, Guido. "Contratto (diritto intermedio)." In *Enciclopedia del diritto*, vol. 9: 759–84.

Auerbach, Erich. *Dante: Poet of the Secular World.* Chicago and London: University of Chicago Press, 1961.

———. "Figura." In *Scenes from the Drama of European Literature: Six Essays*, 11–76. Minneapolis: University of Minnesota Press, 1984.

———. *Literary Language and Its Public in Latin Latin Antiquity and in the Middle Ages.* Translated by Ralph Manheim. Princeton, NJ: Princeton University Press, 1993.

———. *Mimesis: The Representation of Reality in Western Literature.* Princeton, NJ, and Oxford: Princeton University Press, 2003.

Barański, Zygmunt. "*Comedìa*: Notes on Dante, The Epistle to Cangrande, and Medieval Comedy." *Lectura Dantis* 8 (1991), 26–55.

———. "'E cominciare stormo': Notes on Dante's Sieges." In *"Legato con amore in un volume": Essays in honour of John A. Scott*, edited by John J. Kinder and Diana Glenn 175–203. Florence: Olschki, 2012.

———. "Inferno IX." In *Lectura Dantis Bononiensis*, edited by Emilio Pasquini and Carlo Galli, 2:101–26. Bologna: Bologna University Press, 2012.

———. "The 'Marvelous' and the 'Comic': Toward a Reading of *Inferno XVI*." *Lectura Dantis* 7 (1990), 72–95.

———. "'Tres enim sunt manerie dicendi . . .': Some Observations on Medieval Literature, 'Genre,' and Dante, in *"Libri poetarum in quattuor species dividuntur": Essays on Dante and "Genre,"* edited by Zygmunt Barański, 9–60. Reading, UK: University of Reading, 1995.

Barbadoro, Bernardino. "La condanna di Dante e la difesa di Firenze guelfa." *Studi danteschi* 8 (1924), 111–27.

———. "La condanna di Dante e le fazioni politiche del suo tempo." *Studi danteschi* 2 (1920), 5–74.

Barolini, Teodolinda. *Dante's Poets: Textuality and Truth in the Comedy.* Princeton, NJ: Princeton University Press, 1984.

———. "Minos's Tail: The Labor of Devising Hell (*Aeneid* 6.431–33 and *Inferno* 5.1–23)." In *Dante and the Origins of Italian Literary Culture* 132–50. New York: Fordham University Press, 2006.

———. *The Undivine Comedy: Detheologizing Dante.* Princeton, NJ: Princeton University Press, 1992.

Bellini, Piero. "*Dominus totius mundi*: L'imperatore dei romani e i popoli estranei al popolo romano (sec. XII–XIV)." In *Popoli e spazio romano tra diritto e profezia*, 247–71. Naples: Edizioni scientifiche italiane, 1986.

———. *L'obbligazione da promessa con oggetto temporale nel sistema canonistico.* Milan: Giuffrè, 1964.

Beltrami, Piero G. "Metrica e sintassi nel canto XXVIII dell'*Inferno*." *Giornale storico della letteratura italiana* 162 (1985), 1–26.

Berlin, Isaiah. *Liberty*. Edited by Henry Hardy. Oxford: Oxford University Press, 2002.

Bianchi, Luca. "'Cotidiana miracula,' comune corso della natura e dispense al diritto matrimoniale: Il miracolo fra Agostino e Tommaso d'Aquino." *Quaderni storici* 131.2 (2009), 313–28.

Bianchi, Silvana Anna, and Gian Maria Varanini. "Statuti comunali e signoria: Verona e gli Scaligeri." In *Statuti di Verona del 1327*, edited by Silvana Anna Bianchi and Rosalba Granuzzo, 11–62. Rome: Jouvence, 1992.

Birocchi, Italo. *Causa e categoria del contratto: Un problema dogmatico nella cultura privatistica dell'età moderna: I. Il cinquecento*. Turin: G. Giappichielli editore, 1997.

Black, Jane. *Absolutism in Renaissance Milan: Plenitude of Power under the Visconti and the Sforza 1329–1535*. Oxford: Oxford University Press, 2009.

———. "The Visconti in the Fourteenth Century and the Origins of their *Plenitudo Potestatis*." In *Poteri signorili e feudali nelle Campagne dell'Italia settentrionale fra Tre e Quattrocento: Fondamenti di legittimità e forme di esercizio*, edited by Federica Cengarle, Giorgio Chittolini, and Gian Maria Varanini, 11–30. Florence: Firenze University Press, 2005.

Bloch, David J. "Res Sanctae in Gaius and the Founding of the City." *Roman Legal Tradition* 4 (2006), 48–64.

Bognetti, Gian Piero. *Note per la storia del passaporto e del salvacondotto (a proposito di documenti genovesi del Sec. XII)*. Pavia: Tip. Già Cooperativa, 1933.

Bourdieu, Pierre. *Pascalian Meditations*. Translated by Richard Nice. Stanford, CA: Stanford University Press, 2000.

Boureau, Alain. "Privilege in Medieval Societies from the Twelfth to the Fourteenth Centuries; or, How the Exception Proves the Rule." In *The Medieval World*, edited by Peter Linehan and Janet L. Nelson, 621–34. London and New York: Routledge, 2001.

Bowsky, William M. "Medieval Citizenship: The Individual and the State in the Commune of Siena, 1287–1355." *Studies in Medieval and Renaissance History* 4 (1967), 193–243.

———. *Henry VII in Italy: The Conflict of Empire and City-State, 1310–1313*. Lincoln: University of Nebraska Press, 1960.

Boyde, Patrick. *Perception and Passion in Dante's Comedy*. Cambridge: Cambridge University Press, 1993.

Brooks, Peter. *Troubling Confessions: Speaking Guilt in Law and Literature*. Chicago: University of Chicago Press, 2000.

Cachey, Theodore J., Jr. "Dante's Journey between Fiction and Truth: Geryon Revisited." In *Dante, da Firenze all'aldilà: Atti del terzo Seminario dantesco internazionale, Firenze, 9–11 giugno 2000*, edited by Michelangelo Picone, 75–92. Florence: Franco Cesati Editore, 2001.

Calasso, Francesco. *Il negozio giuridico: Lezioni di storia del diritto italiano*. Milan: Giuffrè, 1959.

Campanelli, Maurizio. "Le sentenze contro i bianchi fiorentini del 1302: Edizione critica." *Bullettino dell'Istituto Storico Italiano per il Medio Evo* 108 (2006), 187–377.

Caravale, Mario. *Ordinamenti giuridici dell' Europa medievale*. Bologna: Mulino, 1994.

Carpi, Umberto. "La nobiltà di Dante (A proposito di *Paradiso* XVI)." *Rivista di letteratura italiana* 8 (1990), 229–60.

Carrai, Stefano. "Il doppio congedo di 'Tre donne intorno al cor mi son venute.'" In *Le Rime di Dante: Gargnano del Garda (25–27 settembre 2008)*, edited by Claudia Berra and Paolo Borsa, 197–211. Milan: Cisalpina, 2010.

Casadei, Alberto. "Il titolo della *Commedia* e l'Epistola a Cangrande." *Allegoria* 60 (2009), 167–81.

Cassandro, Giovanni. "Signoria." *Novissimo Digesto Italiano*, 17 vols. Turin: UTET, 1957.

Castagnetti, Andrea, and Gian Maria Varanini, eds., *Il Veneto nel medioevo: Le signorie trecentesche, Verona*. Milan: Mondadori, 1995.

Cassata Contin, Adrina. "Le ferite di Manfredi: Un ipotesi." *Giornale storico della letteratura italiana* 183 (2006), 96–130.

Cassell, Anthony K. *Dante's Fearful Art of Justice*. Toronto: University of Toronto Press, 1984.

Cavallar, Osvaldo. "Regulating Arms in Late Medieval Italy." In *Privileges and Rights of Citizenship: Law and the Juridical Construction of Civil Society*, edited by Julius Kirshner and Laurent Mayali, 57–126. Berkeley: Robbins Collection Publications, University of California, 2002.

Cestaro, Gary. "Pederastic Insemination, or Dante in the Grammar Classroom." In *The Poetics of Masculinity in Early Modern Italy and Spain*, edited by Gerry Milligan and Jane Tylus, 41–73. Toronto: Centre for Reformation and Renaisance Studies, 2010.

Chiamenti, Massimiliano. "Dante Sodomita?" *L'Alighieri* 34 (2009), 133–48.

Chiffoleau, Jacques. "Le crime de majesté, la politique et l'extraordinaire: Note sur les collections érudites de proces de lèse-majesté du XVIIe siècle français et sur leurs exemples médiévaux." In *Le procès politique: XIVe–XVIIe siècle*, edited by Yves-Marie Bercé, 577–667. Rome: École française de Rome, 2007.

———. "Dire l'indicibile: Osservazioni sulla categoria del 'nefandum' dal XII al XV secolo." In *La parola all'accusato*, edited by Jean-Claude Maire Vigueur and Agostino Paravicini Bagliani, 359–481. Palermo: Sellerio, 1991.

———. "'Ecclesia de occultis non judicat?' L'Église, le secret et l'occulte du XIIe au XVe siècle." *Micrologus: Nature, Sciences and Medieval Societies* 13 (2005), 359–481.

Ciccaglione, Federico. "Le lettere arbitrarie nella legislazione angiona." *Rivista italiana per le scienze giuridiche* 28 (1899), 254–89.

Congar, Yves M. J. "Aspects ecclésiologiques de la querelle entre mendiants et séculiers dans la seconde moitié du XIIIe siècle et le début du XIVe siècle." *Archives d'histoire doctrinale et littéraire du Moyen Âge* 36 (1961), 35–151.

Conte, Emanuele, and Sara Menzinger, eds. *La Summa trium librorum di Rolando da Lucca (1195–1234): Fisco, politica, scientia iuris*. Rome: Viella, 2012.

Contini, Gianfranco. "Alcuni appunti su Purgatorio XXVII." In *Un'idea di Dante: Saggi danteschi*, 171–90. Turin: Giulio Einaudi, 1970.

Cornish, Allison. "Messo celeste." In *The Dante Encyclopedia*, edited by Richard Lansing. London and New York: Routledge, 2010.

Cortese, Ennio. "Casi di giustizia sommaria: Le lettere arbitrarie angione." In *Forme stragiudiziali o straordinarie di risoluzione delle controversie nel diritto comune e nel diritto canonico (atti del convegno di studi, Teramo, 21–22 Aprile 2004)*, edited by Piero Antonio Bonnet and Luca Loschiavo, 79–90. Naples: Edizioni scientifiche italiane, 2009.

———. "Nicolaus de Ursone de Salerno: Un'opera ignota sulle lettere arbitrarie angione nella tradizione dei trattati sulla tortura." In *Scritti*, edited by Italo

Birocchi and Ugo Petronio, 2 vols, 379–90. Spoleto: Centro italiano di studi sull'alto Medioevo, 1999.

———. *La norma giuridica: Spunti teorici nel diritto comune classico*, 2 vols. Milan: Giuffrè, 1962.

Corti, Maria. "Dante e la torre." In *Il viaggio testuale*, 245–56. Turin: Einaudi, 1978.

Courtenay, William J. *Capacity and Volition: A History of the Distinction of Absolute and Ordained Power*. Bergamo: P. Lubrina, 1990.

———. *Covenant and Causality in Medieval Thought: Studies in Philosophy, Theology, and Economic Practice*. London: Variorum, 1984.

Dalla Torre, G., Jr., "Infamia (dir. canonico)." In *Enciclopedia del diritto*, vol. 21, 387–91.

Del Giudice, Vincenzo. "Privilegio, dispensa, ed epicheia nel diritto canonico." In *Scritti in Memoria del Prof. Francesco Innamorati*, 227–81. Perugia: Tip. G. Guerra, 1932.

De Stefano, Antonio. *Riformatori ed eretici del Medioevo*. Palermo: Società siciliana per la storia patria, 1990.

De Vergottini, G. "Vicariato imperiale e signoria" and "Signorie e principati." In *Scritti di storia del diritto italiano*, 615–36. Milan: G. Rossi, 1977.

Di Capua, Francesco. "Insegnamenti retorici medievali e dottrine estetiche moderne nel *De vulgari eloquentia* di Dante." In *Scritti minori*, 302–14. Rome: Desclée, 1959.

Di Fonzo, Claudia. "Dante tra diritto, letteratura e politica." *Forum Italicum* 41/1 (spring 2007), 5–22.

Di Salvo, Andrea. "Il signore della Scala: Percezione e rielaborazioni della figura di Cangrande nelle testimonianze del secolo XIV." *Rivista storica italiana* 108 (1996), 36–87.

Douie, Decima L. *The Conflict between the Seculars and the Mendicants at the University of Paris in the Thirteenth Century*. London: Blackfriars, 1954.

Durling, Robert M. "The Primacy of the Intellect, the Sun, and the Circling Theologians." In Dante Alighieri, *Paradiso*, edited and translated by Robert M. Durling. Oxford and New York: Oxford University Press, 2011.

Durling, Robert M., and Ronald L. Martinez, *Time and the Crystal: Studies in Dante's Rime Petrose*. Berkeley and Los Angeles: University of California Press, 1990.

Esposito, Roberto. *Communitas: Origine e destino della comunità*. Turin: Einaudi, 2006.

———. *Immunitas: Protezione e negazione della vita*. Turin: Einaudi, 2002.

Falzone, Paolo. "Psicologia dell'atto umano in Dante: Problemi di lessico e di dottrina." In *Filosofia in volgare nel medioevo: Atti del Convegno della Società italiana per lo studio del pensiero medievale (S.I.S.P.M.), Lecce, 27–29 settembre 2002*, edited by Nadia Bray and Loris Sturlese, 331–66. Louvain-la-Neuve: Fédération internationale des instituts d'études médiévales, 2003.

Favati, Guido. "Il 'Jeu di Dante' (Interpretazione del canto XXI dell'*Inferno*)." *Cultura neolatina* 25 (1965), 34–52.

Ferrante, Joan M. *The Political Vision of the Divine Comedy*. Princeton, NJ: Princeton University Press, 1984.

Ferrara, Sabrina. "Tra pena giuridica e diritto morale: L'esilio di Dante nelle Epistole." *L'Alighieri* 40 (2012), 45–65.

Ferrucci, Franco. "Comedìa." *Yearbook of Italian Studies* 1 (1971), 29–52.

Fiori, Antonia. *Il giuramento di innocenza nel processo canonico medievale: Storia e disciplina nella "purgatio canonica"*. Frankfurt: Klostermann, 2013.

Fiume, Enrico. "Fioritura e decadenza dell'economia fiorentina." *Archivio storico italiano* 30 (1957), 399–401.

Fitting, Hermann. ed. *Juristische Schriften des früheren Mittelalters*. Halle: Buchhandlung des Waisenhauses, 1876.

Foster, Kenelm. "Dante's *Canzone* 'Tre donne.'" *Italian Studies* 9 (1954), 56–68.

Fraher, Richard M. "Conviction According to Conscience: The Medieval Jurists' Debate Concerning Judicial Discretion and the Law of Proof." *Law and History Review* 7 (1989), 23–88.

———. "The Theoretical Justification for the New Criminal Law of the High Middle Ages: 'Rei publicae interest, ne crimina remaneant impunita.'" *University of Illinois Law Review* (1984), 577–95.

Franklin, James. *The Science of Conjecture: Evidence and Probability before Pascal*. Baltimore: Johns Hopkins University Press, 2001.

Freccero, John. *Dante: The Poetics of Conversion*. Edited by Rachel Jacoff. Cambridge, MA: Harvard University Press, 1986.

———. "The Eternal Image of the Father." In *The Poetics of Allusion: Virgil and Ovid in Dante's Commedia*, edited by Rachel Jacoff, 62–76. Stanford, CA: Stanford University Press, 1991.

Gamberini, Andrea. *Lo stato visconteo: Linguaggi politici e dinamiche costituzionali*. Milan: Franco Angeli, 2005.

Garancini, Gianfranco. "'Consuetudo et statutum ambulant pari passu': La consuetudine nei diritti italiani del basso medioevo." *Rivista di storia del diritto italiano* 58 (1985), 19–55.

Garnsey, Peter. *Social Status and Legal Privilege in the Roman Empire*. Oxford: Oxford University Press, 1970.

Gilbert, Allan H. *Dante's Conception of Justice*. Durham, NC: Duke University Press, 1925.

Ginsberg, Warren. "Free Will." In *The Dante Encyclopedia*, edited by Richard Lansing, 425–27. London and New York: Routledge, 2010.

Gittes, Tobias Foster. "'O vendetta di Dio': The Motif of Rape and Retaliation in Dante's *Inferno*." *Modern Language Notes* 120 (2005), 1–29.

Giuliani, Alessandro. "The Influence of Rhetoric on the Law of Evidence." *Juridical Review* 3 (1962), 216–51.

Giunta, Claudia. "Sulla 'vestizione' delle ballate nel medioevo." In *Codici: Saggi sulla poesia del Medioevo*, 239–52. Bologna: Il Mulino, 2005.

Glorieux, Palémon. "Prélats français contre religieux mendicants: Autour de la bulle 'Ad fructus uberes' (1281–1290)." *Revue d'Histoire de l'Église de France* 11 (1925), 309–31.

Glucker, John. "*Probabile, Veri Simile*, and Related Terms." In *Cicero the Philosopher: Twelve Papers*, edited by J. G. F. Powell, 115–43. Oxford: Oxford University Press, 1995.

Gordley, James. "Good faith in contract law in the medieval *ius commune*." In *Good Faith in European Contract Law*, edited by Reinhard Zimmerman and Simon Whittaker, 93–117. Cambridge: Cambridge University Press, 2000.

———. *The Philosophical Origins of Modern Contract Law*. Oxford: Oxford University Press, 1991.

Gouron, André. "La notion de privilège dans la doctrine juridique du douzième siècle." In *Das Privileg im Europäischen Vergleich*, 2 vols., edited by Barbara Döle-meyer and Heinz Mohnhaupt, 1:1–16. Frankfurt am Main: Klostermann, 1999.

Greenblatt, Stephen. *Shakespeare's Freedom*. Chicago: University of Chicago Press, 2010.

Greenidge, A. H. J. *Infamia: Its Place in Roman Public and Private Law*. Oxford: Clarendon Press, 1894.

Grossi, Paolo. *L'ordine giuridico medievale*. Rome and Bari: Laterza, 1995.

———. "Proprietà e contratto." In *Lo Stato moderno in Europa: Istituzioni e diritto*, edited by Maurizio Fioravanti, 128–38. Rome and Bari: Laterza, 2002.

———. "Sulla 'natura' del contratto (qualche nota sul 'mestiere' di storico del diritto, a proposito di un recente 'corso' di lezioni)." *Quaderni fiorentini* 15 (1986), 593–619.

Grossvogel, Steven. "Justinian's *Jus* and *Justificatio* in *Paradiso* 6.10–27." *Modern Language Notes* 127.1 (supplement, January 2012), 130–37.

Guyler, Sam. "Virgil the Hypocrite—Almost: A Re-interpretation of Inferno XXIII." *Dante Studies* 90 (1972), 25–42.

Harrison, Robert Pogue. "Comedy and Modernity: Dante's Hell." *Modern Language Notes* 102.5 (1987), 1043–61.

Hawkins, Peter S. "Descendit ad Inferos." In *Dante's Testaments: Essays in Scriptural Imagination*, 99–124. Stanford, CA: Stanford University Press, 1999.

———. "Dido, Beatrice, and the Signs of Ancient Love." In *The Poetry of Allusion: Virgil and Ovid in Dante's Commedia*, edited by Rachel Jacoff and Jeffrey T. Schnapp, 113–30. Stanford, CA: Stanford University Press, 1991.

Hollander, Robert. *Allegory in Dante's Commedia*. Princeton, NJ: Princeton University Press, 1969.

———. "Dante and the Martial Epic." *Mediaevalia: A Journal of Medieval Studies* 12 (1989), 67–91.

———. "*Purgatorio* II: Cato's Rebuke and Dante's Scoglio." *Italica* 52 (1975), 348–63.

———. "Virgil and Dante as Mind Readers (*Inferno* XXI and XXIII)." *Medioevo Romanzo* 9 (1984), 85–100.

Honig, Bonnie. *Emergency Politics: Paradox, Law, Democracy*. Princeton, NJ: Princeton University Press, 2009.

Hutson, Lorna. "Imagining Justice: Kantorowicz and Shakespeare." *Representations* 106 (Spring 2009), 118–42.

———. *The Invention of Suspicion: Law and Mimesis in Shakespeare and Renaissance Drama*. Oxford: Oxford University Press, 2007.

Iannucci, Amilcare A. "Beatrice in Limbo: A Metaphoric Harrowing of Hell." *Dante Studies* 97 (1979), 23–45.

———. "Dante's Theory of Genres and the *Divina Commedia*." *Dante Studies* 91 (1973), 1–25.

———. "Dottrina e allegoria in *Inferno* VIII, 67–IX, 105." In *Dante e le forme dell'allegoresi*, edited by Michelangelo Picone, 99–124. Ravenna: Longo, 1987.

Jauss, H. R. "Theory of Genres and Medieval Literature." In *Toward an Aesthetic of Reception*, translated by Timothy Bahti, 76–109. Minneapolis: University of Minnesota Press, 1982.

Jussen, Bernhard. "*The King's Two Bodies* Today." *Representations* 106 (2009), 102–17.

Kahn, Victoria. "Political Theology and Fiction in *The King's Two Bodies*." *Representations* 106 (2009), 77–101.

Kantorowicz, Ernst Hartwig. *The King's Two Bodies: A Study in Medieval Political Theology*. Princeton, NJ: Princeton University Press, 1997.

———. "*Pro Patria Mori* in Medieval Political Thought." In *Selected Studies*, 308–24. Locust Valley, NY: J. J. Augustin, 1965.

———. "The Sovereignty of the Artist: A Note on Legal Maxims and Renaissance Theories of Art." In *Selected Studies*, 352–65. Locust Valley, NY: J. J. Augustin, 1965.

Kaser, Max. "Infamia und Ignominia in den römischen Rechtsquellen." In *Zeitschrift der Savigny-Stiftung für Rechtsgeschichte: Romanistische Abteilung* 27 (1956), 220–78.

———. *Roman Private Law*. Translated by Rolf Dannenbring. Pretoria: University of South Africa Press, 1980.

Kay, Richard. *Dante's Swift and Strong: Essay on "Inferno" XV*. Lawrence: Regents Press of Kansas, 1978.

Keen, Catherine. "Fathers of Lies: (Mis)readings of Clerical and Civic Duty in *Inferno* XXII." In Paolo Acquaviva and Jennifer Petrie, eds., *Dante and the Church: Literary and Historical Essays*, 173–207. Dublin: Four Courts Press, 2007.

Kelly, Henry Ansgar. "Inquisitorial Due Process and the Status of Secret Crimes." In *Proceedings of the Eighth International Congress of Medieval Canon Law* (UCSD 1988), edited by Stanley Chodorow, 407–28. Vatican City: Biblioteca Apostolica Vaticana, 1992.

Kelly, J. M. *Studies in the Civil Judicature of the Roman Republic*. Oxford: Oxford University Press, 1970.

Kéry, Lotte. "Non enim homines de occultis, sed de manifestis iudicant: La culpabilité dans le droit pénal de l'Église à l'époque classique." *Revue du droit canonique* 53/2 (2003), 311–36.

Killerby, Catherine Kovesi. *Sumptuary Law in Italy 1200–1500*. Oxford: Oxford University Press, 2002.

Kirshner, Julius. "'Ars Imitatur Naturam': A Consilium of Baldus on Naturalization in Florence." *Viator* 5 (1974), 289–332.

———. "Baldo degli Ubaldi's Contribution to the Rule of Law in Florence." In *VI centenario della morte di Baldo degli Ubaldi 1400–2000*, edited by Maria Grazia, Nico Ottaviani, Carla Frova, and Stefania Zucchini, 313–64 (Perugia: Università degli studi, 2005).

———. "Civitas Sibi Faciat Civem: Bartolus of Sassoferrato's Doctrine on the Making of a Citizen." *Speculum* 48.4 (1973), 694–713.

———. "Custom, Customary Law and *Ius Commune* in Francesco Guicciardini." In *Bologna nell'età di Carlo V e Guicciardini*, edited by Emilio Pasquini and Paolo Prodi, 151–79. Bologna: Il Mulino, 2002.

———. "*Li emergenti bisogni matrimoniali* in Renaissance Florence." In *Society and Individual in Renaissance Florence*, 79–109. Berkeley: University of California Press, 2002.

———. "Genere e cittadinanza nelle città-stato del Medioevo e del Rinascimento." In *Innesti: Donne e genere nella storia sociale*, edited by Giulia Calvi, 21–37. Rome: Viella, 2004.

Klapisch-Zuber, Christiane. *Women, Family, and Ritual in Renaissance Italy*. Translated by L. G. Cochrane. Chicago: University of Chicago Press, 1985.

Kleinhenz, Christopher. "Deceivers Deceived: Devilish Doubletalk in *Inferno* 21–23." *Quaderni d'italianistica* 10 (1989), 133–56.

Korolec, J. B. "Free Will and Free Choice." In *The Cambridge History of Later*

Medieval Philosophy: From the Rediscovery of Aristotle to the Disintegration of Scholasticism, 1100–1600, edited by Norman Kretzmann, Anthony Kenny, and Jan Pinborg, 629–41. Cambridge: Cambridge University Press, 1982.

Kuehn, Thomas. "Fama as a legal status in Renaissance Florence." In Fama: The Politics of Talk and Reputation in Medieval Europe, edited by Thelma Fenster and Daniel Lord Smail, 27–46. Ithaca, NJ: Cornell University Press, 2003.

Kuttner, Stephen. "Ecclesia de occultis non iudicat: Problemata ex doctrina poenali decretistarum et decretalistarum a Gratiano usque ad Gregorium PP. IX." In Acta congressus iuridici internationalis, Romae 1934, vol. 3, 225–46. Rome: Pontificum Institutum Utriusque, 1936.

———. Kanonistische Schuldlehre von Gratian bis auf die Dekretalen Gregors IX. Vatican City: Biblioteca Apostolica Vaticana, 1935.

Landau, Peter. Die Entstehung des Kanonischen Infamienbegriffs von Gratian bis zur Glossa ordinaria. Cologne and Graz: Böhlau Verlag, 1966.

Lear, Jonathan. Radical Hope: Ethics in the Face of Cultural Devastation. Cambridge, MA: Harvard University Press, 2006.

Lefebre, Charles. Les pouvoirs du Juge en droit canonique. Paris: Thèse Droit, 1938.

Lepsius, Susanne. "Public Responsibility for Failure to Prosecute Crime? An Inquiry into an Umbrian Case by Bartolo da Sassoferrato." In A Renaissance of Conflicts: Visions and Revisions of Law and Society in Italy and Spain, edited by John A. Marino and Thomas Kuehn, 131–70. Toronto: Center for Reformation and Renaissance Studies, 2004.

Lieberknecht, Otfried. "A Medieval Christian View of Islam: Dante's Encounter with Mohammed in Inferno XXVIII." Accessed at www.lieberknecht.de/~diss/papers/p_moham.pdf.

Lisini, Alessandro, ed. Il costituto del Comune di Siena volgarizzato nel MCCCIX–MCCCX. Siena: Sordmuti di L. Lazzeri, 1903.

Livingston, John. "Infamia in the Decretists from Rufinus to Johannes Teutonicus." PhD dissertation, University of Wisconsin, 1962.

Lombardi, Giorgio. "Spazio e frontiera. Tra eguaglianza e privilegio: Problemi costituzionali tra storia e diritto." In La frontiera da Stato a Nazione: Il caso Piemonte, edited by C. Ossola, C. Raffestin, and M. Ricciardi, 385–406. Rome: Bulzoni, 1987.

Lopez, Robert S., and Irving W. Raymond, ed. and trans. Medieval Trade in the Mediterranean World: Illustrative Documents. New York: Columbia University Press, 2001.

Lupton, Julia Reinhard. Citizen-Saints: Shakespeare and Political Theology. Chicago: University of Chicago Press, 2005.

Maccarrone, Michele. "Teologia e diritto canonico nella Monarchia III, 3." Rivista di storia della chiesa 5 (1951), 7–42.

Maffi, Alberto. "La costruzione giuridica dell'infamia nell'ordinamento romano." In La fiducia secondo i linguaggi del potere, edited by Paolo Prodi, 41–51. Bologna: Il Mulino, 2008.

Maire Vigueur, Jean-Claude. "Giudici e testimoni a confronto." In La parola all'accusato, edited by Jean-Louis Biget, Jean-Claude Maire Vigueur, and Agostino Paravicini Bagliani, 105–23. Palermo: Sellerio, 1991.

———. "I privilegi della militia." In Cavalieri e cittadini: Guerra, conflitti e società nell'Italia comunale, 207–67. Bologna: Il Mulino, 2004.

Mallette, Karla. "Muhammad in Hell." Dante Studies 125 (2007), 207–24.

Marchesi, Simone. "Distilling Ovid: Dante's Exile and Some Metamorphic Nomenclature in Hell." In *Writers Reading Writers: Intertextual Studies in Medieval and Early Modern Literature in Honor of Robert Hollander*, edited by Janet Levarie Smarr, 21–39. Newark, DE: University of Delaware Press, 2007.

Marchetti, Paolo. *De iure finium: Diritto e confini tra tardo medievo ed età moderna.* Milan: Giuffrè, 2001.

Marrone, John. "The Absolute and Ordained Powers of the Pope: A Quodlibetal Question of Henry of Ghent." *Mediaeval Studies* 36 (1974), 7–27.

Martinez, Ronald L. "Cato of Utica." In *The Dante Encyclopedia*, edited by Richard Lansing, 146–49. London and New York: Routledge, 2010.

——. "Dante between Hope and Despair: The Tradition of Lamentations in the *Divine Comedy.*" *Logos: A Journal of Catholic Thought and Culture* 5, no.3 (2002), 45–76.

——. "'Nasce il Nilo': Justice, Wisdom, and Dante's Canzone 'Tre donne intorno al cor mi son venute." In *Dante Now: Current Trends in Dante Studies*, edited by Theodore J. Cachey Jr., 115–53. Notre Dame, IN: University of Notre Dame Press, 1995.

——. "The Poetry of Schism." In Dante Aligheri, *Inferno*, edited by Robert M. Durling and Ronald R. Martinez. Oxford: Oxford University Press, 1997.

Masi, Gino. *Verso gli albori del principato in Italia: Note di storia del diritto pubblico.* Bologna: N. Zanichelli, 1936.

Massironi, Andrea. *Nell'officina dell'interprete: La qualificazione del contratto nel diritto comune (secoli XIV–XVI).* Milan: Giuffrè, 2012.

Mattingly, Garrett. *Renaissance Diplomacy.* Baltimore: Penguin, 1955.

Mayali, Laurent. "The Concept of Discretionary Punishment in Medieval Jurisprudence." In *Studia in honorem Eminentissimi Cardinalis Alphonsi M. Stickler*, edited by Rosalio José Castillo Lara, 299–315. Rome: Libreria Ateneo Salesiano, 1992.

——. "La coutume dans la doctrine romaniste au Moyen Age." In *La coutume-Custom*, a special issue of *Recueils de la Société Jean Bodin* 52 (1990), 11–31.

Mazzacane, Aldo. "Infamia (storia)." In *Enciclopedia del diritto*, vol. 21, 383–87.

Mazzotta, Giuseppe. *Dante, Poet of the Desert: History and Allegory in the Divine Comedy.* Princeton, NJ: Princeton University Press, 1979.

——. "The Light of Venus and the Poetry of Dante: *Vita Nuova* and *Inferno* XXVII." In *Modern Critical Views: Dante*, edited by Harold Bloom, 189–204. New York: Chelsea, 1986.

——. "Metaphor and Justice." In *Dante's Vision and the Circle of Knowledge.* 75–95. Princeton, NJ: Princeton University Press, 1993.

Meccarelli, Massimo. *Arbitrium: Un aspetto sistematico degli ordinamenti giuridici in età di diritto comune.* Milan: Giuffrè, 1998.

——. "Paradigma dell'eccezione nella parabola della modernità penale: Una prospettiva storico-giuridica." In "Sistemi di eccezioni," a volume of *Quaderni storici* 131 (2009), 493–521.

Menzinger, Sara. "Pareri eccezionali: Procedure decisionali ordinarie e straordinarie nella politica comunale del XIII secolo." In "Sistemi di eccezioni," a volume of *Quaderni storici* 131 (2009), 399–410.

Migliorino, Francesco. *Fama e infamia: Problemi della società medievale nel pensiero giuridico nei secoli XII e XIII.* Catania: Editrice Giannotta, 1985.

Milani, Giuliano. "Appunti per una riconsiderazione del bando di Dante." *Bollettino di Italianistica* 8/2 (2011), 42–70.

————. L'esclusione dal comune: Conflitti e bandi politici a Bologna e in altre città italiane tra XII e XIV secolo. Rome: Istituto Storico Italiano per il Medio Evo, 2003.

————. "Legge ed eccezione nei comuni di Popolo del XIII secolo (Bologna, Perugia, Pisa)." In "Sistemi di eccezioni," a volume of Quaderni storici 131 (2009), 377–98.

Musa, Mark. Advent at the Gates. Bloomington: Indiana University Press, 1974.

Muzzarelli, Maria Giuseppina. Gli inganni delle apparenze. Milan: Scriptorium, 1996.

Najemy, John M. "Dante and Florence." In The Cambridge Companion to Dante, edited by Rachel Jacoff, 80–99. Cambridge: Cambridge University Press, 1993.

Nardi, Bruno. Introduction to Dante Alighieri, Opere minori, 3: 241–69. Milan and Naples: Ricciardi, 1979.

————. Nel Mondo di Dante. Rome: Edizioni di storia e letteratura, 1944.

Oakley, Francis. "The Absolute and Ordained Power of God in Sixteenth- and Seventeenth-Century Theology." Journal of the History of Ideas 59.3 (1998), 437–61.

————. Omnipotence, Covenant, and Order: An Excursion in the History of Ideas from Abelard to Leibniz. Ithaca, NY: Cornell University Press, 1984.

Ortalli, Gherardo. La pittura infamante nei secoli XIII–XVI. Rome: Jouvence, 1979.

Owen, D. D. R. "Hell on the Stage." In The Vision of Hell: Infernal Journey in Medieval French Literature, 224–52. Edinburgh: Scottish Academic Press, 1970.

Pagliaro, Antonio. "La rapsodia dei diavoli." In Ulisse: Ricerche semantiche sulla Divina Commedia, 311–24. Messina and Florence: G. D'Anna, 1967.

Paratore, Ettore. "Analisi 'retorica' del canto di Pier della Vigna." Studi danteschi 42 (1965), 281–336.

————. "Il caso di Brunetto Latini." in Poesia e storia nella "Divina Commedia," edited by Gianfranco Folena and P. V. Mengaldo, 163–200. Vicenza: Neri Pozza editore, 1965.

————. "La Divina Commedia, poema della libertà dell'individuo e il canto XXVII del Purgatorio." In Dante: Raccolta di studi (per il Secentenario della morte di Dante 1321), edited by Alojzij Res, 9–41. Gorizia: Paternolli, 1921.

————. "Lucano e Dante." in Antico e nuovo, 165–210. Rome: Salvatore Sciascia editore, 1965.

Pasquazi, Silvio. "Messo celeste." In Enciclopedia dantesca, vol. 3, 201–7. Rome: Istituto della Enciclopedia Italiana, 1970–78.

Passerin d'Entrèves, Alessandro. Dante as a Political Thinker. Oxford: Oxford University Press, 1952.

Pastore Stocchi, Manlio. "Delusione e giustizia nel canto XV dell'Inferno." Letture classensi 3 (1970), 219–54.

Pennington, Kenneth. The Prince and the Law, 1200–1600: Sovereignty and Rights in the Western Legal Tradition. Berkeley: University of California Press, 1993.

Pequigney, Joseph. "Sodomy in Dante's Inferno and Purgatorio." Representations 36 (1991), 22–42.

Pertile, Lino. "Canto XXIX: Such Outlandish Wounds." In Lectura Dantis: Inferno, edited by Allen Mandlebaum, Anthony Oldcorn, and Charles Ross, 378–91. Berkeley and Los Angeles: University of California Press, 1998.

————. "Canto-cantica-comedìa e l'Epistola a Cangrande." Lectura Dantis 9 (1991), 105–23.

Peters, Edward. "'Crimen Exceptum': The History of an Idea." In Proceedings of the

Tenth International Congress of Medieval Canon Law: Syracuse, New York, 13–18 August 1996137–94. Vatican City: Biblioteca Apostolica Vaticana, 2001.

———. "Wounded Names: The Medieval Doctrine of Infamy." In Law and Mediaeval Life and Thought, edited by Edward B. King and Susan J. Ridyard, 43–89. Sewanee, TN: Press of the University of the South, 1990.

Pézard, André. Dante sous la pluie de feu. Paris: Vrin, 1950.

Piano Mortari, Vincenzo. "Ius singulare e privilegium nel pensiero dei glossatori." Rivista italiana per le scienze giuridiche 9 (1957–58), 271–350.

Piattoli, Renato, ed., Codice diplomatico dantesco. Florence: L. Gonnelli, 1950.

Picone, Michelangelo. "I trovatori di Dante: Bertran de Born." Studi e problemi di critica testuale 19 (1979), 71–94.

Picotti, G. B. "Qualche osservazione sui caratteri delle signorie italiane." Rivista storica italiana (1926), 7–30.

Piergiovanni, Vito. "Diritto commerciale nel diritto medievale e moderno." In Digesto delle discipline privatistiche: Sezione commerciale, 333–45. Turin: UTET, 1989.

Pirandello, Luigi. "Il canto XXI dell'Inferno." In Letture dantesche, edited by G. Getto, 393–414. Florence: Sansoni, 1964.

Porro, Pasquale. "Henry of Ghent on Ordained and Absolute Power." In Henry of Ghent and the Transformation of Scholastic Thought: Studies in Memory of Jos Decorte, edited by Guy Guldenstops and Carlos Steel, 387–408. Leuven: Leuven University Press, 2003.

Potts, Timothy C. "Conscience." In The Cambridge History of Later Medieval Philosophy: From the Rediscovery of Aristotle to the Disintegration of Scholasticism, 1100–1600, edited by Norman Kretzmann, Anthony Kenny and Jan Pinborg, 687–704. Cambridge and New York: Cambridge University Press, 1982.

Queller, Donald E. The Office of Ambassador in the Middle Ages. Princeton, NJ: Princeton University Press, 1967.

Raimondi, Ezio. "I canti bolognesi dell'Inferno dantesco." In Dante e Bologna nei tempi di Dante, 229–49. Bologna: Commissione per i testi di lingua, 1967.

Randi, Eugenio. Il sovrano e l'orologiaio: Due immagini di Dio nel dibattito sulla "potentia absoluta" fra XIII e XIV secolo. Florence: La Nuova Italia, 1987.

Rosoni, Isabella. Quae singula non prosunt collecta iuvant. Milan: Giuffrè, 1969.

Rust, Jennifer. "Political Theologies of the Corpus Mysticum: Schmitt, Kantorowicz, and de Lubac." In Political Theology and Early Modernity, edited by Graham Hammill and Julia Reinhard Lupton, 102–23. Chicago: University of Chicago Press, 2012.

Ryan, Christopher J. "Virgil and Dante: A Study in Contrasts." Italica 59 (1982), 16–31.

Sanfilippo, Mario. "Dante nobile?" Problemi 63 (1982), 89–96 and 190–191.

Santarelli, Umberto. La categoria dei contratti irregolari: Lezioni di storia del diritto. Turin: G. Giappichelli, 1984.

Santner, Eric L. The Royal Remains: The People's Two Bodies and the Endgames of Sovereignty. Chicago: University of Chicago Press, 2011.

Sbriccoli, Mario. "Giustizia negoziata, giustizia egemonica: Riflessione su una nuova fase degli studi di storia della giustizia criminale." In Criminalità e giustizia in Germania e in Italia: Pratiche giudiziarie e linguaggi giuridici tra tardo medioevo ed età moderna, edited by Marco Bellabarba, Gerd Schwerhoff, and Andrea Zorzi, 345–64. Bologna: Il Mulino / Istituto storico italo-germanico in Trento, 2001.

————. *L'interpretazione dello statuto: Contributo allo studio della funzione dei giuristi nell'età comunale*. Milan: Giuffrè, 1969.

————. "'Tormentum idest torquere mentem': Processo inquisitorio e interrogatorio per tortura nell'Italia comunale." In *La parola all'accusato*, edited by Jean-Claude Maire Vigueur and Agostino Paravicini Bagliani, 17–32. Palermo: Sellerio, 1991.

————. "Vidi communiter observari': L'emersione di un ordine penale pubblico nelle città italiane del secolo XIII." *Quaderni fiorentini: Per la storia del pensiero giuridico moderno* 27 (1998), 231–68.

Schioppa, Antonio Padoa. "La coscienza del giudice." In *Italia ed Europa nella storia del diritto: Collezione di testi e di studi*, 251–92. Bologna: Il Mulino, 2003.

Schmitt, Carl. *Political Theology: Four Chapters on the Concept of Sovereignty*. Edited and translated by George Schwab. Chicago: University of Chicago Press, 1985.

Schnapp, Jeffrey T. *The Transfiguration of History at the Center of Dante's Paradise*. Princeton, NJ: Princeton University Press, 1986.

Scott, John A. *Dante's Political Purgatory*. Philadelphia: University of Pennsylvania Press, 1996.

Senior, Matthew. *In the Grip of Minos: Confessional Discourse in Dante, Corneille, and Racine*. Columbus: Ohio State University Press, 1994.

Shapiro, Barbara J. *"Beyond a Reasonable Doubt" and "Probable Cause": Historical Perspectives on the Anglo-American Law of Evidence*. Berkeley: University of California Press, 1991.

Singleton, Charles S. *Dante Studies 2: Journey to Beatrice*. Cambridge, MA: Harvard University Press, 1958.

Sloan, Michael C. "Aristotle's *Nicomachean Ethics* as the Original Locus for the *Septem Circumstantiae*." *Classical Philology* 105 (2010), 236–51.

Spitzer, Leo. "The Farcical Elements in *Inferno*, Cantos XXI–XXIII." *Modern Language Notes* 59.2 (1944), 83–88.

————. "Speech and Language in Inferno XIII." *Italica* 19 (1942), 77–104.

Stabile, Giorgio. "Sì-oc-öil: In signum eiusdem principii. Dante contro le barriere di confini e linguaggi." In *Dante e la filosofia della natura: Percezioni, linguaggi, cosmologie*, 253–70. Florence: SISMEL, Edizioni del Galluzzo, 2007.

————. "Volontà." In *Enciclopedia Dantesca*, vol. 5, 1134–40. Rome: Istituto della Enciclopedia Italiana, 1970–78.

Starn, Randolph. *Contrary Commonwealth: The Theme of Exile in Medieval and Renaissance Italy*. Berkeley: University of California Press, 1982.

Stocchi, Manlio Pastore. "Il canto V del *Paradiso*." *Nuove letture dantesche*, vol. 5, 341–74. Florence: Le Monnier, 1972.

Steinberg, Justin. *Accounting for Dante: Urban Readers and Writers in Late Medieval Italy*. Notre Dame, IN: University of Notre Dame Press, 2007.

Storti Storchi, Claudia. *Scritti sugli statuti Lombardi*. Milan: Giuffrè, 2007.

Taylor, Charles. *A Secular Age*. Cambridge, MA: Harvard University Press, 2007.

Théry, Julien. "Fama: L'opinion publique comme preuve judiciare. Aperçu sur la révolution médiévale de l'inquisitoire (XIIe–XIVe siècles)." In *La preuve en justice, de l'antiquité à nos jours*, edited by Bruno Lemesle, 119–47. Rennes: Presses Universitaires de Rennes, 2002.

————. "'Atrocitas/enormitas': Per una storia della categoria di 'crimine enorme' nel basso Medioevo (XII–XV secolo)." *Quaderni storici* 131.2 (2009), 329–76.

Tierney, Brian. *The Idea of Natural Rights: Studies on Natural Rights, Natural Law,* and *Church Law, 1150–1625*. Grand Rapids, MI, and Cambridge: Eerdmans, 2001.

———. "'The Prince Is Not Bound by the Laws': Accursius and the Origins of the Modern State." *Comparative Studies in Society and History* 5 (1963), 378–400.

Till Davis, Charles. *Dante and the Idea of Rome*. Oxford: Clarendon Press, 1957.

Todeschini, Giacomo. *Visibilmenti crudeli: Malviventi, persone sospette e gente qualunque dal Medioevo all'età moderna*. Bologna: Il Mulino, 2007.

Torri, A., ed. *L'Ottimo commento della Divina Commedia: Testo inedito d'un contemporaneo di Dante citato dagli Accademici della Crusca*, 3 vols. Pisa: N. Capurro, 1827–29.

Ullmann, Walter. "Medieval Principles of Evidence." *Law Quarterly Review* (1946), 77–87.

Vallerani, Massimo. "Il guidice e le sue fonti: Note su inquisitio e fama nel *Tractatus de maleficiis* di Alberto da Gandino," *Rechtsgeschichte: Zeitschrift des Max-Planck-Instituts für europäische Rechtsgeschichte* 14 (2009), 40–61.

———. *La giustizia pubblica medievale*. Bologna: Il Mulino, 2005.

———. *Medieval Public Justice*. Translated by Sarah Rubin Blanshei. Washington: Catholic University of America Press, 2012.

———. "Modelli di verità: Le prove nei processi inquisitori." In *L'enquête au Moyen Âge*, edited by Claude Gauvard, 123–42. Rome: Ecole française de Rome, 2008.

———. "Paradigmi dell'eccezione nel tardo medievo." *Storia del pensiero politico* 2 (2012), 3–30.

———. "Premessa." *Quaderni storici* 131.2 (2009), 299–312.

Valterza, Loren Michael. "Infernal Retainers: Dante and the Juridical Tradition." PhD dissertation, Rutgers University, 2011.

Vanni, Sofia Rovighi. "Arbitrio." In *Enciclopedia Dantesca*, 1:197–208. Rome: Istituto della Enciclopedia Italiana, 1970–78.

———. "Legge e coscienza in San Tommaso." *Vita e pensiero*, n.s., 10 (1971), 787–93.

Varanini, Gian Maria. "Propaganda dei regimi signorili: Le esperienze venete del Trecento." In *Le forme della propaganda politica nel Due e nel Trecento*, 311–43. Rome: École française de Rome, 1994.

Vecchio, Silvana. "Segreti e bugie: I peccata occulta." *Micrologus* 14 (2006), 41–58.

Vernant, Jean-Pierre. *Mortals and Immortals: Collected Essays*. Edited by Froma I. Zeitlin. Princeton, NJ: Princeton University Press, 1991.

Vickers, Nancy J. "Seeing is Believing: Gregory, Trajan, and Dante's Art." *Dante Studies* 101 (1983), 67–85.

Claudia Villa, "Per una tipologia del commento mediolatino: *L'Ars poetica* di Orazio." In *Il commento ai testi: Atti del seminario di Asona 2–9 ottobre 1989*, edited by Ottavio Besomi and Carlo Caruso, 19–42. Basel, Boston, and Berlin: Birkhäuser, 1992.

Volante, Raffaele. *Il sistema contrattuale del diritto commune classico: Struttura dei patti e individuazione del tipo. Glossatori e Ultramontani*. Milan: Giuffrè editore, 2001.

Waelkens, Laurent Leo Jozef Maria. *La théorie de la coutume chez Jacques de Révigny: Edition et analyse de sa repetition sur la loi 'De quibus' (D. 1. 3. 32)*. Leiden: Brill, 1984.

Weigand, Rudolf. *Die Naturrechtslehre der Legisten und Dekretisten von Irnerius bis Accursius und von Gratian bis Johannes Teuononicus*. Munich: Hueber, 1967.

Weil, Simone. *The Need for Roots: Prelude to a Declaration of Duties towards Mankind.* New York: G. P. Putnam's Sons, 1955.

———. *Two Moral Essays by Simone Weil: Draft for a Statement of Human Obligations and Human Personality.* Edited by Ronald Hathaway, translated by Richard Rhees. Wallingford, PA: Pendle Hill Pamphlet, 1981.

Wickham, Chris. "Fama and the Law in Twelfth-Century Tuscany." In *Fama: The Politics of Talk and Reputation in Medieval Europe*, edited by Daniel Lord Small and Thelma Fenster, 15–26. Ithaca, NY: Cornell University Press, 2003.

Yavetz, Zvi. "Existimatio, Fama and the Ides of March." *Harvard Studies in Classical Philology* 78 (1974), 35–65.

Zenatti, Oddone. *Dante e Firenze: Prose antiche con note illustrative ed appendici.* Florence: Sansoni, 1902 (reprint, 1984).

Zimmermann, Reinhard. *The Law of Obligations: Roman Foundations of the Civilian Tradition.* Oxford: Oxford University Press, 1996.

Zorzi, Andrea. "Bien commun et conflits politiques dans l'Italie communale." In *De Bono Communi: The Discourse and Practice of the Common Good in the European City (13th–16th c.)*, edited by Elodie Lecuppre-Desjardin and Anne-Laure Van Bruaene, 267–90. Turnhout: Brepols, 2010.

Index

infamia (*continued*)
177n4, 178n10 (see also under
Paradiso); forms of, 17–21, 178–
79n14; of habitual thieves, 32; *ipso
iure* (by law), 17–18, 41; *ipso iure/
facti*, 28–40, 181n32; *iuris* (infamy
of law), 9, 17; overview of, 8–9,
13–14; performative aspect of, 41;
per sententiam (by sentence), 17,
21–28, 41, 45; through shaming
punishments, 9; social, 9; verisimi-
lar, 34–35, 37, 50, 181n35; as a
wound, 25, 41

Inferno (Dante)
1, 5, 88
2, 21, 93–96, 121, 170
3, 97
5, 72–73, 102
6, 29
7, 103, 110
8–9, 4, 102, 104–7, 110, 141
9, 109–10
13, 71, 75–78
14, 79
15, 36–40
15–16, 35–37
16, 39, 152–53, 155, 157, 159,
182n45
17, 155–57
20, 161
21, 159–63, 166, 203n53
22, 81, 159–63, 165, 191n63
23, 90, 115–19, 162, 164, 196n51,
197n55
26, 4, 142
27, 33, 134, 136–37, 139–40, 143,
156–57
28, 41–50
29, 48
30, 8, 85
32, 44, 71, 79–80, 82
33, 80, 135
34, 81
Alberigo scene in, 80, 135–36;
angelic *tal's* arrival in, 105–6,
108–10; barrators in, 159–61,
165–66; Bertran de Born in,
42–48; blasphemers in, 35–36;
Bocca degli Abati scene in, 71,
79–82; *bolgia*, 43–44, 136; Bru-

netto scene in, 36–40, 182n43;
Caiaphas in, 118–19; Ciacco in,
29; Ciampolo in, 81, 191n63;
confessions in, 71–74, 78; on
contrapasso, 42, 44–46, 48; cord
in Geryon scene in, 159; Dante's
agreements with the damned
in (see under *pactum*); demons
who torture prisoners in, 81–82,
191n63; devil's right to bear arms
in, 48, 184n63; Gates of Dis scene
in, 4, 7, 102, 104–11, 120; Geri
di Bello in, 48, 184n62; Geryon
scene, 12, 154–57, 159; Guido da
Montefeltro scene in, 21, 136–43,
200n21; hypocrites in, 115–16,
117–19, 197nn54–55; Jovial Fri-
ars in, 90, 116–18, 197nn54–55;
justice examined in, 8; as limit
case for studying contracts, 128,
166 (see also *pactum*); Male-
branche pact in, 159–66, 203n53,
203n55; Minos in, 71–73, 97–98,
102, 114; Mohammed in, 42–43,
45–47, 49–50, 52; Pier della Vigna
scene in, 71, 74–79, 135; on pity,
77–79; readers addressed in,
104, 161; sodomites in, 35–39,
135, 182n42, 182n45; St. Francis
scene in, 33, 140, 141; suicides in,
74–77, 79; suspense in, 104–6;
torture and judicial discretion in,
74, 80–82, 191n63; traitors of
Cocytus in, 79–80, 135; usurers
in, 35–36, 155, 156; on vengeance,
48, 184n62; on violence, state-
supported vs. criminal, 80–81;
wounds and speech in, 44–45
Innocent III, Pope, 18–19, 36,
178–79n14
Inquisition of Heretical Pravity, 19
inquisitorial procedure, 19–20, 36
intestabilitas, 21–22
Investiture Controversy, 18
Isidore of Seville: *Etymologies*, 91
Islam, 42
ius commune: and *arbitrium regulatum*,
60; "constitutionalist" tenets
of, 2; freedom as observance of,
57, 185–86n10; immunity from,

Manfred, king of Sicily, 49–52, 71
Marcia (character), 112, 114
Mazzotta, Giuseppe, 196n43
Medusa, 105–6, 110, 195n34
mendicants vs. seculars, 99–102, 194n20
messianism, 105–6, 108–10
military sacrifice, imperative to, 125–26
mimesis: Auerbach's theory of, 50–51; of the *Commedia*, 9, 14, 21, 35, 156; by Nimrod, 64
Minos, 71–73, 97–98, 102, 114
miracle, 6–7, 47, 98, 121, 148
Mohammed, 9, 42–43, 45–47, 49–50, 52
Monarchia (Dante), 1, 58–59, 63, 111, 139, 146–47, 152–53, 195n37
Mosca, 42
mystery plays, 161–63

Najemy, John, 122
natural law: Drittura as personification of, 146; and the light of reason, 71, 189n45; and positive law, 71, 82–83, 189n45; private property as violating, 65
New Jerusalem, 169
Niccolò da Prato, 63
Nicomachean Ethics (Aristotle), 42, 46–47
Nimrod, 64–65, 70, 84
nobility vs. the *popolo*, 122–25, 197–98n63
novella, 133

Oderisi, 83
Ortalli, Gherardo, 29

pactum, 127–66; bindingness of pacts, 130, 199n9; Boniface VIII– Colonna family treaty, 137–38; Church's role re naked pacts, 130; comedy as a naked pact, overview of, 152–54; commerce's role in, 130; consensus vs. contract types, 128–34, 142, 199n3, 199nn5–6; deals and naked pacts in *Inferno*, 27, 127–28, 134–43; definition/ origin of, 8, 200n22; dressed vs.

naked pacts, 127, 129–30, 198n1, 199n6; Geryon pact in *Inferno*, 154–59; and literary genres, 131–33; Malebranche pact in *Inferno*, 159–66, 203n53, 203n55; medieval vs. modern contract law, 11; named/unnamed, 129–31, 199n3; overview of, 8–9, 11–12, 127–28; and poems as naked/ dressed, 143–52, 201–2n37; reader–author contract, 128, 133, 143, 152, 157–59, 161; sacramental, 139–40; *stipulatio*, 129; in "Tre donne intorno al cor mi son venute," 143–46, 150–52, 159, 165
Palinurus, 51
papal power, 99–100, 138, 193n17
Paradiso (Dante)
  1–12, 168
  3, 121
  4, 7–8
  5, 110, 193n17
  10, 32
  13, 31–32
  15, 119–21, 124, 197n58
  15–17, 40, 95, 102, 119–26
  16, 16, 121–25, 197n58
  17, 21, 29, 40, 123
  20, 30, 103
  22, 203n1
  23, 110–11, 153, 204n2
  24, 167–68, 169–70
  24–26, 167–71
  25, 12, 153, 167–71, 173, 204n3, 204n5
  26, 4
  27, 173
  Aquinas on God's justice in, 31–33; Beatrice addresses the host of the Church Triumphant in, 169; Beatrice on Dante's hope, 94–95, 173; Cacciaguida scene in, 28–29, 40, 90, 119–26; Dante is tested in, 167–70; defamatory poetics in, 29; *fama/infamia* in, 28–29; on presumptive justice, 30–32; on rebel angels, 103; "Se mai continga" (homecoming fantasy) in, 12, 168–69, 172–73, 203n1,